Program of Graduate Training and Research
in International Relations
Department of Political Science
Northwestern University
Evanston, Illinois

NATIONAL STUDIES ON INTERNATIONAL ORGANIZATION

PAKISTAN
AND THE
UNITED NATIONS

by

K. SARWAR HASAN

Prepared for the

PAKISTAN INSTITUTE OF INTERNATIONAL AFFAIRS

and the

CARNEGIE ENDOWMENT FOR INTERNATIONAL PEACE

Manhattan Publishing Company
New York
1960

VOLUMES PREVIOUSLY PUBLISHED IN THIS SERIES

PRINTED BY BRÜDER ROSENBAUM, VIENNA (AUSTRIA)

Preface

This volume forms part of a series of studies on international organization initiated by the Carnegie Endowment for International Peace and carried out by private institutions and individuals in more than twenty countries around the world. This particular study has been prepared, under the auspices of the Pakistan Institute of International Affairs, by Mr. K. Sarwar Hasan.

The decision, taken in 1952, to initiate this program reflected both the Endowment's long-standing conviction that international organizations, such as the United Nations, are central to the quest for peace and the assumption that their significance and functioning depend first and foremost upon the attitudes and policies of nations. The fact that the question of Charter review would be on the agenda of the General Assembly in 1955 seemed to afford a unique opportunity for assessing the strengths and weaknesses of the United Nations in terms of national expectations and their fulfillment during the brief but rich testing period of the first ten years. In sponsoring this series of studies the Endowment has sought to encourage an exchange of unofficial national views, with the object of stimulating a closer examination of the past record and future potentialities of the United Nations and of increasing understanding of differences and similarities in national attitudes toward the Organization.

In the pursuit of these objectives, the participants in each country were asked to appraise their national experience in international organization, especially in the United Nations. In doing so they have considered such questions as: What impact has the United Nations had on both the content and the conduct of national policy? To iv

what extent have the purposes and principles set out in the Charter
served as adequate guides to the organs of the United Nations in
their operations? Have developments in the practices and the procedures of the United Nations made the organization more or less
effective as an agency to achieve the purposes for which it was
established? What is, and should be, the relationship of the United
Nations to other forms of international organization, including
regional systems? Does experience suggest the need for formal re-
vision of the Charter?

In exercising its responsibility for the decision to publish the
volumes in this series, the Endowment has been assisted by an advisory review committee, comprising Dr. Alberto Lleras Camargo,
former Secretary General of the Organization of American States
and now President of Colombia; Sir Ramaswami Mudaliar, Vice-
Chancellor of Travancore University, India; and Dr. Bernard H. M.
Vlekke, Secretary-General of the Netherlands Institute of International Affairs. Their faithful and wise counsel is most gratefully
acknowledged.

It should be noted that publication of these volumes does not
necessarily signify endorsement of their contents by either the members of the review committee or the Carnegie Endowment. Responsibility for the views expressed in the studies rests with the authors
alone.

The conclusions of the individual studies have been summarized
and their significance analyzed in two final volumes prepared in-
dependently by Robert M. MacIver, Lieber Professor Emeritus of
Political Philosophy and Sociology at Columbia University in New
York City; and Maurice Bourquin, Professor in the Institut Uni-
versitaire de Hautes Etudes Internationales in Geneva.

No prefatory note which did not exceed its proper dimensions
could possibly acknowledge all the debts which the Endowment
owes to scholars and officials in many parts of the world for the
help which they have graciously given. To the Pakistan Institute of
International Affairs, and especially to Mr. K. Sarwar Hasan, the

author of this study, particular thanks are due for their co-operation in making the present volume possible. The Endowment wishes to record its deep appreciation not only for the scholarship and thought which are reflected in the following pages but also for the patience and unfailing courtesy that have characterized this venture in co-operation over several years.

The Endowment wishes to express its gratitude to the Ford Foundation for providing a grant which, by supplementing funds supplied by the Endowment and the co-operating institutions themselves, made it possible to carry out the project on a broad and comprehensive basis.

March 1960   JOSEPH E. JOHNSON
                                              President
                    Carnegie Endowment for International Peace

Foreword

At the invitation of the Carnegie Endowment for International Peace, this volume has been prepared in the Pakistan Institute of International Affairs for the Endowment's series of National Studies on International Organization. The author of the volume, Mr. K. Sarwar Hasan, has had varied experience of international affairs and has served on delegations to the Security Council and the General Assembly of the United Nations. His task in preparing this study was by no means an easy one. He had to treat adequately of the Kashmir question, which has been Pakistan's principal concern in the United Nations and which has consumed a great deal of its time and effort. In treating of that question, he had also to avoid the pitfalls of prejudice and partisanship.

When Mr. Hasan's research had sufficiently advanced, he drew up, in consultation with me, a questionnaire designed to bring out the Pakistani view of the more outstanding aspects of the working of the United Nations. This questionnaire was considered by a Study Group, which consisted of ex-Prime Minister Chaudhri Mohamad Ali; Mr. Hatim A. Alavi, Director of the State Bank of Pakistan; Mr. M. Ayub, Director of the Pakistan Industrial Development Corporation, formerly Joint Secretary in the Ministry of Kashmir Affairs; Mr. Hasan and myself. The Group was assisted by officials of the Institute and of the Ministries of Foreign Affairs and Economic Affairs. The Group did not cover the entire field of Mr. Hasan's study nor did it see his manuscript. It confined itself to the matters in the questionnaire and formulated its conclusions about them. It should be understood, however, that each member of the Group does not necessarily subscribe to the conclusions of the Group as a whole. Apart from those conclusions, which are set out in appropriate places in Chapters VIII and X, Mr. Hasan alone is responsible for the views expressed in the study which, in its entirety, is based upon his research and has been written by him.

The study was completed just before the revolution took place in Pakistan in October 1958. The new regime has introduced many important reforms in the domestic sphere but the foreign policy of Pakistan and its relations with international organisations have remained unaltered. Consequently, it has not been felt necessary to make any changes in the tenor of the text. However, in respect of some essential matters an attempt has been made to bring the study up-to-date.

It is a pleasure as well as a duty to thank the members of the Study Group and all others who have helped Mr. Hasan in his work. He had the benefit of several long discussions with Mr. M. Ayub on the Kashmir question. In respect of certain points concerning Pakistan's relations with India, he has drawn upon some material on that subject prepared by Mr. H. H. S. Feldman of Karachi. Mr. A. Rashid Ibrahim, Deputy Secretary in the Ministry of Economic Affairs, furnished indispensable guidance in the writing of the chapter on Economic Assistance Programs. Mr. Latif Ahmed Sherwani performed miscellaneous functions incidental to an undertaking of this nature and in particular bore the responsibility for checking the quotations and organising the footnotes. The secretarial staff of the Institute worked ungrudgingly, some times late after office hours. Various chapters of the manuscript were read and useful suggestions for improving it were made by several persons who wish to remain unnamed, some of them on account of their official position. Finally, sincere acknowledgment must be made to the Carnegie Endowment for International Peace and in particular to its Vice President, Mr. Lawrence S. Finkelstein, for the assistance and encouragement given by them in carrying through this project.

Karachi, March 1960   A. B. A. HALEEM
Chairman of Council
Pakistan Institute of International Affairs

Contents

chapter one

Asia and the Emergence of the United Nations

For the people of Asia, World War II had consequences of a very special character. If Japan had stayed neutral or had joined on the side of the Allies, the story would have been different. But Japan—which had by defeating Russia in 1904 given the first blow to the belief that the white man was *ipso facto* a superior kind of being—destroyed that belief altogether in World War II. Indeed, Japan was the only country capable of doing so for, since the Meiji era of the sixties, Japan had progressively adopted the tools of Western civilisation and displayed a dynamism that was far from "oriental." While the rest of Asia remained medieval, Japan had developed not only an industrial economy on the Western pattern but also its concomitant military power. In this and some other respects, Japan was *sui generis* in Asia.

Furthermore, of all the Asian countries, Japan was the only one that counted in international affairs, and counted as one of the great powers of the world. The rest of Asia was not only backward, but most of it was under foreign rule or domination. Indeed, it was this backwardness and political subjection, more than any other factor, that made Asia a continental unit by itself: for many of the peoples of Western Asia, such as those of the littorals of the Caspian, the Mediterranean, and the Black Sea, if judged either by their physical features, or the colour of their skins, or by their historical associations, or their mental attitudes, are more akin to Europeans than to other Asians. Be that as it may, more than half the population of the world that was comprised in Asia had no voice in international affairs. Vast areas, such as those of the Pakistan-Indian subcontinent and of Indonesia, were under European rule. The same was true of the rest of Southeast Asia, barring Thailand. China, rent by internecine warfare, was impotent. The Middle East, with the exception of a sturdy new Turkey, consisted of feeble states, wholly or partly under Western domination. But everywhere there were ferment and brave and defiant efforts to attain freedom. However, that freedom seemed far away.

For Asians, Japan's sensational victories over the Western powers in Southeast Asia probably constituted the most dramatic chapter of the history of World War II. They caused a convulsion that rocked Asia as it had never been rocked before; they electrified its people. In quick succession, one country after another fell before the Japanese. There is no doubt that those successes were facilitated by the co-operation of the people of the conquered countries with the Japanese. This co-operation was offered in the hope that deliverance from Western rule might open the way for deliverance from such rule forever. That hope was eventually justified.

The fall of Singapore, the greatest disaster that befell European arms in Asia, seemed to many people to settle the issue of the war in Asia. But it was not as simple as all that. The war in Asia was interlinked with the war in Europe, where the staying power of the British, the active intervention of the Americans, and the grim determination of the Russians ultimately made their weight felt. Directly confronted with the organisation and the immense technological resources of the United States, the Japanese were unable to develop their initial successes into final victory.

At the time that the Japanese were riding the crest of the wave of their conquests, the leaders of the Congress party of India launched their most aggressive effort to oust the British. The British survived this "stab in the back," as they called it. However, soon after the end of the war and under pressure at home and from all political parties in the subcontinent, they dissolved their Indian empire and, in consequence, the sovereign states of Pakistan and India came into being in 1947. British power withdrew also from Burma and Ceylon.

The British example was not followed by the two other principal European colonial powers in Asia. The Dutch were, however, forced to withdraw from Indonesia by the resistance of its people and by the opposition of the United States and of international opinion generally to the re-establishment of their empire. The French obstinately clung to Indo-China. They were helped by the Americans, who feared the coming of a Communist regime in the area. However, after Dien Bien Phu, the French too had to withdraw, leaving behind a legacy of many intractable problems.

The war brought still another change to Asia: increased contact with foreigners. For the Indian subcontinent this meant increased contact with Americans, who had in earlier times been known almost entirely in the role of educators and missionaries. And in those earlier times the United States had been known, in rather general, vague terms, as a country that had fought a war for its independence and as a supporter of freedom. President Wilson's speeches and his "Fourteen Points," with their emphasis on self-determination, had given a stimulus to freedom movements in Asia. But after World War I the United States had rejected the League of Nations, had become isolationist, and had, except for the Naval Disarmament Conference of 1922 and the "Stimson Doctrine," played little part in the international politics that affected Asia.

In World War II, however, the general requirements of the war, as well as the United States policy of support for Chiang Kai-shek, for the first time brought to the subcontinent a number of Americans —soldiers, airmen, and executives—a great military organization. The subcontinent had become an important Allied military base and, indeed, the only means of communication with China. By 1942, India and its affairs had become sufficiently important to the United States to persuade President Roosevelt to send a personal envoy to New Delhi. The first American diplomatic representative to the subcontinent was Col. Louis Johnson; he was replaced some months later by Mr. William Philips. Little did ordinary people in this region then realise that after the war was over they would have a great deal to do with Americans and that there would come into existence a pattern of international relations in which the United States would play a major role, rivaled only by the Soviet Union.

On the whole, Soviet Russia had been more talked about in prewar Asia than the United States. The Russian Revolution had had its repercussions in Asia. Propaganda by Communists, and the support that the Soviet leaders gave to freedom movements in Asia, combined with the unfriendly treatment that Russia received during the interwar years from "imperialist" governments, created for it a good deal of sympathy. While the United States had no direct interest in Asian affairs, the Soviet Union was actively concerned in Central Asia. After the USSR became involved in World War II, there was more sympathy or, one might say, less apathy for the Allied cause than there had been heretofore. However, about the only non-Soviet Asian country that saw Russian military and civilian personnel during the war was Iran. Very few Russians were in evidence in the subcontinent.

One of the greatest events of the war took place in Asia. This was the use, and the practical demonstration for the first time, of the terrific power of the atom bomb. On the Japanese cities of Hiroshima and Nagasaki, respectively, two of these bombs were dropped, which speeded the exit of Japan from the war. It is sometimes said that the use of the atom bomb was an anti-Asian act and an instance of Western callousness towards Asians. For Asians, who suffer from an anti-Western complex, any stick is good enough to beat the West with. However, no one can genuinely maintain that the United States would not have used the atom bomb against Germany, or that Germany would not have used it, if either had developed it before the end of the war in Europe. One could go further and say that no Asian nation which was engaged in a war and which possessed the atom bomb would hesitate to use it, irrespective of what race or continent the adversary belonged to. And China and India are now believed to be developing the bomb. It is natural for a party to a war to wish to win it and for that purpose to use, if it can, more effective weapons than the other party. The supreme objection to the atom bomb is that it involves unprecedented danger to the lives (and property) of non-combatants, of defenceless people, of women and children, and that it has cumulative and residual effects of an injurious nature, which are not yet precisely known to science. In these respects the atom bomb is far worse than "conventional" air bombing.

While the atom bomb brought about yet another revolution in the art of war, the possession of this most terrible weapon of destruction had far-reaching consequences in international affairs. By 1949 the Soviet Union also had the atom bomb. There had been doubts about the military capacity of the Soviet Union, until it was demonstrated in the war against Germany. But, at the end of the war, the Soviet Union and the United States emerged as the two most powerful nations of the world. The defeated Axis countries— Germany, Italy, and Japan—had ceased to count as powers. Britain, having exhausted its economic resources during the war, and liquidated its Asian empire after it, became dependent upon the United States in more ways than one. France came out of the war utterly shattered, without either the political resourcefulness or the stability of Britain.

So staggering are the extent and variety of human suffering caused by a modern war that men naturally wish that there should be no more of it. Thus, during World War II, as during World War I, the leaders of the prospectively victorious nations started to plan for a postwar international organisation, with the primary aim of maintaining peace. Churchill's idea was to have three regional councils, for the Pacific, the Americas, and Europe, respectively.[1] At Washington, in May 1943, he discussed his plan with Roosevelt, who was inclined to accept it. However, Secretary of State Hull opposed it for fear that such a plan would create spheres of influence.[2] In October 1943 the Foreign Ministers of the United States, the United Kingdom, and the Soviet Union, meeting in Moscow, declared their agreement on the necessity of establishing an international organisation "based on the principle of the sovereign equality of all peace-loving states."[3] On American insistence this declaration was signed also by the Chinese Ambassador in Moscow —an example of the desire of the United Nations to propitiate Chiang Kai-shek. However, no plan for an international organisation had yet emerged. At Teheran, in December 1943, Roosevelt thought of an international organisation to ensure peace which would have had an assembly composed of all member-nations, an executive committee consisting of the Big Four and representative nations from various regions, and a third organ to police the world and prevent or combat aggression.[4] Stalin thought in terms of two organisations, one for Europe and the other for the Far East.[5]

In August 1944 a conference of the representatives of the United States, the United Kingdom, the Soviet Union, and China met at

---

[1] See William Hardy McNeill, *America, Britain and Russia—Their Cooperation and Conflict* (London: Oxford University Press, 1953), pp. 321-23.

[2] For very important arguments against basing international organisations on regional councils, see Cordell Hull, *The Memoirs of Cordell Hull* (New York: The Macmillan Company, 1948), Vol. II, pp. 1644 ff.

[3] *A Decade of American Foreign Policy: Basic Documents, 1941-49* (Washington: U.S. Govt. Printing Office, 1950), p. 12.

[4] Robert E. Sherwood, *The White House Papers of Harry L. Hopkins* (London: Eyre & Spottiswoode, 1949), Vol. II, p. 780.

[5] *Ibid.*, p. 781.

Dumbarton Oaks and drew up proposals for an international organisation. Under these proposals the international organisation was to have a General Assembly and a Security Council, but authority in all matters relating to international peace and security was to be vested in the latter. At Yalta, in February 1945, the Dumbarton Oaks plan was considered by Roosevelt, Churchill, and Stalin, who agreed that each one of the great powers should not only be a permanent member of the Security Council but also a necessary and indispensable party to any substantive decision by that body; in other words, each of the great powers was to have the right of veto in such decisions. The Soviet Union was not prepared to make any compromise in this matter.[6] Stalin was motivated by the fear that the Soviets would be in a permanent minority in the world organisation and "he would never agree to having any action of any of the Great Powers submitted to the judgment of the small Powers."[7] The British favoured the veto as a means of preventing encroachment upon their imperial interests.[8] The United States favoured it as a form of insurance against the commitment by the United Nations of American forces to possible wars.[9] Thus, while planning an international organisation "based upon the sovereign equality of all nations," the great powers decided at Yalta that they were to have the power of decision in world affairs and that there should be no joint decision of which any one of them disapproved.

In other ways, too, the great powers took care to assure their respective interests. At Dumbarton Oaks the Soviet Union had demanded that all its sixteen constituent republics should be admitted to the United Nations. Half of these republics being Asian, one wonders what repercussions their participation in United

---

[6] *Ibid.*, p. 846.

[7] Edward R. Stettinius, Jr., *Roosevelt and the Russians: The Yalta Conference* (Garden City: Doubleday & Company, 1949), p. 112.

[8] Sherwood, *op. cit.*, p. 846.

[9] *Ibid.*

b

Nations debates and activities would have had on their affairs and on Asian affairs generally. However, at Yalta, Stalin scaled down his demand and asked for representation for two republics only. In this he was supported by Churchill, who was influenced by British imperial considerations: India was not self-governing and yet India had been a member of the League of Nations. At Yalta, "Churchill had made it clear that he did not favor Indian independence—and yet India was to have a vote."[10] Roosevelt decided to support the Soviet demand for two extra votes, but suggested that the United States also should have two extra votes. Churchill was agreeable to this parity between the Soviet Union and the United States.[11]

Although Roosevelt finally abandoned the idea of claiming two extra votes for the United States, that does not mean that its government was not taking care that its position in the international organisation and in international affairs generally should be adequately safeguarded. It is true that Hull condemned spheres of influence and European ideas concerning alliances and the balance of power. Yet, in a broader sweep, as one serious student has put it:

> ... American policy in Latin America bore a suspicious likeness to European practices which American statesmen so much deplored. To be sure, the United States gave up coercive methods in Latin America after Roosevelt's introduction of the "Good Neighbour" policy, but economic domination was a good substitute, and made the American republics, with the exception of Argentina, almost always obedient to the diplomatic leadership of the United States.

> America's war-time policy towards China was clothed in similarly idealistic garb, but outsiders could reasonably be pardoned for interpreting America's policy as designed to bring China within the sphere of American influence. An American officer was appointed as Chief of Staff to the Chinese army; emissaries from the President bombarded Chiang Kai-

---

10 Stettinius, *op. cit.*, p. 188.
11 *Ibid.*, p. 283.

shek with good advice; and American pressure compelled Russia and Britain to accord China a courtesy seat amongst the Great Allied Powers. Madame Chiang Kai-shek privately assured Roosevelt in February 1943, that he could be sure China would support American policy at a peace conference after the war, and the President believed he could count upon China as a friend and supporter of the United States.[12]

Thus was a sphere of influence to be consolidated for the United States. However, Roosevelt and Hull were opposed to colonialism. Roosevelt's basic attitude towards colonialism may be judged from the fact that he thought that Hong Kong should be given back to China, or internationalised as a free port, that Indo-China should be made into a trust,[13] and that India should achieve independence.[14]

A lifelong advocate of "Tearing Down Tariff Walls,"[15] Hull saw in the liquidation of colonialism an opportunity for doing away with British empire preferences, establishing free trade policies in the colonies and, also, naturally extending the trade of the United States. Hull also favoured an international administrative organ, with jurisdiction over all the colonies, to prepare them for independence.[16] On the other hand, military leaders in the United States felt that the former Japanese-mandated islands, because of their strategic importance, should be held by the United States either in outright ownership or as a trust.[17] Thus, by the time of the Yalta Conference, the American attitude towards colonial areas had become significantly modified, and consequently also the American plan for trusteeship over those areas. Stettinius was able to explain

---

[12] McNeill, *op. cit.*, p. 317.

[13] Hull, *op. cit.*, Vol. II, pp. 1595-99.

[14] *Ibid.*, pp. 1482-97; Sherwood, *op. cit.*, Vol. II, pp. 515-16, 529-30.

[15] This is the title of a chapter in Hull's *Memoirs*, *op. cit.*, Vol. I (Chap. 26). For Hull's ideas about free trade, see his *Memoirs*, Vol. II, pp. 975 and 1304. *See also* U.S. Dept. of State, *Postwar Foreign Policy Preparation. 1939-1945*, Publication 3580 (Washington: U.S. Govt. Printing Office, 1949), pp. 12 and 34. Cf. McNeill, *op. cit.*, pp. 333 and 367.

[16] *Postwar Foreign Policy Preparation*, *op. cit.*, pp. 471-72.

[17] William D. Leahy, *I Was There* (New York: Whittlesey House, 1950), p. 210.

to Churchill, who had declared that he would "never yield one scrap of Britain's heritage," that trusteeship would apply only to League of Nations mandates, to territories conquered from the enemy, and to territories which might be voluntarily placed under trusteeship.[18] In short: "To the United States, the trusteeship principle afforded a convenient tool for acquiring control over strategically desirable areas without seeming to violate the pledges of the Atlantic Charter."[19]

The Russians were not less interested in colonial dispositions than either the British or the Americans. At Yalta they obtained the consent of the other two big powers for the restoration of the territorial and other rights "violated" by the Japanese after the 1904 war, and these included possession of the southern part of Sakhalin and all adjacent islands and control over the strategic Manchurian Railway and Port Arthur.[20] At Potsdam Stalin raised the question of the former Italian colonies in Africa and demanded that the Soviet Union should be one of the trustees for them. The British did not want the Soviets exercising their authority in the southern and eastern Mediterranean area.[21] At the Council of Foreign Ministers in September 1945, Molotov proposed that each of the big three assume trusteeship over one of the Italian colonies, with the USSR becoming the administering authority over Tripolitania. He claimed that the Soviet Union had experience in establishing friendly relations with different nationalities and also that it needed bases in the Mediterranean for its merchant fleet.[22]

The United States and the Soviet Union were indisputably the greatest powers, whether judged by the extent of their territories or their populations or their economic and military resources.

---

18 Stettinius, *op. cit.*, p. 236.

19 Ernst B. Haas, "The Attempt to Terminate Colonialism," *International Organization*, Vol. VII, No. 1, 1953, p. 6.

20 Sherwood, *op. cit.*, pp. 854-55.

21 Leahy, *op. cit.*, pp. 404-5, 408.

22 Benjamin Rivlin, *The United Nations and the Italian Colonies* (New York: Carnegie Endowment for International Peace, 1950), pp. 9-11.

Britain had less territory, less population, and had depleted its resources during the war. But there was no gainsaying that by standing up to the Axis in solitary battle Britain had played a decisive part in the war. Because of that fact and because of its world-wide interests, Britain was accepted by the United States and the Soviet Union as a great power. Thus, there were three of them. These three, having determined that they would have the decisive voice in world affairs and that nothing would be done of which any one of them might disapprove, proceeded to add to their number some dependable friends. The Americans asked that China should be included in the category of great powers. Stalin was very sceptical about the strength and stability of Nationalist China, and Churchill, too, had no illusions about Chinese power.[23] However, both of them gave way before Roosevelt. The British asked that the same status should be accorded to France, although that country had, morally and materially, ceased to be a great power, with no prospect of becoming one again. But Churchill foresaw the lengthening shadow of Russia across the continent of Europe, and, of all its prostrate nations, France seemed to him to be the only one that could be rebuilt as a bulwark of the old civilisation. Roosevelt and Stalin were persuaded to agree, and France, too, was promoted. Thus, the destinies of the world were committed to the keeping of five powers: two superpowers, one great power, and two middle powers. There would have been six of them, if the proposal urged by the American delegates at Dumbarton Oaks that Brazil, too, should have a permanent seat on the Security Council had not been rejected by the British and the Russians.

Only one of the big five—that is, China—belonged to the continent of Asia. In prewar days, when the imperial rule of the Western powers was supreme over most countries of Asia, China seldom manifested an interest in the affairs of its neighbours. To do so would have been gratuitously to offend the Western powers. Be-

---

[23] Winston Churchill, *The Second World War* (London: Cassell & Co., Ltd., 1951), Vol. IV, Appendix C, p. 837.

sides, China was preoccupied with its own internal troubles. However, during the war, Chiang Kai-shek, who had come to be regarded in the United States as the champion of Asian freedom, sought to "intervene" in Indian affairs. This was resented by the British.[24] Evidently China, although divided, unstable, weak and dependent upon America, was given one of the permanent seats in the Security Council lest there should be an impression abroad that Asia had been excluded from sharing in the direction of world affairs.

At San Francisco, on 25 April 1945, began the United Nations Conference on International Organization. Out of its labours was born the United Nations Charter, which was signed on 26 June. Of the fifty states that were represented at San Francisco, only twelve were truly Asian or African states. These were: China, Egypt, Ethiopia, India, Iran, Iraq, Lebanon, Liberia, the Philippine Republic, Saudi Arabia, Syria, and Turkey. China, India, and Iran had been members of the League of Nations—India, even though it was neither independent nor fully self-governing.

Neither Jinnah nor Gandhi, champions of rival policies for the freedom of the subcontinent, each commanding the allegiance of vast millions, was invited to San Francisco; nor were any of their colleagues. However, to represent India, the British nominated the very able and eloquent Sir Ramaswami Mudaliar, probably the greatest moderate statesman since Gokhale. Sir Ramaswami's stand at San Francisco was not unacceptable either to the Muslim League or the Congress party.

At San Francisco the Asian states joined with other less powerful states in an endeavour to secure a liberalisation of the scheme of the world organisation, as evolved at Dumbarton Oaks and Yalta. In part as a result of this endeavour, the Economic and Social Council was made one of the principal organs of the United Nations. In Article 55, it was recognised that the creation of conditions of

---

[24] *Ibid.*, p. 456.

stability and well-being was necessary for peaceful and friendly relations amongst nations, and the United Nations was committed to promoting higher standards of living, full employment and social progress, as well as universal respect for human rights and fundamental freedoms. There were in the Covenant of the League no comparable provisions, nor any such machinery as the Economic and Social Council. It is interesting to recall that at Dumbarton Oaks the Russians had proposed the creation of two distinct organisations, one for dealing with security problems and the other for economic and social matters.

The Asian states fought hard to put an end to colonialism. As we have seen, the attitude of the United States towards this problem had, because of strategic considerations, undergone a definite change. Consequently, so far as that country was concerned, the idea of a complete transformation of the European colonial empires had been given up; and there was at San Francisco no support by the United States for the demand that all the territories of these empires should be brought under an international trusteeship system and guided to independence. This demand was voiced by practically all Arab-Asian states. Australia and New Zealand, too, were sympathetic towards the trusteeship principle; for they were anxious that there should be stability in the Asian countries to their north, and were therefore desirous that the national aspirations of those countries should be satisfied. But Australia and New Zealand were anxious, also, to consolidate their control over territories that were of strategic importance to them. It suited them to do so under the guise of trusteeship. In this respect, their attitude was identical with the new attitude of the United States. It was finally agreed that there should be two separate categories of dependencies—the non-self-governing territories, which are governed by Chapter XI, and trust territories, which are governed by Chapters XII and XIII of the Charter.

In Article 73, Chapter XI of the United Nations Charter, it was recognised that the interests of the inhabitants of the non-self-governing territories were paramount; and the obligation was imposed on the administering powers to develop self-government in those territories and to ensure the advancement of their people. At San Francisco it was demanded that independence should be the goal for all dependent areas; but it was finally decided that, so far as the territories under Chapter XI were concerned, the objective should be "self-government." For the trust territories, the objective was defined as "progressive development towards self-government or independence, as may be appropriate to the particular circumstances of each territory" (Article 76). A definite stipulation for independence in the case of either category of dependent territories was avoided, obviously because no power that had strategic interests in any such territory was willing to commit itself to the extinction of its authority over it.

Article 77 of the Charter states that the trusteeship system is to apply only to such territories as may be placed under it, including territories held under the mandate of the League of Nations and territories conquered as a result of World War II. In vain did Egypt demand that all mandated territories should *ipso facto* come under the trusteeship system, that the wishes of the people concerned should be considered in the choice of the trustee, and that the General Assembly should have the right to transfer, assign, and terminate trusts.[25] In vain did China press for direct international administration instead of permanent and single nation trusteeships (such as those claimed by the United States over the Pacific Islands).[26] In vain did the Philippines plead that the principle of trusteeship should be applicable to all dependent territories.[27]

Thus, no power that is in possession of a territory can be compelled to bring it under the international supervisory system; and when it does submit it to that system, it does so on terms which,

---

[25] *Documents of the United Nations Conference on International Organization, San Francisco, 1945* (New York: United Nations Information Organizations, 1945), Vol. X, pp. 510-46. Hereinafter referred to as *UNCIO Documents.*

[26] *Ibid.,* p. 439.

[27] *Ibid.,* p. 429.

in effect, it itself determines (Article 79). Further, in any trusteeship agreement, any areas may be designated as strategic areas (Article 82); and, in respect of such areas, the functions of the United Nations will be performed by the Security Council, in which the great powers have the veto, instead of the more popular General Assembly (Article 83). However, the principles of equal rights and self-determination were written into the Charter (Article 1(2)).

The efforts of a number of states, including those of Asia, to bring about a reduction in the special rights of the great powers as envisaged in the Dumbarton Oaks and Yalta proposals, did not meet with success. They did, however, succeed in widening the scope of the activities of the Assembly, in which every member-state is represented, each possessing one vote. The Covenant of the League had made no differentiation between the functions of the Council[28] and the Assembly;[29] though, in actual practice, inasmuch as the Council was in continuous session and the Assembly was not, a differentiation had arisen. For a decision, whether of the Council or the Assembly, the Covenant had required unanimity of their respective members. Thus every member of the League Assembly and of the Council was armed with the veto and, by exercising it, could prevent action by either body. This happened in the case of the Japanese aggression in Manchuria in 1933 and the Italian threat to Ethiopia in 1935.

The Dumbarton Oaks proposals made a clear and emphatic distinction between the functions of the Assembly and those of the Council, the latter to have jurisdiction over matters relating to the maintenance of peace and security. The Assembly was to have general powers of discussion and recommendation with regard to economic and social matters, but no powers of any significance with regard to political matters. However, as a result of the efforts of Asian and other states at San Francisco, Articles 10 and 14 were

---

[28] Article 4(4) of the Covenant.
[29] Article 3(3) of the Covenant.

adopted. Under the former Article, "The General Assembly may discuss any questions or any matters within the scope of the present Charter," and "may make recommendations to the Members of the United Nations or the Security Council, or to both on any such questions or matters." The very important exception to this is that the General Assembly may not make any recommendations with regard to any dispute or situation with respect to which the Security Council is exercising its functions (Article 12). Subject to the same exception, the General Assembly may, under Article 14, recommend measures for the peaceful adjustment of any situation which it deems likely to impair the general welfare or friendly relations amongst nations. Under Article 18, for decisions by the General Assembly on important questions, a two-thirds majority of the members present and voting is required.

As for the Security Council, the efforts of the Asian and other states bore no fruit since the Dumbarton Oaks and Yalta proposals for the Council were incorporated into the Charter without any substantial change. The Security Council has eleven seats; the five permanent members are the United States, the United Kingdom, the Soviet Union, China, and France, while the other six members are elected for a term of two years by the General Assembly. The Council is primarily responsible for the maintenance of international peace and security, and it was visualised that it should have exclusive authority in effecting settlement of disputes, removing threats to peace, and taking enforcement measures. Decisions on procedural questions are made by the vote of any seven members. Upon all other matters decisions are made by an affirmative vote of seven members, including the concurrent votes of the five permanent members. Thus decisions on all questions relating to the maintenance of peace and security must be unanimously supported by the permanent members that are present and voting, a procedure that gives each permanent member of the Security Council the right of veto in such questions. To this power there is one exception; when the Council is seeking pacific settlement of a dispute, *i.e.*, acting under

Chapter VI of the Charter, a member of the Council who is a party to such a dispute has to abstain from voting. But there is no such obligation when the Council is acting under Chapter VII, *i.e.*, considering enforcement action. Such action might be prevented by a member withholding its concurrence, even though that member is a party to the dispute under consideration. Under Article 106, the permanent members have, in consultation with each other, the right to take joint action on behalf of the United Nations.

Strenuous efforts were made at San Francisco either to eliminate the veto or to modify and restrict its application. The great powers resisted all these efforts and made it plain that, unless the scheme as put forward by them was accepted, there would be no United Nations.[30] In this struggle an outstanding part was played by Foreign Minister Herbert Evatt of Australia, Prime Minister Peter Fraser of New Zealand, and Sir A. Ramaswami Mudaliar. If Sir Ramaswami's proposal had been accepted, the concurrence of the permanent members of the Council would not have been required, at least for the amendment of the Charter.[31] However, the will of the permanent members prevailed and the veto went into the Charter.

The justification put forward by the permanent members for their extraordinary rights was that they, and they alone, had the power to enforce peace and that therefore the concurrence of each one of them was necessary in all matters which called for measures to enforce peace, that is, measures involving the employment of their military forces or measures whose consideration might lead to the employment of such forces. This point was elaborated in a statement issued by the delegations of the great powers at San Francisco.[32] In this statement it was also pointed out that the small powers, too, possessed the veto; for without the concurrence of at least two of them,

---

[30] See the statement of Sir Ramaswami Mudaliar, *UNCIO Documents*, Vol. XI, p. 174.

[31] *Ibid.*, p. 175.

[32] *Ibid.*, pp. 711-14.

there could be no substantive decision by the Security Council. The hope was expressed that the big as well as the small powers would use their veto with a sense of responsibility and therefore infrequently. This hope was destined not to fructify.

Thus the San Francisco Charter created what has aptly been described as a directorate of great powers, a directorate that is irremovable and immutable. This has resulted, on the one hand, in rendering illusory the principle of the equality of the member states, and, on the other, in qualifying the sovereignty of all of them, barring the Big Five. In the light of this fact, the declaration in Article 2(1) that "The Organization is based upon the sovereign equality of all its Members" is no less than a prevarication. Furthermore, the Security Council, which is charged with direction and control over the most vital affairs of the world, is not required to act according to any system of law, there being no obligation to follow international law. Consequently, the decisions of that body must rest upon agreement amongst the Big Five, based upon a consideration of what they think best in the circumstances of a given case, which, of course, does not exclude the consideration of their own interests in that case.

No substantive decision of the Security Council can be taken without the concurrence of all the permanent members. Thus, if a decision under Chapter VII is directed against one of the permanent members, that member can veto it. Therefore, such a decision can be taken only against a small power. But if a small power has the backing of a great power, that great power could veto any action by the Council, whether under Chapter VI or Chapter VII. Thus Council action is impossible even against a small power that is supported by a great power. This is borne out by Pakistan's experience in the Kashmir case.

The San Francisco document is less optimistic than the Covenant, whose preamble spoke of "the acceptance [by the members] of obligations not to resort to war." There is no such pious declaration in the United Nations Charter. Indeed, the Charter provides that the member states of the United Nations should place at the disposal of the Security Council armed forces to enable it to prevent war and suppress aggression. That the League of Nations could not command such forces was generally considered to be one of its weaknesses in the preservation of peace. As will be seen later, the provision in the Charter that the United Nations should have its armed forces was destined to remain a dead letter.

The Charter was built on the assumption that the co-operation between the great powers that had made possible the achievement of victory in war would continue. Although serious differences had begun manifesting themselves between the great powers, even before the end of the war in Europe, they co-operated with each other in the first session of the General Assembly, which did take a serious and non-contentious interest in disarmament and which did establish the United Nations Atomic Energy Commission. Thereafter the rift between Moscow and the West became wider and wider and great power co-operation ceased. With the deadlock in the Council of Foreign Ministers in September-October 1945, on the issue of the peace treaties with Italy, Romania, Bulgaria, and Finland, began the "cold war." President Truman's statement of 12 March 1947 and United States military and economic aid to the value of $400,000,000 to Greece and Turkey indicated that the United States was determined not to give in to Soviet Russia. As further evidence of that determination, the Marshall plan for Europe was announced in June 1947. The equally determined Soviet Union excluded itself and the East European countries from this plan.

Such was the international atmosphere when, on 30 September 1947, the new state of Pakistan was admitted to the United Nations. The dealings of that state with the United Nations have been very largely influenced by its relations with India. These we now proceed to consider.

chapter two

Pakistan: Origins and Relations with India

The new sovereign state of Pakistan came into existence on 14 August 1947. Prior to that date, the territories it comprised were a part of what was known as the British Indian Empire, which had extended over the whole of the Indo-Pakistan subcontinent (and which had for some fifty years also included Burma). That empire was peopled principally by two religious groups, the Hindus and the Muslims, whose numbers were roughly in the proportion of four to one.[1] To constitute Pakistan, those contiguous British-Indian provinces in which Muslims were in the majority were separated from the rest.

The British had ruled over some parts of this empire for nearly two hundred years. East Pakistan fell to them in 1757, after the battle of Plassey. However, British rule over some parts had lasted

---

[1] According to the census of 1941 (the last one before partition), out of a total population of 388,997,995, there were 94,389,428 Muslims.

for not much more than a hundred years; the Punjab, for example, was not formally annexed until 1846. For a hundred years after Plassey, the British ruled in the subcontinent through the East India Company which had been established in 1600 as a trading corporation. But after what is known as the Mutiny of 1857, the government of India became the direct responsibility of the British Crown.

Indian governments that preceded the British had maintained important foreign relations. The Mughals had special connections with the countries to the west and the northwest, *i.e.*, Iran, Turkistan, and Afghanistan. Indeed, until the reign of Aurangzeb (1659-1707), Afghanistan was an integral part of the Mughal Empire. The Mughals also had dealings with Europe, notably through the Portuguese, the Dutch, the British, and the French, who in the sixteenth century had started trading with the East. Before the supremacy of the British extended over the entire subcontinent, the Mahrattas in the Deccan and Hyder Ali and his son, Tippu, in the extreme south of the peninsula, had relations with the French. The Mahrattas suffered a decisive defeat at the hands of the Afghan King, Ahmed Shah Abdali, at Panipat in 1761. With the destruction of the power of Tippu and of the Mahrattas and, about the middle of the nineteenth century, of the Sikhs, the British reigned supreme.

Under the East India Company, and subsequently under the Crown, there was no question of any section of the people influencing foreign policy. It was always determined by the British. With the advance of the Russians in Central Asia and with the British becoming involved in wars with Afghanistan, the colonial government in India began playing a part in foreign affairs. But this was a subsidiary role, for all policy decisions were taken in London. However, in World War I the campaign in Mesopotamia was largely a responsibility of the British colonial government in India. Until independence, relations with the so-called Trucial States were managed and British establishments in the Persian Gulf and in the Arabian Sea were controlled by the colonial regime in India. Aden was until 1937 also under that government.

One significant consequence of alien rule in Asia was, generally speaking, to cut off its subjects from all contacts with foreign peoples, languages, and cultures, except those of the ruling power. Thus the Indo-Chinese had contacts only with the French, the Indonesians only with the Dutch. Likewise, the people of the subcontinent had contacts only with the British, and they knew only English for a foreign language. When they started crossing the dreaded ocean, they usually went to Britain. To this general rule the Muslims formed an exception. Because of their belief in the brotherhood of all Muslims, they took a sympathetic interest in the affairs of Muslims in other lands. They made pilgrimages to Mecca and other Holy Places in the Arabian peninsula. Because the Qur'án is in Arabic, they studied that language. They studied Persian also, to whose classics they were devoted and which was the official language of all pre-British regimes and, for some time, of the British administration as well.

The British adopted it as a cardinal principle of policy to suppress the Muslims of the areas which they conquered from them or otherwise took over. This they did in a particularly systematic manner in the vast region of Bengal and the adjoining North Western provinces. Thus, in Bengal, much of which is now in East Pakistan, in contravention to their engagements, the British under the "Permanent Settlement" substituted Hindu landlords for the Muslim landlords of former days, contending that the latter were corrupt.[2] They thus struck a crushing blow at the economic and cultural life of the Muslims. The British destroyed the Muslim system of education.[3] They confiscated Muslim educational trusts or misapplied their income.[4] They kept the Muslims out of the law and other professions.[5] By the middle of the last century the Muslims had

---

[2] Sir William Wilson Hunter, *The Indian Musalmans: Are They Bound in Conscience to Rebel Against the Queen?* (London: Trubner & Co., 1871), p. 159.

[3] *Ibid.*, pp. 183-84.

[4] *Ibid.*, pp. 184-86.

[5] *Ibid.*, p. 168.

been almost wholly excluded from all civil and military services of any consequence. Thus a Calcutta Muslim paper wrote in 1869:

> All sorts of employment, great and small, are being gradually snatched away from the Muhammadans, and bestowed on men of other races, particularly the Hindus. The Government is bound to look upon all classes of its subjects with an equal eye, yet the time has now come when it publicly singles out the Muhammadans in its Gazettes for exclusion from official posts .... In short, the Muhammadans have now sunk so low, that, even when qualified for Government employ, they are studiously kept out of it by Government notifications....[6]

This is confirmed by Sir William Hunter:

> ... The truth is, that when the country passed under our rule, the Musalmans were the superior race, and superior not only in stoutness of heart and strength of arm, but in power of political organization and in the science of practical government. Yet the Muhammadans are now shut out equally from Government employ and from the higher occupations of non-official life.[7]

The result of this policy was not merely that individual Muslims were kept out of lucrative and important positions but, also, that Muslims as a whole were disabled from pursuing any activities which needed influential patronage; and there were no activities that did not. This had a debilitating effect of a far-reaching character on the life of the Muslims as a community. The Hindus, who already had the monopoly of trade and commerce, now also occupied positions of power and influence and were thus provided with opportunities for furthering the advancement of their community. Denied all these advantages, the Muslims were confirmed in their backwardness. Towards the end of the nineteenth century, they began to fight their way back into the government services and the professions. In the face of a persistent demand, the British authorities

[6] *Ibid.*, p. 172.
[7] *Ibid.*, pp. 167-68.

c

were persuaded to abandon their policy of discrimination against the Muslims. But even when the Muslims had the needed qualifications, they had few chances due to lack of patrons. Eventually, as a result of public agitation, quotas were fixed for them in some of the services. Nevertheless, until the time of independence, the unbalance caused by deliberate suppression for over a century had not been redressed. In the private sector of employment the Hindus had a virtually exclusive control of trade, industry, and banking, in which, as a rule, a Muslim was never employed, except for manual work.

After the revolt of 1857 had been successfully put down by the British, the Muslims were in particular punished for it. Indeed, the retribution that was meted out to the Muslims of Eastern and Upper India was terrible. This was the second cycle of repression to which the Muslims had been subjected by the British. For a generation they literally lived in a state of inward terror. But mentally they were still defiant towards the British. To quote Hunter again:

> Had the Musalmans been wise, they would have perceived the change and accepted their fate. But an ancient conquering race cannot easily divest itself of the traditions of its nobler days. . . .[8]

The Hindus, on the other hand, enjoying the patronage of the British, were co-operating fully with them. For the Hindus it merely meant a change of masters, or so it seemed. The Hindus also felt no scruples in taking to English education.

As a result of English education, the twin ideas of nationalism and democracy were introduced into the subcontinent. Both these concepts were born in Europe where they were very much in fashion in the nineteenth century. In India the ideal of government had always been the Good King. The Hindus and the Muslims, who formed the bulk of the population, constituted two distinct communities. Not only their two religions but also their respective

---

[8] *Ibid.*, pp. 175-76.

social systems were antithetical to each other. Islam was mono-theistic, and prescribed a social order based on equality and brother-hood. Hinduism was generally polytheistic and idolatrous and enjoined caste and untouchability.[9] While there was an Indian culture in a wide sense, more significant were the separate cultures of the two communities. There was no intermarriage between Muslims and Hindus and the latter were forbidden to eat with the former. The situation created by two such divergent communities, living side by side, was without parallel in any country, for clearly the differences between them were not to be compared with those prevailing, in a Western country, between Christians and Jews or between Catholics and Protestants or, in an Arab country, between Muslims and Christians.

While the Hindus and Muslims could not have fused into a nation in the Western sense, they might have co-operated politically. As we shall see later, efforts were made to establish such co-operation. But they failed for lack of goodwill between the two communities. The leader of the untouchables, B. R. Ambedkar, ascribes this absence of goodwill to the fact that Hindus and Muslims

> have met as enemies on many fields, and the result of the struggle has often brought them into the relation of con-querors and conquered. Whichever party has triumphed, a great gulf has remained fixed between the two and their en-forced political union either under the Moghuls or the British instead of passing over, as in so many other cases, into organic unity, has only accentuated their mutual antipathy. ... [10]

European liberal ideas, under whose influence British imperialism was condemned in India, led the Hindus to resent intensely past Muslim imperialism over them. This heightened the antagonism between the two communities.

---

[9] See the statement of Mr. Gandhi in *Young India*, 6 Oct. 1921. Reprinted in *Young India, 1919-22* (Madras: S. Ganesan, 1922), Part II, p. 801.

[10] B. R. Ambedkar, *Pakistan or Partition of India* (Bombay: Thacker & Co., 1945), p. 324.

By the end of the nineteenth century the electoral system had been introduced, though to a very limited extent, into the government of the subcontinent. But the elections that were held demonstrated that, since most of the voters were Hindus, either Hindu candidates only were returned, or, here and there, a Muslim candidate, who was not mindful of the special needs of his backward community, and also generally not regarded as representative of it.[11] This led the Muslims in 1906 to demand the right to elect their representatives through their own separate constituencies. After much discussion, this right was conceded by the British government, with the approval of the foremost Congress leader of the time, the liberal G. K. Gokhale, who believed in "slowly evolving a nation out of the heterogeneous elements of which India was composed."[12] In 1906 the All-India Muslim League was also founded.

The principle of separate electorates was clearly not consistent with democracy as it is understood in the West. But in the peculiar conditions of the subcontinent, there was a good deal to be said for it. Among the few Muslims who were opposed to separate electorates was Mohammed Ali Jinnah, a rising young barrister of Bombay,[13] already known for the eloquence, ability, and character with which he was later to impress the pages of history. Mr. Jinnah entered politics in 1906 when he first appeared on the platform of the Indian National Congress party; he was soon to acquire an important place in the Congress. Established in 1885, the Congress party was shunned in body by the Muslims. But the concession of separate electorates to the Muslims allayed their fear of being swamped in the elections by the Hindu majority and removed their hesitation in supporting the Congress demand for freedom. On that basis, in 1916, the

---

11 Aga Khan, *World Enough and Time* (New York: Simon & Schuster, 1954), pp. 106-07; also published as *The Memoirs of Aga Khan* (London: Cassell & Co., 1954).

12 Quoted in Sir Reginald Coupland, *India: A Re-Statement* (London: Oxford University Press, 1945), p. 98.

13 Aga Khan, *op. cit.*, pp. 124-25.

Lucknow pact between the Congress and the League was arrived at, largely through Mr. Jinnah's efforts.

In 1920, the Congress party came under the sway of Mohandas K. Gandhi who, in order to wrest power from the British, introduced bold techniques that were novel in the subcontinent. Unlike some of the earlier westernised leaders of the Congress party, Mr. Gandhi did not keep religion altogether out of politics. He himself led the ascetic life of a Hindu *par excellence* and was venerated as a *Mahatma*, a Hindu holy man. Speaking in Hindu religious metaphors Mohandas Gandhi espoused ancient Hindu ideals, which led him to condemn mechanised industry and transport and to advocate a return to a primitive agricultural economy. He was devoted to the cow. He proclaimed his faith in his "inner voice" and in "soul force" as factors in politics. These attitudes, which won him the allegiance of the vast Hindu masses, eventually alienated the Muslims and were from the beginning repugnant to Mr. Jinnah. In 1921, because of his differences with Mr. Gandhi, Mr. Jinnah resigned from the Congress party.

There were once again important political differences between Hindus and Muslims, on account of the former having denounced separate electorates for the latter. Mr. Jinnah always felt that the easiest way to compel the British to part with power was to resolve Hindu-Muslim differences.[14] He took the view that if the Hindus would not agree to separate electorates for the Muslims, the latter should reconcile themselves to joint electorates, provided that their political and cultural interests were otherwise safeguarded in the constitution. This goal, he proposed, should be achieved through adopting a federal system under which Muslims in the provinces in which they were in the majority would have the benefits of local autonomy. He also suggested other constitutional safeguards similar to those enjoyed by the French minority in Canada. Mr. Jinnah, who had long been a student of federal constitutions, had during a visit

---

[14] Hector Bolitho, *Jinnah* (London: John Murray, 1954), p. 89.

to Canada familiarised himself with the devices that had been adopted in that country to allay the political fears of its French-speaking citizens.

Mr. Jinnah put forward his federal proposals at the All-Parties Convention held at Calcutta in December 1928; but the leaders of the Hindu parties, as well as the Congress, would not look at them. Sir Chimanlal H. Setalvad, liberal Hindu statesman and jurist, laments that through the rejection of Mr. Jinnah's proposals at Calcutta the opportunity was lost to bring about a peaceful settlement of the communal question.[15]

In 1930 a somewhat startling note was heard in the politics of the subcontinent. This note was sounded by Dr. Shaikh Mohammed Iqbal, who was later recognised as the preceptor of Pakistan. A versatile scholar, Iqbal had studied philosophy at Cambridge and Heidelberg. His message, poured forth in soul-stirring Urdu and Persian verse of exquisite beauty, was that Muslims should believe in self-respect and self-reliance, in endeavour and achievement. He denounced the notion of territorial nationalism as inconsistent with the Islamic conception of a universal brotherhood. The far-reaching influence of Iqbal's poetry and philosophy on the thinking of the Muslims of the subcontinent was one of the factors in the emergence of Pakistan.

Called upon to preside over the annual session of the Muslim League held at Allahabad, Iqbal had before him the depressing picture of the events of the preceding years, years of futile search for unity. In his address, he declared that "To base a constitution on the conception of a homogeneous India, or to apply to India principles dictated by British democratic sentiments, is unwittingly to prepare her for a civil war."[16] The Muslims had aspirations of their own. If these aspirations could not be realised within the framework of a

---

15 Chimanlal H. Setalvad, *Recollections & Reflections* (Bombay: Padma Publications, 1947), p. 351.
16 *Indian Annual Register* (Calcutta: Annual Register Office, 1930), Vol. II, p. 344.

united India, Muslims must have a separate homeland of their own. Iqbal had already stated that: "the formation of a consolidated North-West Indian Muslim State appears to me to be the final destiny of the Muslims at least of North West India."[17] He would like to see the Punjab, the North-West Frontier Province, Sind and Baluchistan amalgamated to form a separate state. Although Iqbal was the first front-rank Muslim leader to put forward the idea of a separate Muslim state, it was by no means new. It had been suggested in 1923 by Sardar Mohammed Gul Khan, President of the Islamic Anjuman of Dera Ismail Khan.[18]

The idea was taken up by a small group of Muslim students in England. The leader of this group was Chaudhry Rahmat Ali of Cambridge, who gave to the new state of his dreams the name of Pakistan and kept up the propaganda for it, before Mr. Jinnah and the Muslim League adopted it as their goal.[19] However, Pakistan was still regarded as impractical. Questioned about it in 1933, Sir Zafrulla Khan, later to become Foreign Minister of Pakistan, described it as "a students' scheme."[20]

In 1930 and 1931 two Indian Round Table Conferences were held in London. Amongst the delegates at these Conferences was Mr. Jinnah, and at the second Conference, Mr. Gandhi. The delegates were all agreed on the general principle of self-government. But what was to be done about the Hindu-Muslim problem? Setalvad tells us that the Muslim delegates pledged themselves to agree to

---

[17] *Ibid.*, p. 338.

[18] Ambedkar, *op. cit.*, pp. 326-28.

[19] It is sometimes contended that Chaudhry Rahmat Ali was an agent of British imperialism. A study of his writings would show that he could not have been the agent of any imperialism, least of all British. His principal work is *Pakistan: The Fatherland of the Pak Nation* (Cambridge: Pakistan National Liberation Movement, 1947). On two previous occasions, this study had been circulated in a cyclostyled form. His other works are mostly pamphlets, such as *The Millat of Islam* and *The Pakistan National Movement*.

[20] *Minutes of Evidence Given before the Joint Committee on Indian Constitutional Reform* (London: H.M.S.O., 1933), Vol. 11c, Question 9598.

joint electorates, provided the Hindus would agree to certain safe-guards for the Muslims.[21] The Hindu delegates, barring Setalvad and his liberal colleagues, refused to assent to this proviso. If they had assented to it, says Setalvad, "the subsequent political history of India would have taken a different turn."[22] The sorry story of the first Round Table Conference was repeated at the second, in which Mr. Gandhi had also participated.

However, Mr. Jinnah continued to hope and work for unity. In 1935, speaking before the Indian Legislative Assembly in the debate on the new Constitution Bill, he made yet another impassioned appeal for a settlement of the question of safeguards for the Muslims. The reply of the official leader of the Congress party, Mr. Jinnah reported, was "acquisition first, distribution afterwards."[23] In other words, the Muslims should unconditionally join with the Hindus in the attainment of independence and, after it had been attained, they would talk of safeguards for the Muslims. This attitude, which was adhered to by Pandit Nehru and other Congress leaders throughout, did nothing to allay Muslim apprehensions.

Muslim fears were aggravated by the situation which Sir Percival Griffiths describes in the following words:

> . . . The Congress High Command began to regard themselves as the only guardians of the true faith and Congressmen as the only patriots. From that it was a short step to the belief that only the Congress could claim to represent Indian opinion and feelings. Minorities were entitled to protection, but must seek it within the Congress fold. Spiritual arrogance grew apace and conditioned the approach of the predominantly

---

[21] Setalvad, *op. cit.*, p. 358.

[22] *Ibid.*, p. 359.

[23] Joint Committee Report Debate, Legislative Assembly, New Delhi, 7 Feb. 1935, *The Indian Annual Register* (Calcutta: Annual Register Office, 1935), Vol. I, p. 128. See also Congress resolution passed in March 1940, quoted by W. E. Duffett, A. R. Hicks, G. R. Parkin, *India Today* (New York: The John Day Company, 1942), p. 91. A week after the passing of this resolution Mr. Jinnah advised the League to adopt Pakistan as its goal, *ibid.*, pp. 92-93.

> Hindu Congress to the Muslims at the one time above all
> when conciliation was required. ....[24]

As dissatisfaction with Congress rule in the provinces grew, the number of Muslims in the Congress dwindled still further, the dissidents joining the Muslim League. This could not have been without good reasons. In their writings Congressmen admit that until the middle twenties the Muslims wholeheartedly co-operated with the Congress, and that they also participated in Mr. Gandhi's civil disobedience movement of the early thirties. But they offer no explanation for the general exodus of Muslims from the Congress after 1937, the year in which full self-government was established in the provinces, seven out of eleven of which had Congress governments. Pandit Nehru, who refers to the subject in his autobiography, also significantly refrains from offering an explanation of this phenomenon. He finds that Jinnah "drifted away" from the Congress.[25] Then he records that Maulana Mohamed Ali "drifted away" from the Congress.[26] Later, he observes that the Muslim masses "began to drift away in a separatist direction."[27]

As we have seen, the idea of Pakistan was already there. Says Griffiths:

> Except for a few cranks nobody in India took the Pakistan
> idea seriously until after the inauguration of Provincial au-
> tonomy, and it is undoubtedly true that the real creators of
> the demand for Pakistan were the Congress High Command.
> If they had been prepared to abate their claims to be the sole
> spokesmen for India and had tried to allay Muslim fears even
> slightly, Pakistan might never have come to birth. Unfortu-
> nately, the more moderate Muslim proposals for a federation

[24] Sir Percival Griffiths, *The British Impact on India* (London: MacDonald, 1952), p. 340.
[25] Jawaharlal Nehru, *An Autobiography* (London: John Lane, The Bodley Head, 1936), p. 68; also published as *Toward Freedom: The Autobiography of Jawaharlal Nehru* (New York: The John Day Co., 1942).
[26] *Ibid.*, p. 19.
[27] Jawaharlal Nehru, *The Discovery of India* (London: Meridian, Ltd., 1951), p. 418; also published as *Discovery of India* (New York: Meridian Books, Inc., 1951).

in which the balance of power would be in the provinces rather than in the centre received no serious consideration from the Congress. . . .[28]

Jinnah did not adopt the Pakistan idea in any haste. It went counter to much that he had stood for, and struggled for, in the course of his long political career. The argument for Pakistan was that the Muslims would have a homeland, an independent state of their own, comprising those areas of the subcontinent in which they were in the majority. The Muslims in the rest of the subcontinent, where they were a minority, would in any event be a minority. In any case, if there were two principal cultures in the vast region of the subcontinent, each one of them should have the assurance of preservation that only a state can give. Mr. Jinnah advised the League at its Lahore session of March 1940 to adopt Pakistan as its goal. The die was now cast.[29]

Setalvad, himself a declared opponent of Pakistan, sums up its origin as follows:

> The real parentage of the Pakistan movement can be traced to the Congress leaders, who, by the wrong way in which they handled the communal questions and by their behaviour when they were in power, created great distrust in the minds of the Muslim community which has driven them to advocate Pakistan. In the beginning, Congress leaders said that there was no communal problem in India and if there was, it could be settled after India got independence, forgetting that for the very purpose of getting independence, communal unity was essential. Then there is the tragic perversity which the Congress displayed when they assumed office under the Act of 1935. . . . They dealt unjustly with the Muslim community and made them hostile.[30]

If the upheaval of 1857 had resulted in the destruction of British power, doubtless several Muslim and Hindu states, presumably under the hegemony of the Mughal Emperor, would have come

---

[28] Griffiths, *op. cit.*, p. 342.

[29] *The Statesman* (Delhi), 24 March 1940.

[30] Setalvad, *op. cit.*, p. 414.

into existence. There would then have been no need for Pakistan. But that did not happen. The British, after suppressing the revolt with a heavy hand, initiated a process of developing self-governing institutions, which, it was evident, would one day lead to the establishment of a fully democratic system of government. To that the Muslims were not opposed. But they were not prepared to become another permanently depressed minority, dominated politically and culturally by the exclusive Hindu community. Because they were backward, because they desired to preserve their way of life, because they did not wish to be swamped by the Hindu majority, they constantly sought an arrangement with the Congress party whereby their political and cultural rights would be safeguarded in a democratic constitution. When they became convinced that such an arrangement would not be achieved, they demanded a separate homeland, a state of their own to "get rid of the present slavery of the British and the contemplated future caste Hindu domination, . . ."[31]

The last attempt to resolve the constitutional deadlock without partition was made in 1946. In May of that year certain proposals for the transfer of power were put forward on behalf of the British Cabinet;[32] proposals which, while avoiding partition, would have given a large measure of autonomy to the predominantly Muslim areas. The Muslim League accepted the proposals, as they stood, in the hope that they would ultimately result in the establishment of a sovereign Pakistan;[33] the Congress according to its own interpretation.[34] The failure of the two parties mutually to agree on the terms of the proposals rendered them unfruitful.

---

[31] Cited in *Keesing's Contemporary Archives* (London: Keesing's Publications, 1946-48), Vol. VI, p. 8080.

[32] *India (Cabinet Mission): Correspondence and Documents connected with the Conference between the Cabinet Mission and His Excellency the Viceroy and Representatives of the Congress and the Muslim League, May 1946* (London: H.M.S.O., 1946), Cmd. 6829, pp. 9-10.

[33] *India (Cabinet Mission): Correspondence with the Congress Party and the Muslim League 20th May - 29th June 1946* (London: H.M.S.O., 1946), Cmd. 6861, pp. 7-8.

[34] *Ibid.*, pp. 24-25.

On 3 June 1947, after consultations with the leaders of the Congress and the Muslim League, Lord Mountbatten, as the new Viceroy, announced a new plan which provided for the liquidation of the British Indian Empire. Out of this empire were to emerge the states of India and Pakistan, the former to comprise Hindu majority areas and the latter, Muslim majority areas.[35] This plan was assented to by the leaders of the various political parties, including Pandit Nehru.[36]

Unfortunately, from the moment of their birth in August 1947, relations between the new states of Pakistan and India have been bad. This fact has had far-reaching influence on their respective foreign policies and their attitudes towards international organisations. Objective considerations required close and continuing co-operation between the two countries. Hitherto they had constituted one political entity. Their economies, too, were interdependent. In the areas forming Pakistan there had been no industrial development worth the name; in fact the economic backwardness of these areas was one of the arguments for Pakistan. East Pakistan produced the bulk of the subcontinent's jute and all its jute of finer quality. But at the time of partition, the western boundary of East Pakistan was so drawn as to leave all the jute mills just a little way in India. In West Pakistan, where all the good quality cotton of the subcontinent was grown, there were but two small cotton mills. This cotton was utilised in the colossal textile industry of India or exported. Hides and skins came from Pakistan, which did not have a single tannery. A good deal of the wheat consumed in India was grown in West Pakistan. India produced all the high grade coal for railways and other purposes in Pakistan. Moreover, India was well established as a manufacturer of steel while the iron ore resources of Pakistan had not even been surveyed.

The defence system of the subcontinent had been conceived and built on the assumption of its unity. Necessarily as a result of

---

[35] *Indian Policy: Statement of 3rd June 1947* (London: H.M.S.O., 1947), Cmd. 7136.

[36] *The Statesman* (Delhi), 4 June 1947.

partition, there was to be a division of the army, the navy, and the air force, so that the two states should each have its own armed forces, both as a symbol of sovereignty and as an indispensable means for its preservation. But it was the hope of Mr. Jinnah that Pakistan and India would together evolve a "Monroe Doctrine" of their own.[37]

However, even before the date of independence, events took place that showed that neither in matters of political policy, economics, nor defence, was there to be co-operation between Pakistan and India. As Sir Zafrulla Khan was later to point out:

> Their very situation, their economy, the considerations of their defence and security demand that they ought to stand in friendly, cooperative relationship with each other. But at the moment they are deadlocked.[38]

Sir Zafrulla declared:

> From what might have been a position of positive and constructive beneficence for the human race, they have been pushed into one that threatens the peace and prosperity of the whole of South Asia and, in its turn, constitutes a grave menace to international security.[39]

The demand for the creation of Pakistan had been vigourously resisted by the Congress party, as it was by the Hindu community generally. But, of all the arguments advanced against it, the only one that has turned out to be correct was that adduced by Dr. Rajendra Prasad, now President of the Indian Republic. Writing in 1946, Dr. Prasad said:

> ... Whatever the position may be as far as the Muslims are concerned, the Hindus and Sikhs have declared their unequivocal

---

[37] *Some Recent Speeches and Writings of Mr. Jinnah* (Lahore: S. M. Ashraf, 1952), Vol. I, p. 241.
[38] Sir M. Zafrulla Khan, *Pakistan's Foreign Relations* (Karachi: Pakistan Institute of International Affairs, 1951), p. 8.
[39] *Ibid.*

determination to resist partition. . . . It is difficult to forecast what shape this conflict may take in the future. One thing is certain: partition is not likely to be attained with the goodwill of those most concerned, and this illwill is bound to persist on both sides, even if the proposal succeeds, even after the separation is effected. Distrust which is the basis of the proposal is bound to grow and any hope that after separation things will settle down and the independent states will soon become friendly will have been built on sand. . . .[40]

It is a melancholy fact that things have not settled down, and the two independent states of India and Pakistan are far from being friendly. Dr. Prasad's prophecy has come true to the last detail.

When Dr. Prasad wrote the words that have been quoted he undoubtedly knew the mind of his people. Yet no official explanation has ever been given of why the leaders of the Congress party agreed to the creation of Pakistan by rejecting Jinnah's federal proposals and the British Cabinet Mission's plan, either of which would have avoided partition. That they agreed to it with mental reservations is evident, on the one hand, from the policies that have been followed in India in respect to Pakistan and, on the other, from statements of Indians occupying the highest places in their country. That Pandit Nehru "found it difficult to recognize the very existence of Pakistan" is the judgement of Josef Korbel, who had discussions with him on the subject of Kashmir.[41] The late Sardar V. Patel, Deputy Prime Minister of India, in his message on India's first Independence Day, referred to "the bitterness and sorrow which partition has brought to those who cherished unity," and expressed "the full hope and confidence that sooner or later we shall again be united in common allegiance to our country."[42] More naively, Mrs. Vijaya Lakshmi Pandit, the sister of the Prime Minister of India, in the course of a

---

[40] Rajendra Prasad, *India Divided* (Bombay: Hind Kitabs, 1947), p. 337.

[41] Josef Korbel, "The Kashmir Dispute After Six Years," *International Organization*, Vol. VII, No. 4, Nov. 1953, p. 501.

[42] *Amrita Bazar Patrika* (Calcutta), 15 Aug. 1947.

statement in America, declared that her people had agreed to Pakistan only as a means of getting rid of the British.[43]

In its complaint to the Security Council in 1948, the government of Pakistan claimed that "India has never wholeheartedly accepted the partition scheme and has, since June 1947, been making persistent attempts to undo it" and that the object of those in power in India was "to paralyse Pakistan at the very start."[44] Nothing could have been better calculated to bring about this paralysis than the vast refugee movement that swept Pakistan on the morrow of its establishment, while it was still without a properly organized administration.[45] As is well known, this movement was the result of the large scale massacre of Muslims in the East Punjab. Under the partition scheme, this area had gone to India. The massacre was planned[46] and carried out by the Sikhs who, along with Hindus, had, to use the words of Dr. Prasad, "declared their unequivocal determination to resist partition." The Sikhs were assisted by the Rashtriya Swayam Sewak Sangh (RSS), the secret Hindu paramilitary organisation which proclaimed "doctrines that would have warmed the heart of Rosenberg."[47] The RSS, whose aim was the extermination of Muslims, did not fall from official grace in India until it was found to have been involved in the assassination of Mr. Gandhi.

In an official letter written at the time that the massacres in the Punjab were at their worst, Field Marshal Auchinleck recorded:

---

[43] Interview with Dorothy Brandon on behalf of the *New York Herald Tribune*, reported in *Dawn* (Karachi), 22 Aug. 1951.

[44] Security Council, Official Records (S.C.O.R.): 3rd Year, Supple. for Nov. 1948, pp. 72-73.

[45] The number of Muslim refugees from India in Pakistan is past the 8,000,000 mark. *Pakistan, 1953-54* (Karachi: Pakistan Publications), p. 196.

[46] This matter was discussed in detail in the Security Council. For a statement of the Pakistan case, see S.C.O.R., 3rd Year, No. 64, 289th and 290th Mtgs., 7 May 1948, pp. 16-32; for a statement of the Indian case, see pp. 37-47.

[47] Alan Campbell-Johnson, *Mission with Mountbatten* (London: Robert Hale, 1951), p. 282.

The massacre, arson and disorder which started in Amritsar
before the Boundary Commission had made its award had
nothing to do with the boundary or anything connected with
it. The whole movement was undoubtedly planned long before-
hand and soon gave rise to inevitable repercussion in the West
Punjab.[48]

To the undying shame of Pakistanis, there followed killing of Hindus
and Sikhs. Said Sir Zafrulla:

And whenever I have made a reference to this double tragedy,
I have never sought to excuse either the one side or the other.
Nevertheless, it is true that it was started on the other side.[49]

The government of Pakistan reported to the Security Council that
it had made repeated efforts to persuade the government of India
to arrest the course of "genocide" in the East Punjab and the
neighbouring areas, but without success.[50] In the words of Pakistan's
official declaration to the Security Council:

... it became clear that they [the government of India] were
determined to leave no Muslims in East Punjab. The Pakistan
Government appealed to the Governments of the British
Commonwealth to arrange a conference to find ways and
means of removing this serious threat to the peace and security
of the sub-continent, but the India Government opposed this
proposal on the ground of outside interference. The Pakistan
Government also proposed that United Nations observers
should immediately visit the disturbed areas but this too was
opposed by India.[51]

Finally, the government of Pakistan asked the Security Council to
appoint a commission or commissions "to investigate the charges
of mass destruction of Muslims" in India and to bring the rulers,
officials, and other persons responsible for it to trial before an
international tribunal and:

---

[48] John Connell, *Auchinleck* (London: Cassell & Co., 1959), p. 911.

[49] Sir M. Zafrulla Khan, *op. cit.*, p. 18.

[50] S.C.O.R., 3rd Year, Supple. for Nov. 1948, p. 77.

[51] *Ibid.*, pp. 77-78.

> To devise and implement plans for the restoration to their homes, lands and properties of Muslim residents of the Indian Union who have been driven out of or compelled to leave the Indian Union and seek refuge in Pakistan; ...[52]

This plea was rejected by the government of India, which absolutely refused to consider any proposal for the return of the refugees to their homes or the restoration to them of their properties. The government of India rejected the demand for an inquiry into the massacres, even though Pakistan was willing that similar charges made against Pakistan by India should also be investigated. "We do not shirk any inquiry,"[53] Sir Zafrulla Khan told the Security Council. In the same speech he declared: "Pakistan would welcome reciprocal investigation, arrangements, and settlements for achieving the objectives that we have set out here."[54] The matter was, however, referred to the United Nations Commission on India and Pakistan which was directed "to study and report to the Security Council when it considers it appropriate on the matters raised in the letter of the Foreign Minister of Pakistan, dated 15th January 1948,..."[55] Against this the government of India through its letter of 5 June 1948 protested and refused to acquiesce in it.[56]

There was also the matter of the division of government supplies between the two states. In a report written in September 1947, Field Marshal Auchinleck, who had been appointed Supreme Commander for India and Pakistan to effect a division of the armed forces and defence equipment, recorded as follows: "I have no hesitation whatever in affirming that the present India Cabinet are implacably determined to do all in their power to prevent the establishment of the Dominion of Pakistan on a firm basis."[57] The Field Marshal

---

[52] *Ibid.*, p. 74.
[53] S.C.O.R., 3rd Year, No. 64, 289th and 290th Mtgs., 7 May 1948, p. 21.
[54] *Ibid.*, p. 32.
[55] S.C.O.R., 3rd Year, 312th Mtg., 3 June 1948, p. 21.
[56] S.C.O.R., 3rd Year, Supple. for June 1948, p. 78.
[57] Connell, *op. cit.*, p. 920.

d

then referred to the campaign in India to "prevent Pakistan receiving her just share or indeed anything of the large stocks of reserve arms, equipment, stores, etc. held in the arsenals and depots in India."[58] This again was regarded in Pakistan as significant of India's intentions. There is no doubt that a certain amount of canteen equipment, saddlery and barrack room furniture was delivered, but practically no arms or ammunition. It was obvious that the motive was to keep Pakistan defenceless. As a consequence, Pakistan was compelled to buy arms at prices considerably higher than those at which India had acquired them from the British government's stores lying in India after World War II. This imposed an extraordinary strain on Pakistan's foreign exchange resources.

In September 1949 Pakistan was compelled to stand by itself, isolated from India, in financial and commercial matters. It was a very grave situation but Pakistan was able to face it. Following Britain's decision to devalue the pound sterling, India announced the devaluation of its rupee. The Pakistani rupee was not devalued. No country in the world questioned Pakistan's right to take this decision. But India declined to recognise the new par value of the Pakistani rupee. As a result all trade between the two countries came to a standstill.

The loss of the Indian market meant a serious threat to the jute growers of East Pakistan. The government of Pakistan immediately took steps to meet the situation. A Jute Board was set up and it fixed minimum prices for raw jute. Almost overnight the National Bank of Pakistan was brought into existence, one of its principal objects being the financing of the Jute Board's trade. The export facilities of the Indian port of Calcutta being no longer available, measures were taken to improve the Chittagong port. Plans were made for establishing jute spinning and weaving mills. Since Indian purchases of Pakistan cotton had also ceased, buyers for it were sought and

---

58 *Ibid.*, p. 921. This matter was referred to in Pakistan's complaint to the Security Council. See also Mr. Liaquat Ali Khan's telegram to Pandit Nehru, *Dawn* (Karachi), 27 July 1951.

found in the United Kingdom, China, the Soviet Union, France, Italy, Spain, and later in Japan.

In 1950 the International Monetary Fund examined the position of the Pakistani rupee and upheld its par value. Subsequently it was accepted by India also. In August 1953 Pakistan devalued its rupee, bringing it on par with the Indian rupee, *vis-à-vis* the dollar and the pound sterling, the Finance Minister explaining that this was done primarily to facilitate the export of the products of Pakistan's new textile industry.[59]

Trade between Pakistan and India was resumed in 1951 and since then successive trade agreements have been entered into between the two countries. However, the nature of the economic relationship between them has changed to such an extent that while India's share of Pakistan's trade in 1948-49 was about 47 per cent, in 1956-57 it had fallen to about 7 per cent.[60]

In the meanwhile, Pakistan, which had started with practically no industries, built up several significant ones, including a substantial cotton textile and jute industry.[61] Pakistan has no coal, except of a very low grade, and its natural supplier of coal is its next door neighbour. As a result of the stoppage of trade with India, however, Pakistan has taken to importing coal from such distant countries as South Africa, Poland, the Soviet Union, and China. There was, however, the expectation that in the long run Pakistan would have to depend upon India, at least for coal. But as a result of the discovery of natural gas in vast quantitites in both West Pakistan and East Pakistan, this will not be so in the future. Thus, the complementary character of the economies of Pakistan and India is diminishing.

The differences between the two countries to which we have referred are important in themselves; but they pale into insignificance before the disputes over Kashmir and the canal waters. Neither of

---

[59] Reported in *Dawn* (Karachi), 2 Aug. 1955.

[60] Percentages worked out in the Pakistan Institute of International Affairs.

[61] In 1947 the country started with no jute mills and 177,000 cotton spindles. In 1958 there were 6,500 jute looms and 1,844,000 cotton spindles.

these disputes would have arisen but for the wrongful award to India of certain Muslim majority areas of the Punjab.

To delimit the frontiers between India and West Pakistan and between India and East Pakistan, two Boundary Commissions were appointed. The princely states apart, the Commissions were to separate contiguous Muslim majority areas from contiguous non-Muslim majority areas, the former to go to Pakistan, the latter to India.[62] The Commissions were also permitted to take "other factors" into consideration. Owing to differences between Muslim and non-Muslim members, the Awards of the Commissions were given by Sir Cyril (afterwards Lord) Radcliffe, who was Chairman of both the bodies. Radcliffe gave away large contiguous Muslim majority areas to India, both in the west and the east, without so much as bothering to give his reasons for doing so. About some of such areas of the Punjab, all that he said in his Award was:

> I have hesitated long over those not inconsiderable areas east of the Sutlej River and in the angle of the Beas and Sutlej Rivers in which Muslim majorities are found. But on the whole I have come to the conclusion that it would be in the true interest of neither State to extend the territories of the West Punjab to a strip on the far side of the Sutlej and that there are factors such as the disruption of railway communications and water systems that ought in this instance to displace the primary claims of contiguous majorities.[63]

Disruption of railway lines is not irreparable, for these could be realigned. But so far as the water systems were concerned, the effect of the Award was not to save them from disruption but, as we shall see, to disrupt them with disastrous consequences. Radcliffe, a trained lawyer, could not but have known what he was doing.

Included in the Punjab areas given by Radcliffe to India were two Muslim majority *tehsils* (subdistricts) of the Gurdaspur district. We

---

[62] *Partition Proceedings* (Superintendent, Govt. Printing, West Bengal Govt., Alipore, West Bengal, 1950), Vol. VI, p. 9.
[63] *Ibid.*, p. 304.

have it on the authority of Lord Birdwood, an Indian Army officer of long experience, that

> ... It was Radcliffe's award to India of the Gurdaspur and Batala *tehsils*, with Muslim majorities, which rendered possible the maintenance of an Indian force at Jammu based on Pathankot as railhead, and which enabled India to consolidate her defences southwards all the way from Uri to the Pakistan border.[64]

The Radcliffe Award not only facilitated the Indian invasion and occupation of Kashmir, it also put India in a position to interfere with the flow of irrigation waters to Pakistan. The agricultural prosperity, indeed the very existence of the people of West Pakistan, depends upon its rivers and canals. The West Pakistan canal system irrigates some twenty million acres of land, growing wheat, rice, cotton, sugar cane, and other food and cash crops. Three of the rivers whose waters flow into Pakistan, namely, the Sutlej, the Beas, and the Ravi, originate in India. The other three rivers, the Chenab, the Jhelum, and the Indus, flow into Pakistan from Kashmir. If India had not been in occupation of Kashmir, there would have been no threat, at any rate, to the waters of the Chenab, the Jhelum, and the Indus.

The Boundary Commission had assumed that arrangements would be made to assure that a proportionate share of waters would continue to be supplied to the West Pakistan canals that originate in India, without variation or interruption.[65] Nevertheless, India has, on the one hand, been following a policy of large scale development of canals and hydro-electricity based upon the Sutlej and, on the other hand, claiming exclusive proprietary rights in the rivers and headworks lying in its territory.

India did not raise the matter of the waters before the Arbitral Tribunal that had been set up to decide disputed claims arising out

---

[64] Lord Birdwood, *A Continent Decides* (London: Robert Hale, 1953), p. 236.
[65] *Partition Proceedings, op. cit.,* Vol. VI, pp. 304-05.

of partition. India must therefore be presumed to have acknowledged the obligation to continue supplying water to Pakistan. However, on 1 April 1948, *i.e.*, on the morrow of the dissolution of the Tribunal, India during the sowing season cut off supplies in the Central Bari Doab and the Dipalpur Canals, the headworks of both of which had been placed by Radcliffe in India. The position for Pakistan was critical. On 4 May 1948 Pakistan obtained restoration of the flow of water by signing a provisional agreement with India, undertaking to pay seigniorage as well as a share of the carrying charges and recognising that the two canals were not as of right entitled to the waters of the Sutlej. This agreement was registered by India with the United Nations Secretariat.[66] However, Pakistan registered a certified statement to the effect that the agreement had been exacted under duress, as was obvious. Of course, registration with the United Nations does not confer on an agreement any more legitimacy than it intrinsically possesses. It is significant that the agreement of May 1948 concerns only the Central Bari Doab and the Dipalpur Canals and is irrelevant in respect of India's general claim of exclusive proprietary right in the waters that flow out of India into Pakistan.

The Pakistan case is based upon the recognised rules of international law governing riparian rights. According to these rights, an upper riparian cannot deny water to a lower riparian and Pakistan is entitled to continue drawing its historic supplies. This position is not affected by the fact that there is now an international boundary cutting across the rivers and canals, for the pre-existing servitude is not thereby extinguished. According to a study of the problem published in the Chatham House journal, *The World Today*:

> ... Two principles emerge from the decisions of the Supreme Court (of the United States), as well as, incidentally, from the decisions of the highest tribunals of other countries. The first is the principle of "equitable apportionment" of the waters of international rivers, and the second is that a State may not

66 *United Nations Treaty Series* (New York: United Nations, 1950), Vol. 54, No. 794, pp. 46-49.

unilaterally divert the waters of such rivers so as to prejudice and injuriously affect the rights of other riparian States.[67]

The waters dispute being obviously a justiciable one, Pakistan in 1950 suggested that it should be referred to the International Court of Justice at The Hague. This suggestion was rejected by Pandit Nehru on the plea that it would be a "confession of our continued dependence on others. That would hardly be becoming for proud and self-respecting independent nations."[68] Pandit Nehru must have known that no court would uphold India's claim to exclusive proprietary rights in the waters of the rivers that flowed out of its territory into Pakistan. In any event India's acceptance of the jurisdiction of The Hague Court had always excluded disputes with other members of the Commonwealth and now India has totally ceased to accept that jurisdiction. In 1952 India again reduced the supply of water during the important crop season of April to September, attributing this action to shortage of rainfall.[69] In June 1958 the flow of water again stopped, causing a great deal of hardship and alarm in Pakistan.[70]

The grave situation with which Pakistan was faced as a result of this dispute could not be better described than in the vivid words of David E. Lilienthal, former Chairman of the Tennessee Valley Authority, written after a study of the problem on the spot:

> No army, with bombs and shellfire, could devastate a land so thoroughly as Pakistan could be devastated by the simple expedient of India's permanently shutting off the sources of water that keep the fields and people of Pakistan alive.[71]

In 1953, on the invitation of Mr. Eugene Black, President of the International Bank for Reconstruction and Development, nego-

---

[67] "The Eastern Rivers Dispute between India and Pakistan," *The World Today*, Vol. 13, No. 12, Dec. 1957, p. 543.

[68] *No War Declaration and Canal Waters Dispute* (Karachi: Govt. of Pakistan, Ministry of Foreign Affairs and Commonwealth Relations, n.d.), p. 19.

[69] *Dawn* (Karachi), 7 June 1958.

[70] *Ibid.*, 21 June 1958.

[71] David E. Lilienthal, "Another Korea in the Making," *Collier's*, 4 Aug. 1951.

tiations began between the two countries for the sharing between them of the waters of the six rivers of the Indus system. During the negotiations India unilaterally decided that it would in 1962 stop the flow of the waters into Pakistan.[72] Nevertheless, the negotiations continued. On 1 March 1960 the World Bank announced that it hoped that final agreement would be reached within two months on all points outstanding between India and Pakistan over the Indus basin waters question and that a treaty embodying that agreement would be signed by the two countries. The announcement stated further that the treaty would be based on a division of the Indus waters on the lines of proposals made by the Bank to the two governments in 1954: the three eastern rivers of the Indus system (Sutlej, Beas, and Ravi) would be for the use of India and the three western rivers (Indus, Jhelum, and Chenab) would be for the use of Pakistan. This arrangement would necessitate the construction of works to transfer from the three western rivers supplies to meet the irrigation uses in those areas of Pakistan which had hitherto depended for supplies from the three eastern rivers. Total cost of the works is estimated to be $1,000 million, partly in foreign exchange and partly in local currencies. It was intended that the Bank should give loans to India and Pakistan of the order of $103 million. Foreign exchange grants by friendly governments would be:

Australia	£	6,964,286
Canada	$	22,100,000
Germany	M	126,000,000
New Zealand	£	1,000,000
United Kingdom	£	20,860,000
United States	$	177,000,000

The United States would also provide $103 million in loans and the equivalent of $235 million in local currency. The programme, whose cost would be spread over approximately ten years, would be generally supervised by the Bank.[73]

[72] *Dawn* (Karachi), 6 June 1958.

[73] International Bank for Reconstruction and Development, Press Release No. 626, 1 March 1960, re: Indus Waters.

The success so far achieved in the negotiations for the settlement of this dispute between India and Pakistan is a tribute to the patience and skill of the officials of the World Bank. This success brings into bold relief the role of the United Nations in the settlement of difficult international questions, the Bank being one of the specialised agencies of the United Nations. The government of Pakistan, in a statement issued on 1 March 1960, recorded its thanks to the Bank for its endeavours and expressed its gratitude to the nations that had given assurances of financial assistance for the implementation of the proposed settlement.[74]

It may well be true that India would not have assented to an arrangement more satisfactory from Pakistan's point of view than the one which has emerged from the negotiations conducted under the auspices of the World Bank. Public opinion in Pakistan has not yet assessed the full implications of that arrangement. One might, however, be permitted to make a comment or two. It must be realised that so long as India is in possession of Kashmir, it will be in a position to interfere with the flow of water in the three western rivers, on which Pakistan is to depend exclusively in the future. Thus the proposed treaty, which seeks to settle one of the two major disputes that have embittered relations between India and Pakistan, cannot bring full satisfaction to the people of the latter country unless the other dispute, *i.e.*, the one over Kashmir, is also speedily settled. A just solution of the waters dispute would have been to get India to respect international law and to continue to supply Pakistan with the latter's historic share of the waters of the eastern rivers, leaving India also free to draw its historic share of those waters. That solution would also have been more economical and more simple than the one devised by the World Bank, which involves the construction of works over a long period of time and at an enormous cost. It might be pointed out that West Pakistan is a low rainfall area and needs its share of the waters of the eastern rivers. India

---

[74] *Dawn* (Karachi), 1 March 1960.

does not need more than its historic share of those waters, for the areas to which it is now diverting them have heavy rainfall and/or could be served by the Jumna and the Ganges. What the effect of the proposed treaty will be on Pakistan's legal right to its historic share of the waters of the eastern rivers will depend on how the relevant clauses of the treaty are worded.

The years since independence have thus been agitated ones. Nevertheless, Pakistan has tried to work out ways of peaceful settlement of conflicts with India. Thus, the government of Pakistan welcomed the Indian proposal of December 1949 that the two governments should make a joint declaration condemning resort to war as a means of settling disputes between them. This proposal led to correspondence between the Prime Ministers of the two countries which continued for over a year but without yielding any results. The terms of the declaration proposed by the government of India were as follows:

> The Government of India and the Government of Pakistan ... declare that they condemn resort to war for the settlement of any existing or future disputes between them. They further agree that the settlement of such disputes between them shall always be sought through recognised peaceful methods, such as negotiation, or by resort to mediation or arbitration by special agency set up by mutual agreement for the purpose, or by agreed reference to some appropriate international body recognised by both of them.[75]

When welcoming the proposal Prime Minister Liaquat Ali Khan said that "the declaration as proposed by India might appear to be a rather unnecessary repetition of certain portions of the United Nations Charter," to which both India and Pakistan were committed. Writing to Pandit Nehru on 14 February 1950 he proposed that, in addition to the declaration, there should be a clear-cut procedure with an agreed timetable, which would make it binding on both governments to carry through the settlement of the disputes to a peaceful conclusion.[76]

---

[75] *No War Declaration and Canal Waters Dispute*, *op. cit.*, p. 12.
[76] *Ibid.*, pp. 4-5.

According to the procedure that Mr. Liaquat Ali Khan proposed, all the disputes between the two countries would be taken up one by one and attempts made to settle them, first through negotiation; but if in any case negotiation did not lead to a settlement within a specified period of time, mediation was to be automatically resorted to; and if mediation also did not yield results within a specified period of time, the matter was automatically to go to arbitration. He declared that Pakistan was willing ultimately to accept the decision of an arbitrator in all its disputes with India.[77] However, Pandit Nehru was not prepared to go beyond an expression of sentiments, such as was contained in his draft. To this, Mr. Liaquat Ali Khan, who probably had in his mind the fate of the Kellogg Pact, saw no purpose in agreeing.

It is a depressing picture that we have presented of the relations between India and Pakistan. But because the two states have come into existence as the result of a territorial partition, should their relations necessarily be bad? Spain and Portugal together constitute the Iberian Peninsula, and there are between them no natural boundaries. Norway separated from Sweden. More recently and nearer home, Burma, which was a part of the British Indian Empire, was separated from it and is now an independent sovereign state. Yet there is normality in the relations of Spain and Portugal and of Sweden and Norway. Nor is there bad feeling between Burma and Pakistan, or Burma and India. For the bad feeling between Pakistan and India, the logic of partition is not to blame. The relations between India and Pakistan have been bad because there are specific disputes between them. Unless those disputes are resolved, there can be no hope of improvement in their relations or assuagement of Pakistan's fear of Indian intentions.

Robert Schuman, former Prime Minister of France, once observed that since 1871 the foreign policy of his country had "been continuously dominated by one main preoccupation, that of ensuring

---

[77] *Ibid.*

her security and independence from her neighbour, Germany."[78]
Unfortunately, the foreign policy of Pakistan has in a similar manner
been dominated by considerations of security and independence from
its neighbour, India.

---

[78] Robert Schuman, *French Policy Towards Germany Since the War* (London:
Oxford University Press, 1954), p. 1.

chapter three

Regional Arrangements

Having achieved their new state after a great struggle, both against the alien ruling power and against the preponderant Hindu majority, and having paid the price of that triumph in blood and suffering of every imaginable kind, the people of Pakistan are naturally very jealous of its integrity and freedom. Whatever they may think of themselves, and whatever others may think of them, any judgement on the affairs of Pakistan which is not based upon a recognition of this fact would be wholly unreal.

To preserve Pakistan, to safeguard and to defend it, has throughout been the first consideration of its policy makers. The urgency of this consideration will be appreciated when one recalls that the neighbouring state of India has followed a policy which, to put it mildly, is unfriendly towards Pakistan. It is against this background that Pakistan's foreign policy and in particular its policy in respect of regional alliances should be understood.

Pakistan consists of two territories, West Pakistan and East Pakistan, separated from each other by over a thousand miles of India. West Pakistan has a common border with Iran and Afghanistan and is separated from Soviet Asia by a narrow belt of Afghan territory which is nowhere more than fifty miles across. At one point, the Wakhan tongue, as this belt is sometimes called, is only eight miles wide, and it is possible to look across from Pakistan to the USSR. As the crow flies, Karachi, the first capital of Pakistan, is less than a thousand miles from the Soviet frontier.

Pakistan controls the northwest mountain passes through which alone a physical invasion of the subcontinent has been considered possible. It was through these passes that Cyrus in the sixth century B.C. and Alexander in the fourth century B.C. invaded the subcontinent. They, in turn, were followed by other invaders, Turki, Persian, and Afghan. It was through these passes that the British, in the nineteenth century, feared an invasion of the subcontinent by the Russians, who were extending their empire in Central Asia. Except for the border areas and the extensive wastes of Baluchistan, West Pakistan is generally level country, with a railway system connecting its principal towns and linking the Khyber Pass and other fortified points on the frontier with the port and city of Karachi.

East Pakistan is flat and tropical, with large torrential rivers and a criss-cross of smaller streams. It has a common frontier with Burma but the lush jungle here is mountainous and, as was demonstrated in World War II, extremely difficult country. To the northeast, with Burmese territory intervening, is the vast Chinese perimeter. To the east and south of Burma lie Thailand and Malaya. Both the Pacific and the Indian Oceans wash their shores. The Indo-Chinese frontier beyond Thailand is less than five hundred miles from the eastern frontier of East Pakistan.

Such, then, is the geographical setting of Pakistan. This situation places Pakistan in both the Middle East and Southeast Asia and is of considerable military importance. However, until some time after the creation of Pakistan, the Western powers evinced no apparent interest in this situation. It is hard to believe that they did not regard it as important. The British had a long tradition of dealing with this region. The Americans, too, had during World War II acquired military experience in this area and amplified their knowledge of the territory. It may be that the Western powers were waiting to see whether the new state of Pakistan would collapse, as was predicted in India. So far as the United States was concerned, its main centre of interest in Asia was still China, and American hopes and endeavours were concentrated on the prevention of a Communist victory over Chiang Kai-shek.

We have noticed the proximity of the northern frontier of West Pakistan to the Central Asian territories of the USSR. The creation of a new state so close to their borders must have made an immediate impression on the Soviet leaders. They had devoted a great deal of attention and effort to consolidating and developing their Central Asian territories. They had a systematic understanding, partly inherited from the previous Czarist regime, of the demarcation of the southern approaches to their frontiers, and generally of the areas that lie between those frontiers and the Arabian Sea. Take just one sentence uttered by Georghi Vasilievich Chicherin in 1923: "The old English policy was to make Russian-English conflict impossible by the interposition of barriers—a closed Dardanelles at the one side, and an independent Afghanistan at the other."[1] The Soviet Commissar also had some ideas about "the ridge of the Hindu Kush"[2] on the Pakistan side of Wakhan. The significance of Karachi, seaport and airport, as a strategic base and a nerve centre of communications, could not have been lost upon the Soviet

---

[1] Jane Degras, ed., *Soviet Documents on Foreign Policy* (London: Oxford University Press for the Royal Institute of International Affairs, 1951), Vol. 1, p. 420.

[2] In referring to the Hindu Kush, Chicherin said: "You are uneasy because our horsemen have reappeared on the heights of the Pamirs, and because you no longer have to deal with the half-witted Tsar who ceded the ridge of the Hindu Kush to you in 1895." *Ibid.*, p. 350.

leaders. In any event, they were not slow in manifesting their interest in Pakistan. In 1949, even before the two countries had exchanged diplomatic representatives, there came an invitation to Prime Minister Liaquat Ali Khan to visit Moscow. Mr. Khan did not go to Moscow.

Ideologically, an alliance with the Soviet Union could have had no attraction for Mr. Liaquat Ali Khan or for any other Pakistani statesman. It is doubtful that such an alliance had ever been favourably contemplated by them. They may have feared that if they entered into such an arrangement with the Soviet Union they would ultimately have to change their political and economic systems, adopt Communism, and identify themselves wholly with the USSR in matters of foreign policy. Furthermore, Pakistanis were deeply disappointed by the Soviet attitude in the Security Council towards the Kashmir question, which in its earlier stages was apparently one of sheer indifference and later became one of positive antipathy to the Pakistan case. The Soviet government's part in the creation of the state of Israel, too, made a most unfavourable impression in Pakistan. Thus, Pakistanis had seen that Soviet policies could be just as opportunistic and unprincipled as those of the other imperialist powers.

Pakistanis were profoundly interested in the republics of Central Asia, the Turkistan of the pre-Soviet days, with which they had not only religious but deep racial, cultural, and historical ties. Were not the arches and domes of Samarkand the prototypes of those of Lahore? And Turkistan was just a few miles from Pakistan's frontier. Pakistanis had respect for the impressive agricultural and industrial development that had taken place there amid social conditions similar to their own.[3] But development is not everything. In December 1917 Lenin and Stalin had issued their famous appeal to the "toiling and disinherited Moslems of Russia and the East." Through this appeal all those whose mosques and prayer houses were destroyed, and whose religion and customs were trampled on by the Russian

---

[3] *Dawn* (Karachi), 29 April 1958 (editorial).

Czars and tyrants were assured: "Henceforward your beliefs and customs, your national and cultural institutions, are declared free and inviolable! Build your national life freely and without hindrance."[4] Pakistanis wondered to what extent the faith and customs and national and cultural institutions of the Muslims of Turkistan were free and whether they had really been able to build up their national life unhindered. The Republics of the Soviet Union were supposed to possess the right to diplomatic representation in foreign countries. No representative came to Pakistan from any of the Central Asian Republics. To say the least, it was all very bewildering.

In 1950 Mr. Liaquat Ali Khan went to America. His speeches in the United States and Canada left no room for doubt that, ideologically, Pakistan was pro-West and put an end to all speculation about the possibility of an alliance with Russia. However, there was no urgency for forging any formal bonds with the West. The foreign policy of Pakistan remained independent. Thus, speaking in March 1951, Mr. Liaquat Ali Khan said that:

> Pakistan was neither tied to the apron-strings of the Anglo-American bloc, nor was it a camp follower of the Communist bloc. It steered clear of the inter-bloc rivalry, and had an absolutely independent foreign policy. Pakistan had all along been uninfluenced by the inter-bloc struggle going on in the world, and had supported the cause which it considered to be just. The records of the U.N. debates bear testimony to this fact. Sometimes we agreed with the Western bloc and sometimes with the Communist bloc, as the situation and the matter under discussion demanded. Pakistan could pursue such an independent course because it was not under the obligation of any foreign Power. We have not been assisted by any country in the world and whatever we have achieved has been through our own resources. Therefore, the question of subservience in foreign policy did not arise.[5]

In July 1951, some three months before Mr. Liaquat Ali Khan's

---

[4] *Soviet Documents on Foreign Policy, op. cit.*, p. 16.
[5] *Dawn* (Karachi), 9 March 1951.

e

assassination, came the threat of an Indian invasion, with almost all of India's forces and its armoured divisions concentrated on the borders of Pakistan. Although the threat did not develop, it showed vividly, as nothing else had done before, that even an outright full scale attack by India on Pakistan was not beyond the range of possibility. This made Pakistani statesmen reflect on some hard facts, the very facts which negated the Indian allegation that Pakistan intended to invade India. India had nearly five times the population of Pakistan and far greater resources. India had in 1951 at least twice the armed strength of Pakistan and, to sustain it, a relatively industrialised economy, which Pakistan lacked. India had also been fortunate in inheriting all the arsenals and ordnance factories that the British had established in the subcontinent. Pakistan had none of these although it was building some. On the other hand, India had denied to Pakistan the latter's share of the military stores left by the British in the subcontinent. Although Pakistan had made extensive purchases of arms at high prices in foreign markets, risking a severe strain on its finances and in particular on its foreign exchange resources, it was far weaker than India.

The tortuous steps by which India had sought to consolidate its hold over Kashmir were in themselves alarming evidence of India's attitude towards Pakistan. India had spent vast sums of money in fighting a war in Kashmir, and was spending similar large amounts in maintaining its military occupation of that state. India's refusal to allow a plebiscite was a violation of international agreements to which it was committed, and a defiance of the United Nations. This stand had given India a bad name throughout the world. Why was India enduring all this ? Not, as Pakistanis appraised the situation, for a small bit of territory, but rather because, with India in possession of Kashmir, Pakistan would be strategically encircled. Indian occupation of Kashmir means political and financial stresses for Pakistan. But Pakistan cannot abandon its stand on Kashmir.

In the event of possible war-like action against Pakistan by a superior power like India, how was Pakistan to protect itself?

Clearly its own armed strength would not be sufficient. Nor could reliance be placed in the United Nations, for it had failed to develop into an effective instrument for the maintenance of world peace. Recognition of this fact had led to the establishment of regional defence arrangements such as NATO and ANZUS. Countries like Britain and France and less-developed ones, like Yugoslavia and Turkey, were taking military aid from the United States. Should Pakistan do likewise in its desperate situation? The United States, as we shall presently see, was keen on having a defence pact with Pakistan.

The collapse of Chiang Kai-shek's authority in China and the establishment of a Communist regime in that country changed the entire aspect of international relations in Asia. It meant an immeasurable accession to the strength of the Soviet Union and the Communist world and an equally great setback for the Western powers. It meant that the United States, the leader of the West, should re-examine its position in Asia. Up to that point, the Americans had taken steps to bolster Turkey at the western end of the Russian "barrier" in Asia. South of that barrier lay the greatest oil resources of the world—in Iran, Bahrein, Saudi Arabia, Kuwait, and Iraq. There were in these oil fields vast wealth and vast resources of industrial power. The safeguarding of the oil resources of the Middle East as well as the preservation of their communications through it was an urgent necessity for the Western powers. Hitherto, they had depended mainly on the base at Suez, whose efficacy had been demonstrated in World War II. But in view of pressing Egyptian claims, the future of Suez was uncertain; and, in any event, the nature of war had changed to such an extent that Suez was no longer sufficient. What was needed was a larger and a different structure in which the people of the area themselves could participate (under the patronage of the West).[6]

---

[6] See the statement of the British Minister, Mr. Anthony Head, *Chronology of International Events and Documents* (London: Royal Institute of International Affairs, 1954), Vol. X, p. 490.

In October 1951 the Western powers and Turkey put forward a proposal for an Allied Middle East Command. This was rejected by Egypt. Nearly a year later came the plan for a Middle East Defense Organization. The proposal was abandoned because of Britain's disputes with Egypt and Iran, and hostility between the Arab nations and Israel.[7] Britain's dispute with Egypt related to the latter's demand for the evacuation of the Suez Canal zone. The dispute with Iran arose out of the nationalisation of that country's oil industry, which was run by a British company. Pakistan fully appreciated and sympathised with the Arab and Iranian claims. As regards the Arabs' dispute with Israel, Pakistan had completely identified itself with the former. If the Arabs and the Iranians, after settling with the British, had agreed to join the Middle East Defense Organization, it was conjectured that Pakistan would also join it. This raised a storm of protest in India[8] and was denounced, both officially and unofficially, as a threat to the security of India. This was the first occasion when Indian opinion plainly declared its resentment of any increase in the defence potential of Pakistan.

In the winter of 1952-53 Pakistan was faced with severe difficulties in the form of a serious economic crisis and a desperate food shortage, the latter due partly to a drought and partly to India's not allowing Pakistan, in the judgement of Pakistanis, its full share of water in the canals that originated in India. There had been "a catastrophic fall in the country's revenues. Heavy and drastic cuts had been imposed on Government expenditure, including that on defence, which had to be curtailed at the risk of security."[9] The leaders of Pakistan were, however, still following the late Liaquat Ali Khan's policy of not placing their country under obligation to a foreign power. In the spring of 1953 the United States came forward with a gift of 610,000 tons of wheat, of the value of

---

[7] *The Statesman* (New Delhi), 1 June 1952.

[8] *Dawn* (Karachi), 20 Jan. 1953; *The Eastern Economist* (New Delhi), 16 Jan. 1953.

[9] See the statement of Prime Minister Mohammed Ali, *Dawn* (Karachi), 2 March 1954.

$67,200,000. The friend in need began to be looked upon as a friend indeed. This went a long way towards removing the hesitation of Pakistani leaders in agreeing to further arrangements with the United States, arrangements that were indicated by Pakistan's ideological affinities and calculated to insure it against aggression and to lighten its financial burdens.

When, for lack of support, the plan for a Middle East Defense Organization was abandoned, the United States began looking for some alternative arrangement for the region. That country was, as we have seen, giving aid to Turkey at the western end of the Russian barrier in Asia. At its eastern end was Pakistan. Following the logic of former British policy in the area, to which Mr. Chicherin had referred in 1923, it seemed imperative to strengthen Pakistan. If Pakistan and Turkey could be persuaded to enter into an agreement with each other, they would provide the core in a substitute for the abortive Middle East Defense Organization. Iraq and Iran had been sounded and there was hope that they would join the new arrangement. The Turco-Pakistani Pact was announced on 19 February 1954. A week later President Eisenhower revealed the decision to give military aid to Pakistan. This was confirmed the same day by Prime Minister Mohammed Ali of Pakistan.

Explaining why Pakistan had entered into the aid agreement with the United States, the Prime Minister said:

> Hitherto, Pakistan has striven to build up her defences with her own unaided resources. But under rapidly changing requirements of modern warfare, the demands of adequate defence are becoming progressively heavy and are imposing an increasingly burdensome strain on the country's economy. In consequence, the development of the country's resources has, to a considerable degree, had to be sacrificed to the primary need of building up its defences. Assured thus of the adequacy of its defence for safeguarding its security and preserving its independence, Pakistan will be able to devote its resources increasingly to the development of its human and material wealth, so as to achieve greater economic stability and pros-

perity. It must be emphasized that the decision to obtain
military aid from the United States is not aimed against any
country whatsoever. Pakistan has never entertained, and does
not entertain, any aggressive intentions.[10]

In Pakistan the pact with Turkey was welcomed as an alliance
between two Muslim countries; and, of all the Muslim countries,
none was respected more than Turkey. The Prime Minister of
Pakistan referred to the pact as "the first major step towards
strengthening the Muslim world," and said that it was "in the interest
of all the people of the region."[11] While no reference was made by
Turkish statesmen to the Islamic character of the arrangement, there
was no doubt that it was very popular in Turkey also. There was
a precedent for it in the Sa'adabad Pact of 1937, entered into by
Turkey, Iraq, Iran, and Afghanistan. Between the two instruments
there are many points of similarity, both emphasising the need for
the maintenance of friendly relations between the contracting parties
and of international peace generally. Under both there is a promise
of non-intervention in the internal affairs of the participants. While
the Sa'adabad Pact declared allegiance to the League of Nations,
the Turco-Pakistan Pact affirms faith in the purposes and principles
of the United Nations Charter. Under the Sa'adabad Pact the
contracting parties undertook to refrain from "any act of aggression
directed against the other"; under the Turco-Pakistani Pact "from
participating in any alliance or activities directed against the other."
Both contain provisions for consultation and co-operation, those in
the later document being of a more specific nature, extending to
such matters as technical experience and progress and the production
of arms and ammunition.

The agreement between the United States and Pakistan aims at
fostering "international peace and security within the framework
of the Charter of the United Nations"; at promoting "individual
and collective self-defence" in support of the purposes and principles

---

[10] *Ibid.*, 26 Feb. 1954.
[11] *Ibid.*

of the Charter. It reaffirms determination to give full co-operation "to the efforts to provide the United Nations with armed forces as contemplated by the Charter."[12] Assistance to Pakistan is to be governed by the provisions of the Mutual Defense Assistance Act of 1949 and the Mutual Security Act of 1951 of the United States. Explaining the requirements of the relevant provisions of those Acts, President Eisenhower said:

> ... equipment, materials or services provided will be used solely to maintain the recipient country's internal security and for its legitimate self-defense, or to permit it to participate in the defense of the area of which it is a part. Any recipient country also must undertake that it will not engage in any act of aggression against any other nation.[13]

Does the acceptance of American military aid make it obligatory for Pakistan to take sides with the United States in the event of a war? That there is no such obligation was categorically stated by Prime Minister Mohammed Ali.[14] This was confirmed by the American Ambassador to Pakistan, Horace A. Hildreth.[15] The same was the assertion of Foreign Minister Zafrulla Khan in an interview on 12 April 1954 with an American journalist, Norman Cliff. But the Foreign Minister was careful to point out that:

> ... the possibility of remaining neutral does not depend merely upon the desire of a people or a government. Left to themselves, no people or government would wish to invite the miseries and horrors of war to their areas. Should, however, a conflict between the Great Powers become unavoidable, the choice of neutrality might become an illusion.[16]

Nor did the pact imply the granting of military bases by Pakistan

---

12 *United Nations Treaty Series* (New York: United Nations, 1954-1955), Vol. 202, No. 2736, p. 301.

13 U.S. Dept. of State *Bulletin*, Vol. XXX, No. 768 (15 March 1954), p. 401.

14 *Dawn* (Karachi), 23 Feb. 1954.

15 *Ibid.*, 1 April 1954.

16 *Ibid.*, 13 April 1954.

to the United States. This was reiterated by the government of
Pakistan in its note of May 1954, rejecting the Soviet protest against
Pakistan accepting American aid.[17]

Did the acceptance of American military aid make Pakistan
subservient to the United States in matters of foreign policy?
Answering this question, Sir Zafrulla Khan said:

> Certain values that we share, we shall continue to share;
> where our policies differ, we shall continue to differ. If the
> feeling of sharing together deepens, then there will be greater
> accord. For instance, on the question of colonial domination,
> Pakistan has often opposed the stand taken by the Western
> Powers and has been supported by the U.S.S.R. and the
> Eastern Group. We continue determined to press our point
> of view.[18]

In the neighbouring country of India, the proposal for American
aid to Pakistan was not only received with disfavour, but every
effort was made to prevent its finalisation. As early as 15 November
1953, Pandit Nehru had stated: "We are deeply concerned at the
consequences that will follow from Pakistan joining an American
sponsored defence organization."[19] On 31 December 1953, he stated:
"The cold war comes to India's borders."[20] Three days later, he
declared: "It is a step not only towards war, even world war, but
one that will bring the war right up to our doors."[21] Pandit Nehru
expressed the fear that American military aid "might possibly be
used against India."[22] In the meanwhile, in violation of the Indian
undertaking to hold a plebiscite in Kashmir, steps were being taken
to integrate that state with India. On 22 February Pandit Nehru,
speaking about the plebiscite in Kashmir, said: "American aid to

---

17 *Ibid.*, 5 May 1954.
18 *Ibid.*, 13 April 1954.
19 *Ibid.*, 16 Nov. 1953.
20 *The Statesman* (New Delhi), 1 Jan. 1954.
21 *Ibid.*, 4 Jan. 1954.
22 *Dawn* (Karachi), 24 Jan. 1954.

Pakistan would change the context of events."[23] Finally, he made the astonishing announcement that:

> American military officers serving as United Nations observers in Kashmir could no longer be treated by India as neutrals, in view of the American military aid to Pakistan, which was foreign intervention in Pakistan-Indian problems.[24]

Indian contentions against Pakistan's military aid pact with the United States were answered by Foreign Minister Zafrulla Khan. Referring to the view that India's acceptance of large scale economic assistance from the United States had not brought the cold war any nearer to the subcontinent, Sir Zafrulla Khan wondered how it could be argued that United States military aid to Pakistan was an invitation to cold war, especially considering the strict limitation that such aid could not be used for aggression. That in effect there was no difference between military aid and economic aid, such as India was receiving, was not exclusively a Pakistani view.[25] It was held in other quarters, too, and was advanced, for example, by Sir Alexander Clutterbuck, the British High Commissioner in India.[26]

Regarding United Nations observers of American nationality in Kashmir, Pakistan's Foreign Minister said that they had discharged their duties with absolute impartiality. By impeaching their loyalty, Pandit Nehru was merely seeking:

> . . . excuses, however flimsy, for not proceeding with the implementation of the international agreement with regard to the settlement of the Kashmir problem and of his own undertaking that the plebiscite administrator shall be appointed by the end of April.

Referring to Pandit Nehru's statement that military aid was obtained by a country "either for making war, or for preparation for war," Sir Zafrulla Khan said that if that argument was correct:

---

23 *Ibid.*, 23 Feb. 1954.
24 *Ibid.*, 5 March 1954.
25 *Ibid.*
26 *Ibid.*, 9 Feb. 1954.

> . . . then the mere maintenance of any defence force could be characterised as maintenance of forces for the purpose of making war, or as a preparation for war. If that were accepted, it must follow that the very maintenance of an army by India, on Pandit Nehru's own reasoning, is for the purpose of making war, or is it peaceful preparation for war?

India, a vast country, was able by its own resources to maintain military forces at a very much higher level of effectiveness than any other country in southern Asia. The Foreign Minister asked:

> Does this mean that India's object in maintaining such effective military forces is war, or preparation for war? If not, then how does it follow that if any other country seeks to maintain its armed forces in a state of effectiveness, to ensure its security, by procuring from outside what it cannot supply itself, such effort must be for the purpose of making war, or preparing for war?

He made it clear that Pakistan's relations with China and the USSR were friendly.[27]

One of the grounds on which Pandit Nehru bases his opposition to pacts with the West is that they go counter to his conception of "non-alignment." It is difficult to understand what exactly that conception means, for clearly it is not identical with genuine neutrality such as is practised, for example, by Switzerland. India does not denounce China for its pact with the Soviet Union, nor the Soviet Union for its military alliances with East European countries, nor even for the presence of Soviet forces in those countries. It has been India's consistent policy to do everything to build up the prestige and influence of the Communist powers. On the other hand, India has done everything possible in the international sphere to checkmate the policies of the Western powers. It is not suggested that everything that the Soviet Union does is bad, nor that everything that the Western powers do is good. But India does certainly promote the belief that everything that the Soviet Union does is good and everything that the Western powers do is bad. At the same time,

[27] *Ibid.*, 5 March 1954.

India has, year after year, obtained grants and loans on a most generous scale from the Western powers. That is one explanation of the strange kind of "neutralism" that India follows. But there is another one too, which is linked with India's stand on the Kashmir question. According to an American writer:

> ... The possibility that one day India might have to fall back on the Kremlin's veto in the Security Council, or its nine votes in the General Assembly, goes far to explain Nehru's policy of neutralism in the cold war.[28]

The logic of the pact with the United States led Pakistan to join the South East Asia Defense Organization. In this instance, too, the United States was prompted to step in by the fear of the expansion of Communism, which had established itself as the state system of the vast area of China and which had waged a successful war with French colonialism in Indo-China. The British had the wisdom to withdraw from India, Pakistan, Ceylon, and Burma. The French obstinately insisted upon remaining in Indo-China. Pakistan was throughout very critical of French policies in that area. Foreign Minister Zafrulla Khan condemned the French war in Indo-China and said: "It may now be difficult to convince Indo-China and large sections of the people of South Asia that a conflict is being waged in Indo-China's interest."[29] The war in Indo-China involved the most senseless waste of human life and money. From 1946 to 1954 it cost the French 2,385,100,000,000 francs. The United States gave France arms supplies of the value of 200,000,000,000 francs in 1954, and of an equivalent value in 1952 and 1953.[30] It might be pointed out that a major part of the expenditure incurred by the French government was paid for by the United States in dollars. Indeed, the Indo-Chinese war was, in the later stages, to a great extent an

---

[28] William R. Frye, *A United Nations Peace Force* (New York: Oceana Publications, Inc. for the Carnegie Endowment for International Peace, 1957), p. 37.

[29] *Dawn* (Karachi), 13 April 1954.

[30] For a historical background of the Indo-Chinese conflict, see *Keesing's Contemporary Archives* (London: Keesing's Publications, 1952-1954), Vol. IX, pp. 13741-43.

American effort. However, nothing could prevent the fall of Dien Bien Phu after a siege of 55 days. Viet Minh pressure against the French continued to increase, until the armistice agreement was concluded at Geneva on 20 July 1954. The main provision of the Geneva Agreement was that Vietnam was to be partitioned by a demarcation line near the 17th Parallel, the northern part to be under the control of the Viet Minh government and the southern part under the control of the Vietnamese government. It was further provided that an election should be held simultaneously in both parts by 20 July 1956, with the aim of establishing a unified government. It is difficult to say whether a genuine French settlement with Ho Chi Minh in 1946 would have prevented the establishment of a Communist regime. However, after the Geneva decisions of 1954, with international consent, a Communist regime did come into existence in North Vietnam, the first one of its kind in Southeast Asia. This was an unmistakable defeat for the United States in the region.

At Manila on 6 September 1954, the representatives of Australia, France, Great Britain, New Zealand, Pakistan, the Philippines, Thailand, and the United States met to evolve a South East Asia Defense Organization. Speaking for the United States, Secretary of State Dulles said that his country was concerned in opposing the spread of Communism, which could take the form of open aggression, subversion, or indirect aggression. Against the first of these dangers, it would not be possible to ensure defence by stationing adequate land forces at selected points. The United States would, therefore, think in terms of mobile striking power with strategically placed reserves.[31] Sir Zafrulla Khan stressed Pakistan's view that the Conference should be concerned with resisting aggression of every description and from any quarter and said that it was a mistake to imply that one kind of aggression, rather than another, required speedier action.[32] It was reported in *The New York Times* of

[31] Cited in *ibid.*, p. 13763.
[32] Cited in *ibid.*

3 September 1954 that the United States delegation had desired the pact to be of an exclusively anti-Communist character, whilst all the other delegations had favoured a pact against aggression in more general terms. The Conference ended on 8 September with the signing by all the delegates of a Southeast Asia Collective Defense Treaty, which was accompanied by a unilateral United States declaration in the form of an "Understanding," and a general statement of principles by the eight signatories in the form of a "Pacific Charter."[33] The "Understanding" declared that United States adherence to the pact was directed against Communist aggression, with the stipulation that in the event of other aggression, the United States would consult with the other signatory countries.

Each party to the Manila Treaty, in the event of an armed attack in the treaty area, is "to meet the common danger in accordance with its constitutional processes." Thus, it does not provide for automatic military action against aggression, which would mean that if one member were the victim of aggression, the others would automatically come to its aid. Such a provision was demanded by Philippine and Thai spokesmen.[34] But this demand was resisted by the United States on the ground that Congressional sentiment had hardened against such commitments.[35] The treaty, however, does establish a Council with wide powers for military and other defence planning. The "treaty area" is defined as

> ... the general area of Southeast Asia, including also the entire territories of the Asian parties and the general area of the Southwest Pacific not including the Pacific area north of 21 degrees 30 minutes north latitude. . . .[36]

Thus, the area in respect of which the treaty is effective includes both East Pakistan and West Pakistan and excludes Formosa, about

---

[33] *United Nations Treaty Series* (New York: United Nations, 1955), Vol. 209, No. 2819, pp. 23-37.

[34] *The New York Times*, 3 Sept. 1954.

[35] *Ibid.*

[36] *United Nations Treaty Series, op. cit.*, Vol. 209, No. 2819, pp. 23-37, Art. VIII.

which the United States has a special attitude, not shared by all the other signatory countries.

In Pakistan the Manila Treaty was received without enthusiasm. There was disappointment at the United States "Understanding" that the pact was directed against Communist aggression only. The United States and the other signatories to the treaty, Pakistan included, were all conscious of the Communist danger. But so far as Pakistan was concerned, it was primarily perturbed about its troubles with India. Clearly it was illogical and inconsistent with the principle of peace that one kind of aggression should be considered less reprehensible than another kind. Nor was Pakistan alone in taking this view; for the Australian statesman, Dr. Herbert V. Evatt, too, "criticised the United States' insistance that her obligations under the treaty were limited to countering Communist aggression."[37]

In general, criticism of the Manila Treaty, in its provision of an organisation for Southeast Asia, centred on the fact that the important states of the region were not parties to it and that others that did not belong to the region were members. Needless to say, the treaty was condemned in several parts of Asia. Pandit Nehru condemned it on the ground that it would add to unrest in Southeast Asia and convert it into an area of war.[38] Similar comments were officially made in China and Indonesia.

In Southeast Asia, two other patterns of international relations were developing. One was the Panch Shila, or the "Five Principles," which for the first time found expression in the treaty between India and China on Tibet, concluded on 29 April 1954.[39] These principles were also accepted by the Prime Minister of Indonesia, Ali Sastroamidjojo, when he visited New Delhi in September 1954.[40]

---

[37] *The Pakistan Times* (Lahore), 5 Nov. 1954.

[38] *Ibid.*, 30 Sept. 1954.

[39] *Keesing's Contemporary Archives*, *op. cit.*, Vol. IX, p. 13588.

[40] *Keesing's Contemporary Archives* (London: Keesing's Publications, 1955-1956), Vol. X, p. 13977.

The other pattern of international relations in Southeast Asia was represented by the Conference of the Prime Ministers of Ceylon, India, Pakistan, Burma, and Indonesia, the so-called Colombo powers. They first met in Ceylon from 28 April to 2 May 1954. However, the area of agreement that the Conference achieved was not very large. Pandit Nehru refused to accept a proposal on the Kashmir dispute by Mr. Mohammed Ali, who described it "as the biggest potential danger to peace in South-East Asia." Pandit Nehru also refused to accept a proposal, made by Sir John Kotelawala and supported by Mr. Mohammed Ali, declaring that international Communism was a danger to South and Southeast Asia. In this, Pandit Nehru was supported by Dr. Ali Sastroamidjojo. Eventually, the five Prime Ministers issued a compromise statement condemning colonialism and interference by all external agencies, Communist or anti-Communist; asking for the admission of Communist China to the United Nations; supporting self-determination in Tunisia and Morocco; and expressing sympathy for the Arabs of Palestine. Certain proposals relating to mutual economic co-operation were also considered. The most important achievement of the Conference was the constructive influence that it exerted on the negotiations which were at that time proceeding at Geneva and which led to the cease-fire in Indo-China. The five Prime Ministers also considered a proposal for holding a conference of Asian and African nations and asked the Prime Minister of Indonesia (who was the author of the idea) to explore the possibility of holding such a Conference.[41] A second meeting of the Colombo powers, held at Bogor in Indonesia, in December 1954, decided that the Asian-African Conference should be held at Bandung in the same country in April 1955.

A third meeting of the five powers took place at Bandung in April 1955. At the fourth meeting held in November 1956 in New Delhi to consider the Suez situation, Pakistan was not represented.

---

[41] *Keesing's Contemporary Archives, op. cit.,* Vol. IX, p. 13577.

Prime Minister H. S. Suhrawardy was at that time in Teheran con-
ferring with the representatives of the Asian members of the Baghdad
Pact.

The purposes of the proposed Asian-African Conference were
defined at Bogor as the promotion of goodwill and social, economic,
and cultural co-operation between all nations of Asia and Africa.
Special problems, such as racialism and colonialism, and the contribution that the two continents could make to world peace were
also to be discussed.[42] Countries not to be invited to the Conference
were Korea (because it was "in a fluid state"), Israel (because of
the hostility of the Arab States), and Central Asia (because "it was
politically part of a European unit, namely, the Soviet Union").
Also to be excluded were Formosa (because it was "not a State")
and South Africa ("because of her very aggressive racial policy").
But because the Colombo powers had a special responsibility in
regard to Indo-China (even though the situation there was also
fluid), all the states of that region were to be invited.[43]

The Asian-African Conference was one of the most spectacular
as well as one of the most important international conferences ever
held. It was the largest official conference to have been held on
Asian soil and it contained a record number of heads of governments. The great powers and the powers of the West, that had
hitherto dominated all international discussions, were excluded
from it.

The responsibility for organising the Conference was borne entirely
by Asians. This responsibility required the making of elaborate
preparations and providing the requisite accommodation and equipment for the Conference, its Secretariat, the over 2,000 delegates,
observers, pressmen, and cameramen who came to the Conference.
The Secretary-General of the vast organisation was an Indonesian,
Ruslan Abdulgani, who was guided by a committee consisting of
the envoys in Djakarta of the five sponsoring powers. The principal

---

[42] *Keesing's Contemporary Archives*, *op. cit.*, Vol. X, p. 13977.
[43] *Ibid.*, p. 13978.

responsibility of the Conference proper rested on the shoulders of an Indian and a Pakistani. This responsibility consisted chiefly in the preparation and circulation of background papers on the questions to be discussed at the Conference, and in the preparation and circulation of its documentation, almost from hour to hour; and in keeping the machinery of the Conference running. Other departments of the organisation were headed either by Indians or Pakistanis or Indonesians, valuable assistance being given by officials from Burma and Ceylon. The bulk of the Secretariat, however, consisted of Indonesian men and women. The Conference was in every respect a very large undertaking. If it had been held in Europe or America, it would have presented far fewer problems in respect of accommodation, equipment, and staff than it did in Indonesia. But, largely because of the determination and resourcefulness of the government of that country, the direct personal interest of President Sukarno, and the co-operation of the governments of the other four sponsors, these problems were overcome. Indeed, the Conference was an object lesson in co-operation amongst countries, some of which had deep political differences.

The countries that participated in the Bandung Conference were 29 in number, namely, Afghanistan, Burma, Cambodia, Ceylon, the People's Republic of China, Egypt, Ethiopia, Gold Coast, India, Indonesia, Iran, Iraq, Japan, Jordan, Laos, Lebanon, Liberia, Libya, Nepal, Pakistan, the Philippine Republic, Saudi Arabia, the Sudan, Syria, Thailand, Turkey, the Democratic Republic of Vietnam, the State of Vietnam, and Yemen. Many of them had until recently been under the domination, in one way or another, of the West. They were united, said President Sukarno who inaugurated the Conference, by their desire to see colonialism disappear altogether. The Prime Minister of Ceylon saw for the Asian and African nations a mediator's role in the world conflict between Communism and anti-Communism. In the words of the leader of the Cambodian delegation, the Conference shattered the frontiers which separated the Communist world from the non-Communist world. Pandit

f

Nehru, who had through his speeches worked up a great deal of
enthusiasm for the Conference, hoped it would record a verdict
against Asian and African nations entering into alliances with the
Western powers. Countries like Pakistan that had entered into such
alliances were anxious to obtain a recognition of their right to do
so as a means of warding off possible aggression and of assuring
peace. The Arab states were there to canvass support for their
demands in respect of Palestine and North Africa. Mr. Chou En-Lai,
the Chinese Premier, stood for peaceful co-existence.

So far as the problems of cultural and economic co-operation
between the Asian and African countries were concerned, and these
were dealt with in two separate committees, there were no significant
differences between the participants. In respect, however, of political
problems, there was inevitably very great divergence. In effect, this
divergence arose out of the differing attitudes of the participating
countries towards the proposal of the Prime Minister of Pakistan
that the Conference accept "seven principles of peace," namely:

(1) Sovereignty and territorial integrity of all nations;
(2) Equality of all independent and sovereign nations;
(3) Non-interference in the internal affairs of one country
    by another;
(4) Non-aggression;
(5) Right of self-defence of each country, to be exercised
    singly or collectively;
(6) Self-determination for all peoples and abhorrence of
    colonial exploitation in every shape;
(7) Settlement of internal disputes through peaceful means,
    that is, by negotiation, mediation and arbitration.

The fifth of these principles, giving recognition to the right of a
state to enter into alliances with other states for the purpose of
self-defence, was condemned by Pandit Nehru in the strongest
possible language. He declared that Mr. Mohammed Ali had introduced it to shield the recently concluded SEATO alliance, and
criticised Pakistan for aligning itself with the Western world. Pandit
Nehru said that it was intolerable humiliation for any Asian or

African country to degrade itself by becoming the camp follower of any great power.[44] Mr. Nehru took his stand on the "Five Principles." However, Mr. Chou En-Lai, also committed to the "Five Principles," saw nothing sacrosanct in numbers, and said that he was prepared to add to or subtract from them.[45] Mr. Chou revealed that the Pakistan Prime Minister had assured him that Pakistan had no fear of aggression by his government. This was confirmed by Mr. Mohammed Ali. In the final communiqué of the Conference, "the right of each nation to defend itself singly or collectively, in conformity with the Charter of the United Nations" was recognised.

While all the participants in the Conference were prepared to record their condemnation of colonialism, there was a difference of opinion on whether this should be taken to include Soviet colonialism. Sir John Kotelawala, the Prime Minister of Ceylon, referred to the Russian satellites in Europe and asked for the condemnation of colonialism, old and new. The charges against Russia were denied by Mr. Chou En-Lai and by Pandit Nehru, who affirmed that the so-called Russian satellites were independent states.[46] While the Pakistan Prime Minister supported his colleague from Ceylon, he made it clear that Pakistan did not regard China as imperialistic, for China had no satellites.[47] It was eventually agreed that "colonialism in all its manifestations was an evil and should speedily be brought to an end."

The Conference recorded its approval of the principles of self-determination and human rights and its condemnation of racialism with special reference to South Africa. Support was given to the rights of the Arab people of Palestine, the position of Indonesia in the dispute over West Irian, and that of Yemen in respect of Aden. The Conference asked for universality in United Nations

---

[44] *Dawn* (Karachi), 23 April 1955.
[45] *Ibid.*, 24 April 1955.
[46] *The Pakistan Times* (Lahore), 23 April 1955.
[47] *Ibid.*, 24 April 1955.

membership and for greater Asian-African representation in the Security Council. This was proposed by Pakistan. The Conference called for disarmament and prohibition of nuclear and thermonuclear weapons.

Inasmuch as the Bandung Conference recognised the right of a country to enter into collective defence arrangements, and did not consider the "Five Principles" sufficient, it was a major defeat for Pandit Nehru. These decisions were made possible by several factors, foremost among them being the determination of Mr. Chou En-Lai to "seek a common ground,"[48] despite differences in ideology. At the same time, Mr. Chou, the leader of the world's largest nation, was not prepared to let go the opportunity of destroying the impression that he was but a *protégé* and "yes-man" of Pandit Nehru. In contrast to the Pandit, Mr. Chou adopted an attitude of "sweet reasonableness" and "real give and take."[49]

It will have been observed that the Bandung Conference did not redraw the map of the world: nor did its decisions instantaneously affect the fate of mankind. Nevertheless, those decisions have had a far-reaching influence on thinking about world affairs, especially on Western thinking about the affairs of Asia and Africa. Significant also was the fact that the Bandung Communiqué permitted collective defence pacts, a fact which is too often forgotten by "neutralist" statesmen who were parties to and swear by that communiqué.

A year after the signing of the Turco-Pakistani agreement came the Turkish-Iraqi Treaty of 25 February 1955 which led to the so-called Baghdad Pact. The parties to the treaty were Iran, Iraq, Pakistan, Turkey, and the United Kingdom. Under Articles I and V of the pact, states acceding to it may conclude special agreements amongst themselves for the purpose of giving effect to the purposes of the pact. On 4 April 1955 Britain and Iraq concluded such an agreement and Britain acceded to the Baghdad Pact. This agreement took the place of the Anglo-Iraqi Treaty of 1932 which was ter-

---

48 *The Statesman* (New Delhi), 20 April 1955.
49 *Ibid.*, 21 April 1955.

minated. The effect of the new treaty was that the pre-existing defence arrangements between Britain and Iraq would continue. Sir Anthony Eden explained to the House of Commons that there would be joint planning and exercises in peacetime and effective help would be given to Iraq in case of aggression. Assistance would also be given in establishing an air defence organisation. Britain would be entitled to stock military stores and equipment in Iraq. British instructors would train the Iraqi Army and facilities for overflying, landing, and servicing aircraft would continue. British air bases at Habbaniya and Shaiba would pass under Iraqi control and British squadrons stationed there would be progressively withdrawn. Installations at the airfields, required for British use, would remain British property. Eden was careful to point out that "no aspect of the treaty could possibly be directed against Israel."[50]

In effect the new agreements confirmed Britain in its position of power in the Middle East. It will be recalled that British policies in that region, particularly those which led to the establishment of the state of Israel, had caused much bitter resentment in Egypt and the other Arab countries. Having failed in their efforts to prevent the Baghdad Pact, those countries denounced it as aiding Western imperialism and giving implied recognition and support to Israel.

Realising that the pact would be extremely unpopular in the Arab countries, the United States did not formally join it and contented itself with being represented at the meetings of the pact Council by observers, though it is a full member of its Committees. Nevertheless in the Arab countries, the United States is as much blamed for its support of the pact as it would have been if it had become a formal party to it.

Generally, the pacts with the West have resulted in three distinct disadvantages to Pakistan. First, Pakistan has suffered a setback in the position that it enjoyed among the Asian-African states in the United Nations, most of those states being themselves uncommitted

---

[50] *Keesing's Contemporary Archives, op. cit.*, Vol. X, p. 14137.

in the inter-bloc rivalry and opposed to close alignment with the West. Secondly, Pakistan has fallen in the estimation of the Arabs, who are all strongly opposed to alignment with the West. Pakistan's participation in the Baghdad Pact has been strongly condemned by them, a typical Arab reaction being that of Radio Mecca, which said:

> Is it therefore possible for any person to believe that an Is-lamic State such as that of Pakistan should accede to those who have joined hands with Zionist Jews ... Whatever may be the case, Pakistan, a country so dear to us and to other Arab countries, cannot be expected to put her hand in the hands of those who have bad intentions towards the Arabs.[51]

The Baghdad Pact undoubtedly divided the Arab world: Pakistan by its membership in that pact was held responsible for contributing to that division. By destroying Arab unity and by making the Arabs more suspicious of Western intentions, the Baghdad Pact increased instability in the region. If the intention of the Western powers was to keep out, through the pact, instability and Soviet influence from the Middle East, they have succeeded in achieving just the opposite. Thirdly, the pacts with the West, far from bringing any advantage to Pakistan in respect of its disputes with India, in particular, the all-important dispute over Kashmir, are believed to have made the position worse for Pakistan. Hitherto, whenever a resolution on that dispute came before the Security Council, the Soviet Union had always abstained on it. But subsequent to Pakistan's entry into the pacts, every resolution proposing effective action in Kashmir has been vetoed by the Soviet Union. In 1955, Messrs. Bulganin and Khrushchev went to the extent of declaring that they looked upon Kashmir as a part of India.[52] Wrote *Dawn* of Karachi:

> Never would Russia have used her veto and actively partici-pated on the side of Bharat in the matter of Kashmir if

---

[51] *The Pakistan Times* (Lahore), 26 Sept. 1955.
[52] *The New York Times*, 11 Dec. 1955.

Pakistan had not aligned herself so closely with the Anglo-American bloc.[53]

For their part, the western Powers, after their pacts with Pakistan, have been less keen to exert themselves about Pakistan's case than they were before. In fact, they have tried to keep Pakistan quiescent over Kashmir.[54]

Nevertheless, each successive government of Pakistan has seen wisdom in continuing firmly to adhere to the pacts. In 1958, revolutions took place in Iraq and Pakistan. As a consequence of the revolution in Iraq, that country withdrew from the Baghdad Pact, which was renamed Central Treaty Organisation, for short, CENTO. The new regime in Pakistan, headed by Field Marshal Muhammad Ayub Khan, made no change in the country's foreign policy and it has maintained Pakistan's alignment with the West. The value of the pacts as a means of collective security and a safeguard against aggression has been greatly enhanced by the Pakistan-United States Bilateral Agreement of Cooperation, signed at Ankara on 5 March 1959. According to Article I of that agreement, the government of the United States will, in the event of aggression against Pakistan, take appropriate action, including the use of armed forces. In Article II, the government of the United States reaffirms that it will continue to furnish, on an agreed basis, military and economic assistance to Pakistan with a view to helping in the preservation of its national independence and integrity and the promotion of its economic development.

Speaking in March 1960, Foreign Minister Manzur Qadir said that the alliance with the West was the sheet anchor of Pakistan's foreign policy and that Pakistan regarded her alignments as the guarantee of her independence and sovereignty. He claimed: "We are not being so much misunderstood about those alignments now as we were some years ago."[55]

[53] *Dawn* (Karachi), 27 June 1958.
[54] Frye, *op. cit.*, p. 37.
[55] *Dawn* (Karachi), 12 March 1960.

True, Pakistan has entered into the pacts with the Western powers in its own interest. But it is equally true that under those pacts Pakistan has undertaken grave and risky obligations. India has undertaken no obligations and staked nothing. Yet in every respect India is in a more advantageous position with regard to those powers than Pakistan. Nor is this due to the fact that India is the larger country or more "democratic." The aid offers of the two great powers have little to do with ideologies. The United States is giving aid to Yugoslavia which is Communist. The Soviet Union is giving aid to some states that are monarchical and altogether feudal. The "neutralist" countries, whatever their size or their political and economic systems, are able to make exactions on both sides. Thus, "neutralism" is better business for countries looking for assistance.

In the prevailing political climate of a world divided into two frankly hostile camps, it was inevitable that each one of them should seek to protect its far-flung interests through regional defence arrangements. The powers that made these arrangements have now gone beyond them and are engaged in a neck-to-neck race for purchasing either support or "neutralism." "Countries get cold war economic aid because they can be influenced toward or away from one side or the other or because of their strategic location."[56] However, the altruistic motive of the countries that give this aid is being more and more recognised by the countries that receive it.

For their part Pakistani leaders and diplomats have sometimes taken too much for granted. Having entered into the pacts with the West, they believed they had entered a new millennium in which matters would be determined according to ethical principles. They forgot that the essential nature of diplomacy had not changed, that astute and rugged defiance still achieved better results than unqualified consistency. But when is the millennium, which is promised in the United Nations Charter, going to be ushered in?

---

[56] A. G. Mezerik, ed., "Economic Aid for Underdeveloped Countries," *International Review Service*, Vol. III, No. 35, July 1957, p. 6.

chapter four

Kashmir Dispute: The Issues

The Kashmir question has not only been the principal factor in the attitudes of Pakistan (and India) towards foreign policy questions, but also one of the major questions with which the United Nations has been concerned. In its essence, the problem today is that India refuses to permit the holding of a plebiscite in Kashmir to enable its people to decide whether their state should accede to Pakistan or India. To the holding of such a plebiscite, India is committed by its own declarations and by its acceptance of the resolutions of the United Nations Commission for India and Pakistan. The issues of fact and law involved in the dispute have again and again been debated in the Security Council. It is necessary to consider what those issues are and how they arose.

It will be remembered that, as a result of the plan of 3 June 1947, to which the leaders of the Congress and the Muslim League had assented, the sovereign states of Pakistan and (residuary) India came into existence. These two states were to comprise, respectively, contiguous Muslim majority areas of the subcontinent and its contiguous non-Muslim majority areas. Explaining the basis of partition, the Viceroy, Lord Mountbatten, pointed out: "there can be no question of coercing any large areas in which one community has a majority to live against their will under a Government in which another community has a majority."[1]

The plan of 3 June contained express provisions for the partition of what was known as British India—that is, the eleven provinces which were directly under British rule. But, in addition, comprised in the British Indian Empire, were the Indian states—that is, those territories which were ruled by Indian princes under the suzerainty of the British Crown, the Crown exercising on their behalf all powers in respect to their foreign relations and defence. The number of these Indian states was over 550, some of them with areas and populations as large as those of average European countries; while others were no bigger than private landed estates. With regard to the states, it was decided that on the withdrawal of British power, the suzerainty of the Crown over them would lapse and that they would be free to accede to India or to Pakistan or remain independent.[2] However, Lord Mountbatten, addressing the Chamber of Princes on 25 July 1947, advised the princes to accede to India or to Pakistan, bearing in mind the geographical situation of their respective states, the composition of their population, and the wishes of their people.[3]

There were three states, the question of whose accession became the subject of dispute, namely, (1) Junagadh, which had a Hindu majority population but a Muslim ruler, and which acceded to Pakistan; (2) Hyderabad, which had a Hindu majority population but whose ruler was a Muslim and which wished to retain a measure of inde-

---

[1] *Keesing's Contemporary Archives* (London: Keesing's Publications, 1946-48), Vol. VII, p. 8633.
[2] *Cf.* Mr. Gopalaswami Ayyangar's statement in Security Council, Official Records (S.C.O.R.): 3rd Year, 227th Mtg., 15 Jan. 1948, p. 13.
[3] *The Statesman* (Delhi), 26 July 1947.

pendence; and (3) Kashmir, which had a Muslim majority but a Hindu ruler, who acceded to India (under circumstances which will be examined later). It would be helpful first to examine Indian transactions in respect to Junagadh and Hyderabad.

The government of Pakistan accepted the accession of the state of Junagadh (area about 4,000 square miles, population about 800,000) and informed the government of India of this acceptance on 12 September 1947. The latter most vehemently denounced that arrangement, on the ground that Junagadh was geographically contiguous to India, and that Hindus formed the majority of its population. The government of India furthermore insisted that the question of the accession of Junagadh to either of the two dominions should be decided by a plebiscite to be held under the joint supervision of the governments of India and Junagadh.[4] Pakistan, to whom Junagadh had acceded, was not to participate in the organisation and holding of the plebiscite. If this principle were accepted, India should have nothing to do with the organisation and holding of the plebiscite in Kashmir and that plebiscite should be held under the joint supervision of the governments of Pakistan and Kashmir, for the majority of Kashmiris are Muslims and Kashmir has a far longer common border with Pakistan than with India.

On 22 September 1947 the Governor-General of India telegraphed to the Governor-General of Pakistan:

> ... Such acceptance of accession by Pakistan cannot but be regarded by Government of India as an encroachment on India's sovereignty and territory and inconsistent with friendly relations that should exist between the two Dominions. This action of Pakistan is considered by Government of India to be a clear attempt to cause disruption in integrity of India by extending influence and boundaries of Dominion of Pakistan in utter violation of principles on which partition was agreed upon and effected.[5]

---

[4] Government of India's telegram of 22 Sept. 1947 to the Governor-General of Pakistan quoted by Sir Muhammad Zafrulla Khan in S.C.O.R., 3rd Year, 250th Mtg., 18 Feb. 1948, p. 193.

[5] *Ibid.*

Clearly, the principles referred to are those of separating contiguous Muslim majority areas from contiguous non-Muslim majority areas and incorporating them respectively into the sovereign states of Pakistan and India. If these principles were applied to the case of Kashmir, the acceptance by India of the accession of Kashmir would be *ab initio* invalid and an unwarranted encroachment by India upon the sovereignty and territory of Pakistan.

No mention of the communications of the government of India to the government of Pakistan in regard to Junagadh is made by Mr. V. P. Menon in his book, *The Story of the Integration of the Indian States*. Mr. Menon, it should be noted, played a leading part in the evolution and implementation of the government of India's policy with regard to the states and Kashmir. However, it is clear from his book that in the case of other states also the government of India insisted upon the principles on which it challenged the accession of Junagadh to Pakistan. Thus, the Maharajah of Jodhpur wished to accede to Pakistan. To dissuade him from doing so, he was summoned for an interview with Lord Mountbatten. Menon records:

> ... Lord Mountbatten made it clear that from a purely legal standpoint there was no objection to the ruler of Jodhpur acceding to Pakistan; but the Maharajah should, he stressed, consider seriously the consequences of his doing so, having regard to the fact that he himself was a Hindu; that his State was populated predominantly by Hindus and that the same applied to the States surrounding Jodhpur. In the light of these considerations, if the Maharajah were to accede to Pakistan, his action would surely be in conflict with the principle underlying the partition of India on the basis of Muslim and non-Muslim majority areas; and serious communal trouble inside the State would be the inevitable consequence of such affiliation.[6]

---

[6] V. P. Menon, *The Story of the Integration of the Indian States* (Bombay: Orient Longmans, 1956), p. 117.

Jodhpur was compelled to accede to India. By the same token, Kashmir ought to have acceded to Pakistan.

To return to Junagadh: the Prime Minister of Pakistan, in his telegram dated 23 October 1947, proposed to the Prime Minister of India that the two governments should discuss and settle the conditions for the holding of a plebiscite or a referendum in the states where there were disputes with regard to accession.[7] To this proposal there was no reply from the government of India. Obviously, in view of the steps that it contemplated taking in Junagadh, Kashmir, and Hyderabad, the government of India was not prepared to enter into any parleys with the government of Pakistan, such as might lead to the affirmation of principles for the accession of states, or the devising of provisions for the holding of plebiscites in cases of disputed accession.

There had been no disturbances of any kind in Junagadh and no opposition by the people of the state to their ruler's decision to accede to Pakistan. But, after that decision, a severe economic blockade was imposed by India on Junagadh, lines of communication were cut, and a campaign of terror was inaugurated. Indian troops surrounded the state. A "Provisional Government" of Junagadh was set up in Bombay; later it moved to Rajkot, a town outside Junagadh State, which was the headquarters of the Regional Commissioner of the government of India. To Pakistan's protests, the government of India first gave evasive replies and subsequently no replies at all. The so-called "Provisional Government" seized Junagadh property at Rajkot and organized raids into Junagadh territory. Indian forces penetrated into some parts of the state. On 7 November 1947, a force of 20,000 calling itself Azad Fauj (Liberation Army), equipped with tanks, armoured cars, and other modern weapons obviously supplied by the government of India, marched into Junagadh. The government of India promptly assumed control over the entire state and, under conditions which it itself determined, held

---

7 Quoted by Sir Muhammad Zafrulla Khan in S.C.O.R., 3rd Year, 250th Mtg., 18 Feb. 1948, pp. 198-99.

a plebiscite in the course of which the majority of voters was reported to have voted for accession to India. Pakistan considered this referendum to be farcical and refused to recognise its validity.

This was the Junagadh story that Pakistan laid before the Security Council. By a strange coincidence the alternate delegate of India in the Security Council was Mr. M. C. Setalvad. Sir Zafrulla Khan read to the Council two letters written to the *Times of India* of Bombay by Mr. Setalvad's father, the Indian elder statesman and jurist, Sir Chimanlal H. Setalvad. With rare courage and devotion to truth—of which we have already noted instances in this book—Sir Chimanlal in his letter of 3 November 1947 said:

> . . . The so-called "Provisional Government" of Junagadh was openly formed in Bombay, and for days it proclaimed its intention of marching to Junagadh to overthrow the Junagadh Government as by law established. The leaders of that "Provisional Government" have openly raised a volunteer army and have captured several villages in Junagadh territory. Junagadh House in Rajkot was forcibly seized by the "Provisional Government", and Rajkot State, which has acceded to India, and the Indian Government themselves have remained passive spectators of all unfriendly and hostile acts against a State which is, together with the Dominion to which it has acceded, at peace with India.[8]

The Security Council heard the statements of the representatives of Pakistan and India on Junagadh, and through its resolution of 3 June 1948 directed the United Nations Commission of India and Pakistan "to study and report to the Security Council when it considers appropriate"[9] on the Junagadh dispute, this being one of the matters raised by the Foreign Minister of Pakistan in his letter of 15 January 1948. This was never done.

Let us next consider the case of Hyderabad (area over 82,000 square miles and population about 20,000,000). This state, as we

---

[8] Quoted by Sir Muhammad Zafrulla Khan in S.C.O.R., 3rd Year, 244th Mtg., 11 Feb. 1948, pp. 103-04.

[9] S.C.O.R., 3rd Year, 312th Mtg., 3 June 1948, p. 21.

have seen, had a Hindu majority population and a Muslim ruler, known as the Nizam. The Nizam did not wish to accede either to India or to Pakistan and desired a special treaty relation with the government of India, preserving a limited measure of independence for his state. [10] Pending the negotiation of such a treaty, the Nizam entered into a Standstill Agreement with the government of India.[11] The government of India complained that Hyderabad had violated the Standstill Agreement. The Nizam, denying this, offered that the matter be arbitrated as provided by Article 4 of the Standstill Agreement. The government of India refused to agree to arbitration.[12] Thereafter the government of India demanded that the Nizam accede to India unconditionally. With a view to ascertaining the wishes of the people in the matter, the Nizam offered to hold a plebiscite under suitable supervision, a proposal which he had earlier refused to consider. The government of India rejected this offer and insisted that the accession should take place first and the plebiscite be held later, the people to vote only on the issue of accession to India (and not the alternative of partial independence).[13] An interim government was also demanded. The government of India said: "plebiscite without an interim government representative of and satisfactory to the majority population in Hyderabad will only be a fraud on the people."[14] This was yet another principle, as we shall see later, whose application to the case of Kashmir was resolutely resisted by India. Eventually, the government of India subjected Hyderabad to a crippling economic blockade[15] and, on 11 September 1948, marched

[10] Nizam's letter dated 8 Aug. 1947 to the Crown Representative, *Hyderabad's Relations with the Dominion of India* (Hyderabad: Govt. Press, April 1948), Vol. I, pp. 3-6.

[11] *White Paper on Hyderabad 1948* (New Delhi: Govt. of India, 1948), pp. 25, 45.

[12] Letter dated 15 May 1948 from the Secretary to the Government of India, Ministry of States, to the Prime Minister of Hyderabad, *Hyderabad's Relations with the Dominion of India, op. cit.*, Vol. II, p. 23.

[13] *Ibid.*, p. 55.

[14] *White Paper on Hyderabad 1948, op. cit.*, p. 37.

[15] Cablegram dated 24 Aug. 1948 from the Hyderabad Government to the President of the Security Council, S.C.O.R., 3rd Year, Supple. for Sept. 1948, p. 5.

its armies into the state and occupied it. This happened while Hyderabad's complaint was pending before the Security Council. It is still pending.

We now turn to the dispute about Kashmir. The State of Jammu and Kashmir, to give it its full name, has an area of 84,471 square miles. It is bounded on the north by Sinkiang and the narrow Wakhan strip of Afghanistan, beyond which lies the Soviet Union. To its west and southwest is Pakistan; to the southeast is India; and to the east is Tibet. The state is also contiguous to Sinkiang which is a part of the People's Republic of China and adjoins the Soviet Union.

It has never been denied that between Kashmir and Pakistan there are strong affinities, far stronger than between Kashmir and India. The extent of Kashmir's common border with Pakistan is 902 miles, and with India 317 miles. The only two roads that linked Jammu and Kashmir with the outside world lay through Pakistan. The three main rivers of West Pakistan, namely, the Indus, the Jhelum, and the Chenab, come down from Kashmir. Upon these rivers depends the agricultural prosperity of the people of West Pakistan. The export and import trade of Kashmir was mostly with Pakistan. Indeed, the timber of Kashmir, its largest source of revenue, was exported by being floated down the rivers into Pakistan. Strategically, Kashmir is important to Pakistan, for, with India in possession of Kashmir, West Pakistan would be encircled, and India's intentions towards Pakistan are none too friendly. Further, Pakistan's main road and rail communications to the North-West Frontier, the historic defence line of the subcontinent, pass within 30 miles of the Kashmir boundary. Entrenched in Kashmir, India could disrupt these communications with possibly disastrous consequences to Pakistan.

Cultural links between Kashmir and Pakistan are as manifold as those between Kashmir and India are meagre. According to the 1941 census, the total population of the state was about 4,000,000, 77 per cent of whom were Muslims. In the Kashmir province, Muslims were 93 per cent, in the Jammu province 61 per cent, and in Gilgit which, though sparsely populated, is a very large area, 100 per cent. In respect of their background, habits, customs, manners, dress, food, and their way of life generally, there is no difference between the Muslims of Kashmir and those of West Pakistan. The communities living on either side of the long border between the two are racially the same and speak the same language or dialects. For centuries there have been intermarriages between Pakistanis and Kashmiris, more commonly among those who live near the border, but also among those whose homes are farther away.

The State of Jammu and Kashmir came into existence in 1846, as a result of the Treaty of Amritsar, by which the British sold this territory to Gulab Singh, a petty chieftain of the Hindu Dogra tribe, for the sum of Rs. 7,500,000. Lord Lawrence, who negotiated this sale deed of a people, himself referred to it as a

> ... very questionable stroke of policy, which had been ar-
> ranged beforehand and which has brought woes innumerable
> on the happy Kashmiris ever since, we handed it over to the
> Dogra Rajput, Gulab Singh, who paid us down at once in
> hard cash which he had stolen from the Lahore Durbar.[16]

Lord Lawrence again speaks of "The iniquitous arrangement by which Kashmir and its ill-fated inhabitants were to be transferred without their consent, as though they were so many logs of wood, to Gulab Singh, a Dogra Rajput, who had nothing in common with them."[17]

The Dogra Maharajahs proved to be the worst kind of despots. They were alien, incompetent, dissolute, and tyrannical. Under their rule, the Kashmiri Muslims for a whole century eked out an utterly miserable existence. It was grinding poverty for a most gifted people, inhabiting a land renowned the world over, not only for its natural beauty but also for its natural wealth. The Maharajah and his officialdom were mercilessly extortionate. Public offices were held

---

[16] Letter quoted in S.C.O.R., 3rd Year, 239th Mtg., p. 337.
[17] *Ibid.*

g

only by Dogras or other Hindus. The Muslims were suppressed and discriminated against in every sphere. The slaughter of the cow, which animal is sacred to the Hindus, was a criminal offence for which the punishment was death (later reduced to seven years' imprisonment).[18]

It was inevitable that sooner or later the people should rise against this state of affairs. This they did in the early 1930's when the All-Jammu and Kashmir Muslim Conference was established and a demand for elementary political rights, not exclusively for Muslims, was put forward. The Maharajah tried to suppress this movement. There was shooting; there were arrests. To help their Kashmiri brethren as many as 30,000 Muslims from the Punjab went into Kashmir and courted arrest. This shows that Pakistani sympathy for the aspirations of the Muslims of Kashmir is not a new phenomenon.

As a result of this movement some rights were granted to the people of Kashmir and a Legislative Assembly, partly elected, was created. In the first elections, held in 1933-34, the Muslim Conference captured 16 out of 21 elected seats. In the 1938 elections, that party won 20 out of 21 seats.

The solidarity of the Muslims of Kashmir caused alarm to the Maharajah and the Hindus generally, who saw power slipping out of their hands. The leaders of the Muslim Conference were persuaded that they should throw open the doors of their movement to non-Muslims. They decided to do so in 1939 and changed the name of their organisation to the National Conference. There were some Muslim leaders who had misgivings about this move, but generally they confidently hoped that their Hindu brethren would co-operate with them in the fight for freedom. Soon they realised their mistake. The Hindus of Jammu and Kashmir did not really desire that democratic government should supersede the Maharajah's rule, under which they, although in a minority, were the sole beneficiaries of

18 Statement of Sir Muhammad Zafrulla Khan in S.C.O.R., 3rd Year, 228th Mtg., 16 Jan. 1948, pp. 65-66.

official patronage.[19] The Hindu members of the Conference, in following what they thought to be their interests, undermined the revolutionary character of the organisation.[20] This view is supported by the Hindu Kashmiri leader, Pandit Prem Nath Bazaz, in his remarkable book, *The History of the Struggle for Freedom in Kashmir*. Bazaz, it might be mentioned, had played a leading part in bringing about the transformation of the Muslim Conference into the National Conference and was in the forefront of the Kashmir liberation movement until he was exiled in 1949 to Delhi, where he suffered imprisonment for his fearless criticism of the Indian government's Kashmir policies.

In brief, under the influence of its non-Muslim members (controlled behind the scenes by Mr. Gopalaswami Ayyangar, who was Prime Minister from 1936 to 1943), the National Conference tended to become on the one hand an instrument of the Maharajah's government and on the other an appendage of the Indian Congress party.[21] This was hardly calculated to make it popular with the predominantly Muslim masses of Kashmir. After giving the National Conference a trial, most of the Muslim leaders left it in 1941 and, under the leadership of Ghulam Abbas, revived the Muslim Conference. Outstanding amongst the Muslims who remained with the National Conference was Sheikh Mohammad Abdullah who had been in the forefront of the struggle of the Muslim Conference since 1931.

Sheikh Abdullah persevered in his efforts to popularize the National Conference amongst the Muslim masses, but without success. Seeing that they stood solidly behind the demand for Pakistan, he tried to curry favour with Mr. Mohammed Ali Jinnah. Sheikh Abdullah went to Delhi and saw Mr. Jinnah and, during the latter's visit to Kashmir in 1944, made public speeches in his praise. However, Mr. Jinnah refused to recognise the National Conference as the

---

[19] Prem Nath Bazaz, *The History of the Struggle for Freedom in Kashmir* (New Delhi: Kashmir Publishing Co., 1954), p. 177.

[20] *Ibid.*

[21] *Ibid.*, p. 190.

representative organisation of the Muslims of Kashmir.[22] This marked the beginning of Sheikh Abdullah's hostility to Mr. Jinnah and his utter dependence upon Pandit Nehru, which eventually led him to support the accession of Kashmir to India. The Pandit visited Kashmir in 1945 in an effort to build up some prestige for the National Conference and Sheikh Abdullah. But as the Pakistan movement was now in full swing, Pandit Nehru was not the man that the masses of Kashmir cared for and he was received with black flags.[23]

It has repeatedly been claimed on behalf of India that its government and leaders took no interest at all in the affairs of Kashmir until the Maharajah, after the incursion of the tribesmen from Pakistan, offered to accede to India.[24] On the other hand, certain clearly established facts leave no room for doubt that the leaders of the Congress party, including those in the government of India, were actively concerned about Kashmir from the time it was decided that there would be partition. Pakistan, of course, has always maintained that there was a conspiracy between the government of India and the Maharajah to bring about the accession of Kashmir to India. As a first step in pursuance of this conspiracy, a campaign to massacre or drive out the Muslims of Kashmir was started. This was a well considered move. The thinking behind it is revealed by V. P. Menon, who records that he told Sardar V. Patel, Indian Deputy Prime Minister and Minister for States, "that [the] communal flare-up in north India had made the non-Muslim rulers turn away from Pakistan and . . . that we should use this development to our advantage."[25] As will be presently seen, a "communal flare-up" was

---

[22] *Ibid.*, p. 211.

[23] *Ibid.*, p. 245.

[24] Telegram dated 31 Oct. 1947 from the Prime Minister of India to the Prime Minister of Pakistan, *White Paper on Jammu and Kashmir* (Delhi: Govt. of India, n.d.), p. 50. (This is the first White Paper on Kashmir published by the Government of India.)

[25] Menon, *op. cit.*, p. 97.

organised in the state of the non-Muslim ruler of Kashmir and advantage taken of it to obtain his accession to India.

We also learn from Menon that some of the rulers were used to persuade their brother princes to accede to India.[26] This standard technique was employed also in the case of Kashmir. Menon mentions in particular the services rendered by the Maharajah of Patiala in procuring the accession of some of the states. One such state was Kashmir, which was visited by the Maharajah of Patiala.

As we have seen, the partition plan was publicly announced on 3 June 1947. But it had already been decided on, since a fortnight earlier the Maharajah of Kashmir had received a visit from the President of the Congress party, Acharya Kripalani. Speaking in Srinagar, Kripalani had publicly declared that it was absurd to denounce the Treaty of Amritsar or to demand that the Maharajah should quit. In fact, he had argued that the dynasty had properly acquired the state.[27] What was the purpose for which the Indian leaders wanted to retain the Maharajah, if it was not to use him for obtaining the accession of Kashmir? It is easy to conjecture what advice Kripalani must have given to the Maharajah on the question of accession.

After the announcement of the partition plan, the Maharajah of Kashmir was visited in turn by the Maharajahs of Patiala, Kapurthala, and Faridkot. Early in August Mr. Mohandas K. Gandhi himself went to Srinagar and conferred with the Maharajah. These were significant pointers, for clearly during those fateful weeks these gentlemen could not have left their political pre-occupations, which, in view of the unprecedented problems created by the impending transfer of power, must undoubtedly have been pressing, and gone to Kashmir just to breathe the mountain air and look at the flowers. No official record is available of what transpired between the Maharajah and the Mahatma. But a safe guess might be made on the basis of the fact that Pandit Nehru told his Parliament on

[26] *Ibid.*, pp. 122-23.
[27] Bazaz, *op. cit.*, p. 272.

8 March 1949 that all steps which he had taken in Kashmir had Mr. Gandhi's blessings.[28] The "Apostle" of non-violence might also be presumed to have blessed the idea of India seizing Kashmir by waging a war. Speaking at his prayer meeting on 26 September 1947, he had said: "If Pakistan Government persistently refused to see its error and continued to minimise it, the Indian Government would have to go to war against it."[29]

As early as July, there were rumours, too many to be ignored, that the Maharajah of Kashmir was privately seeking pretexts for acceding to India.[30] But he knew that an overwhelming majority of the people of his state desired accession to Pakistan. He could have had no doubt about it and, if he did have any, it must have been removed when 14 August was celebrated as Pakistan Day. Throughout every town and hamlet the Pakistan flag was raised and saluted by the people. In the face of such universal enthusiasm for Pakistan, the Maharajah could not precipitately accede to India. However, the ruthless pro-Indian Jan Singh, who after Mr. Gandhi's visit to Srinagar had been appointed Prime Minister of Kashmir, made no effort to conceal his inclination. Under the Standstill Agreement, the postal system of Kashmir was being run by Pakistan. Consequently, on 15 August, which was Independence Day, the Pakistan flag was hoisted over the post offices. It was ordered to be removed. The *Daily Hamddard*, which criticised this action, was made subject to pre-censorship.[31]

In a previous chapter we have seen that the entire Muslim population of the East Punjab was wiped out through massacre or forcible expulsion to Pakistan. The same thing happened in the East Punjab States of Patiala, Faridkot, Jind, Kapurthala, and Nabha, as well as the States of Bharatpur and Alwar, all of which had either Sikh

---

[28] *The Statesman* (Delhi), 9 March 1949.
[29] Sir Muhammad Zafrulla Khan in S.C.O.R., 3rd Year, 228th Mtg., 16 Jan. 1948, pp. 60-61.
[30] Ian Stephens, *Horned Moon* (London: Chatto & Windus, 1953), p. 107.
[31] Bazaz, *op. cit.*, pp. 320-21.

or Hindu rulers. This fact was stated in the Security Council on behalf of Pakistan and was naturally not denied on behalf of India.[32] Kapurthala had a 64 per cent Muslim majority, the number being 235,000. Every one of them was killed or driven out. Kapurthala acceded to India; there was none to raise a voice of protest against it. Likewise, if the Maharajah of Kashmir, through massacre and expulsion, could substantially reduce the number of his Muslim subjects, if not totally eliminate them, that would facilitate his accession to India. As a consequence of the transfer of power and in order that there should be no disturbance in the life of the state, the Maharajah entered into a "Standstill Agreement" with Pakistan. This agreement placed upon Pakistan, in respect to Kashmir, the same responsibilities as were formerly borne by the Crown or the pre-partition government of India.[33] Hyderabad had entered into a Standstill Agreement with India leading to India's claim that Hyderabad was under an obligation (a) to have no relations with any country other than India, and (b) to accede to India.[34] *Pari passu*, because of the Standstill Agreement between Kashmir and Pakistan, Kashmir was (a) debarred from having any relations with any country other than Pakistan, and (b) under an obligation to accede to Pakistan. This would render Kashmir's accession to India invalid.

Both in Kashmir and India, in view of the intended accession of the former to the latter, certain necessary preparations were taken in hand. Clearly, there must be surface communications between them. Even before the district of Gurdaspur was given to India under the Radcliffe Award (which was not announced until after the middle of August) Kashmir had some common border with India. It lay athwart high mountains through which there had hitherto been no communications of any kind. The Maharajah started negotiations with two minor princes, whose states were situated on the Indian side of that border, for the building of a road

---

[32] S.C.O.R., 3rd Year, 228th Mtg., 16 Jan. 1948, pp. 43-46.

[33] *Ibid.*, p. 66.

[34] Menon, *op. cit.*, pp. 340, 343.

which would debouch into India.[35] However, when certain low-lying portions of the Gurdaspur district, contiguous to Jammu, were given by Radcliffe to India, it was no longer necessary to proceed with that project and it was abandoned. Steps were now taken to build a road linking Pathankot with Jammu. In order that Pakistan should not be alarmed, this was done secretly. When the news appeared in a local Kashmiri paper, the censor prohibited its circulation both within the state and outside it.[36] Without this road Kashmir's accession to India would have made no sense. Equally, if it was not intended that Kashmir should accede to India, the road made no sense.

We have referred to the Standstill Agreement with Pakistan. Under this Agreement the postal and telegraphic services of Kashmir were to be run by the government of Pakistan. The government of India, on 1 September 1947, sent to the General Post Office in London a list of places for which mails should be sent to India. This list included places in Jammu and Kashmir, as if that state formed a part of India. A similar directive was issued to all foreign postal administrations with regard to air mail. On 9 September 1947 the government of India appointed one of its officers to take charge of the Kashmir Postal Division. The government of Pakistan protested against this step but no reply was ever received to that protest. Documentary proof of these facts was put forward in the Security Council by Pakistan and not challenged by India.[37]

Towards the end of July the Maharajah ordered his Muslim subjects to deposit all arms in their possession. This was followed by an order for the disarming of the Muslim personnel of the Maharajah's army. In the latter half of August the Rashtriya Swayam Sewak Sangh (RSS) and Sikh murder gangs began to pour into

---

[35] Wilfrid Russell, *Indian Summer* (Bombay: Thacker, 1951), pp. 101-02.

[36] Josef Korbel, *Danger in Kashmir* (Princeton: Princeton University Press, 1954), pp. 60-61.

[37] S.C.O.R., 3rd Year, 229th Mtg., 17 Jan. 1948, p. 101.

Jammu.[38] Simultaneously, appeals were made by the government of Pakistan to the Maharajah of Kashmir, as well as by his Muslim subjects, that he should abandon his plans of massacring them.[39] As a direct result of the activities of the imported murderers, feelings ran high, particularly in the area of Poonch. A good many of the soldiers of the Pakistan Army were drawn from this area, which was also the home of no less than 65,000 veterans of World War II. In Poonch resentment against the Maharajah was greater than in other parts of the state. Here, every cow, buffalo, and sheep was taxed, and even every wife. A further tax had recently been imposed to meet the cost of tax collection.[40]

For self-preservation in the face of repression, the Poonchees organised a movement of resistance and sent messengers asking for help to the tribal areas of the North-West Frontier Province, where rifles have always been manufactured. The leader of this movement was a young London-trained barrister, Sardar Mohammed Ibrahim Khan, who, sensing that the Maharajah would accede to India, had been since June travelling the length and breadth of the state, rousing the spirit of the people. Three months later, when the Maharajah's forces had been defeated, the *Azad* (Free) Kashmir government was established, with Ibrahim Khan at its head.

Richard Symonds, the British Quaker who served on a mercy mission in the strife-torn areas, describes the origin of the revolt in Kashmir as follows:

> As August 15 and the partition of India drew near, there were many meetings and demonstrations in Poonch in favour of

---

[38] Lord Birdwood, *India and Pakistan: A Continent Decides* (New York: Frederick A. Praeger, 1954), p. 219; also published as *A Continent Decides* (London: Robert Hale, 1953). In addition, see Korbel, *op. cit.*, p. 55. The RSS and the Sikhs were already in action in Sept. 1947. (See S.C.O.R., 3rd Year, Supple. for Nov. 1948, Annex 6, Doc. III, para. 17, p. 81.)

[39] Telegram dated 19 Oct. 1947 from the Foreign Minister of Pakistan to the Prime Minister of Kashmir quoted in *White Paper on Jammu and Kashmir*, *op. cit.*, p. 11. Also *cf.* Bazaz, *op. cit.*, p. 325.

[40] See article by Richard Symonds, *The Statesman* (Calcutta), 4 Feb. 1948.

Kashmir joining Pakistan. Martial law was introduced and meetings fired on. After one such incident on August 27 in Nila But, Abdul Qayyum, a young *zamindar*, started the revolt with a few friends. Substantial men told me that they would never have joined such a rash enterprise but for the folly of the Dogras who burnt whole villages where only a single family was involved in the revolt. Rapidly most of the Muslim ex-servicemen joined Qayyum and in six weeks the whole district, except for Poonch city itself was in rebel hands.[41]

That was how the "trouble" in Kashmir began. This was confirmed by Sheikh Abdullah, who had meanwhile been released from prison. Speaking in New Delhi on 21 October 1947, Sheikh Abdullah, then regarded as a friend by Pandit Nehru, said:

> ... the present troubles in Poonch, a feudatory of Kashmir, were caused by the unwise policy adopted by the State. The people of Poonch ... had started a people's movement for the redress of their grievances. It was not communal. Kashmir State sent its troops, and there was panic in Poonch. But most of the adult population of Poonch were ... ex-servicemen in the Indian Army with close connections with the people of Jhelum and Rawalpindi ... [in Pakistan].

> They evacuated their women and children, crossed the frontier, and returned with arms supplied to them by willing people. The present position was that the Kashmir State forces were forced to withdraw in certain areas.[42]

Sheikh Abdullah pointed out that the Muslims of Kashmir were in fear of being exterminated like the Muslims of Kapurthala, where, despite their majority, they had been wiped out. He continued:

> ... Not a single Muslim would be found in that State now. The same fate had been meted out to them in Alwar, Bharatpur, and Kapurthala, where the Muslim population had either been killed or expelled, but obviously the fear was that the same thing might be enacted in Kashmir.[43]

---

[41] *Ibid.*

[42] Quoted by Sir Muhammad Zafrulla Khan, S.C.O.R., 3rd Year, 228th Mtg., 16 Jan. 1948, p. 68.

[43] *Ibid.*, p. 69.

In the Security Council India denied that there had been a spontaneous revolt against the Maharajah. However, Mr. V. P. Menon in his book repeatedly refers to what he in one place describes as "the spontaneous desertion of the entire Muslim element of the Kashmir State Forces."[44] Further, the fact that there was ferment against the Maharajah's government, long before the tribesmen entered Kashmir, was admitted in a statement issued by that government on 12 September 1947. It said:

> On 24 August 1947 ... large and highly excited mobs collected in West Bagh Tehsil, and on 25th August, disregarding all efforts to persuade them to disperse, marched on Bagh, a town in the vicinity where they reached the number of some 5,000, which swelled considerably during the next two days. These mobs were armed with firearms of various patterns, axes, spears and other weapons.[45]

This was nearly two months before the tribesmen went into Kashmir. There is no mention here of instigation by Pakistan.

The people did not take to arms until the Maharajah had started putting into effect his massacre-*cum*-expulsion plan. This he did in broad daylight and on a grand scale in the Poonch and Jammu areas. In the process, the technique adopted in the East Punjab and the East Punjab States (including Patiala, Kapurthala and Faridkot, whose Maharajahs had visited the Maharajah of Kashmir) was followed, the Maharajah's police and soldiers participating in the mass killing.[46] Town after town, and village after village, were ordered to be evacuated and the evacuees to leave for Pakistan. But they were not all allowed or able to get away. Sometimes hundreds, sometimes thousands of evacuees were all at once shot down with automatic weapons. People were killed in their homes, in the streets, in the fields. Whole villages were burnt down, their inhabitants

---

44 Menon, *op. cit.*, p. 414.
45 Quoted by Sir Muhammad Zafrulla Khan in S.C.O.R., 5th Year, 464th Mtg., 8 Feb. 1950, p. 11.
46 Bazaz, *op. cit.*, p. 325.

roasted to death.[47] In one area, wrote the London *Times* of 10
October 1948, "237,000 Muslims were systematically exterminated,
unless they escaped to Pakistan along the border, by the forces of the
Dogra State, headed by the Maharajah in person." The number of
those who had escaped to Pakistan was already over 100,000 before
the tribesmen went into Kashmir. Ian Stephens, formerly editor of
the British-owned *Statesman* of Delhi and Calcutta, and later Fellow
of King's College, Cambridge, speaking of the fate of the Muslim
population of Jammu, records:

> ... these, half a million or so, had almost totally disintegrated
> in the autumn of 1947. About 200,000 simply vanished, being
> presumably butchered or killed by epidemics and exposure
> while seeking to get away; the rest had fled into Pakistani
> Punjab.[48]

Addressing the Hindus of Jammu in November 1947, Abdullah said:
"You have emptied this area of Muslims."[49]

The news of the atrocities in Poonch and Jammu spread like wild-
fire to the far corners of the state and to the adjoining regions of
Pakistan, including the tribal area. The Muslims of Kashmir rose as
one man to defend themselves, their women and children and their
hearths and homes, to throw off once and for all the tyranny under
which they had suffered for a century. The Maharajah's forces were
engaged by the patriots and everywhere routed and scattered. On
22 October, Pathan tribesmen from the North-West Frontier areas
of Pakistan entered Kashmir and joined the fight against the Maharajah. In the words of the Special Correspondent of *The Daily Tele-
graph* of London (12 January 1948): "It was undoubtedly tales of
horrible cruelties against their co-religionists in Jammu, coupled
with heartening news of the insurrection, which first set them on
their course of invasion." However, in the Security Council India

---

[47] Sir Muhammad Zafrulla Khan in S.C.O.R., 3rd Year, 228th Mtg., 16 Jan.
1948, pp. 69-75; 235th Mtg., 24 Jan. 1948, pp. 249-53.

[48] Stephens, *op. cit.*, p. 138.

[49] Quoted in Bazaz, *op. cit.*, p. 331.

argued at length that the tribal incursion was instigated and organised by Pakistan authorities. This has throughout been the main basis of the Indian charge that Pakistan was an aggressor in Kashmir. But this has never been proved. Nor has the contention ever been accepted by the Security Council or by any of its members. According to Lord Birdwood, who has carried out an independent investigation of the Kashmir question:

> . . . The tribes had let it be known that whatever attitude the Pakistan Government took, they would not be deterred from moving to the assistance of their brothers in distress. The earliest contacts between Kashmir and the tribes must almost certainly have taken place in August, when ex-servicemen in Western Poonch began collecting money to buy arms and ammunition from the Frontier Province factories in tribal territory. At that time the State troops had established a blockade along the southern border, destroying the Jhelum River ferries and placing pickets on the bridges. A few of Ibrahim's men, however, managed to cross the Jhelum in rafts and were able to make for the frontier and purchase arms and ammunition with hard cash. It is reasonable to believe that the plans for tribal action were initiated in these first contacts.[50]

Was Pakistan to blame for not trying to stop the tribesmen from entering Kashmir? Lord Birdwood throws interesting light on this question. He says:

> The first news of actual movements reached the Governor [of the Frontier Province] on 20th October, when it was reported that 900 Mahsuds had left Tank in lorries for Kashmir. He immediately ordered their advance to be blocked at Kushalgarh, but they were already across the Indus. Simultaneously, news came from General Ross McCay, who commanded the Peshawar Division, that tribesmen in lorries were crossing the Attock Bridge. McCay was then asked by the Governor to take preventive action, but he was quite unable to do so, since at the time he had no formed units ready. . . .[51]

---

[50] Birdwood, *op. cit.*, pp. 221-22.

[51] *Ibid.*, p. 222.

Mr. Gopalaswami Ayyangar, presenting India's complaint in the Security Council, gave gruesome details of the atrocities allegedly perpetrated by the tribesmen in the town of Baramula, and described how a convent there had been desecrated and some nuns shot down by the tribesmen.[52] Sir Zafrulla Khan could neither admit nor deny these charges because Pakistan was not in control in the area and therefore had no knowledge of the events that had taken place there. However, he read out a letter written by the Mother Superior of the Sisters of St. Joseph's Hospital, Baramula, in which she thanked two Pakistani ladies for having "risked your lives to save us from Baramula when bombing and machine-gunning from the air made our situation there dangerous and impossible." The bombing and machine-gunning of the hospital were evidently done by the Indian forces, for it has never been alleged that the tribesmen had aircraft. The Mother Superior concluded: "We hope to go back to Baramula soon. Otherwise, I think we shall all join the *Azad* Kashmir forces."[53]

The allegations made in the Security Council against the tribesmen have since been repeated by Indian spokesmen, including Pandit Nehru. Commenting on the misconduct of the tribesmen, Bazaz observes: "reports of these excesses have been exaggerated by the Hindu publicists and the Nationalist renegades."[54] Bazaz, throughout the period of the tribal action, was in the Valley and therefore in the vicinity of the scene of action. Comparing the behaviour of the tribesmen with that of the Indian troops in Kashmir, he says: "If undisciplined and unorganized Muslim tribesmen are condemnable for what they did, the trained Indian soldiers who were members of regular armies deserve harsher criticism."[55] He demands: "Some

---

[52] Mr. Gopalaswami Ayyangar in S.C.O.R., 3rd Year, 227th Mtg., 15 Jan. 1948, p. 17.

[53] Quoted by Sir Muhammad Zafrulla Khan in S.C.O.R., 3rd Year, 229th Mtg., 17 Jan. 1948, pp. 115-16.

[54] Bazaz, *op. cit.*, p. 328.

[55] *Ibid.*, p. 337.

day when the people of Kashmir attain freedom, an enquiry shall have to be made into the conduct of the Indian armies while they remained in occupation of the State."[56]

It was the contention of the representative of India in the Security Council that the trouble in Kashmir began with the incursion of the tribesmen. He denied that there had been any killing at all of Muslims in the state before that date, or any attempt to expel them. The representative of India did not say that the representative of Pakistan had given an exaggerated picture of what had happened in Kashmir. He said: "That is a totally untrue picture."[57] Without imputing motives to the Indian representative, one might say that it was easier totally to deny the atrocities perpetrated by the Maharajah than to justify them. However, the representative of India could not altogether conceal the fact that he himself felt that there would have been justification for the tribesmen to enter Kashmir if the process of denuding it of its Muslim population had been going on. The representative of India said: "If there was no killing by the Dogras before that date of invasion, there can be no question of the invaders rushing to the aid of their distressed brethren in Kashmir."[58]

The government of Pakistan never denied that a certain number of Pakistani nationals might have been involved in the fighting in Kashmir. Some of them might even have been members of the Pakistan armed forces who had taken leave, or gone away without leave. In the words of Sir Zafrulla Khan, these men, according to the Indian view, ought to have said to themselves, "My brother may have been killed, my father may have been killed, my wife may have been raped and my children butchered, but I am a member of the Pakistan forces and must not retaliate." Sir Zafrulla added:

> That kind of thing might be expected of angels, but it cannot be expected of human beings. I will say that a man would be

---

[56] *Ibid.*
[57] Mr. Setalvad in S.C.O.R., 3rd Year, 234th Mtg., 23 Jan. 1948, p. 214.
[58] *Ibid.*, pp. 214-15.

a despicable coward, if, under those circumstances, he did nothing to help.[59]

According to Lord Birdwood:

> There are many precedents in history for unofficial support of a movement on foreign soil from sympathisers from another country. Englishmen have fought within recent years on both Spanish and Finnish territory in sympathy with their friends. Naturally there are protests. But the answer has usually been that it is not possible to control the movements of those who offer their services in a cause in which they passionately believe.[60]

According to the Pakistani view another part of the Maharajah's plan of "conspiracy" with the Indian government was to start disputation and pick a quarrel with Pakistan, this quarrel to be used as an excuse for not acceding to that country and for acceding to India. The Maharajah's government made a number of complaints to the government of Pakistan. It was alleged that there had been infiltration of armed people from Pakistan into Kashmir and that Pakistan had been withholding supplies of such articles as foodgrains, cloth, salt, and petrol. The government of Pakistan sent one of its senior Foreign Office officials, Major A. S. B. Shah, "immediately to discuss the whole question, with a view to arriving at a satisfactory solution."[61] The Maharajah's government refused to have any discussions with this official. Its intention evidently was to find fault with Pakistan, not to obtain redress of any genuine grievances. On 18 October the Maharajah's government proposed to the government of Pakistan "an impartial enquiry into the whole affair."[62] At the same time it said that if this request were not heeded, it would

---

[59] S.C.O.R., 3rd Year, 229th Mtg., 17 Jan. 1948, p. 109.

[60] Lord Birdwood, *Two Nations and Kashmir* (London: Robert Hale, 1956), p. 54.

[61] Telegram dated 6 Oct. 1947 from Foreign Minister, Karachi, to Prime Minister, Srinagar, *White Paper on Jammu and Kashmir*, *op. cit.*, p. 8.

[62] *Cf.* Telegram dated 19 Oct. 1947 from Foreign Minister, Karachi, to the Prime Minister, Kashmir, *ibid.*, p. 11.

ask for "friendly assistance."[63] The government of Pakistan was quick to recognise in this threat the warning that Kashmir was preparing to accede to India. However, the government of Pakistan agreed that a committee of enquiry be appointed and undertook to nominate its representative as soon as the Maharajah's government had nominated its representatives. The Maharajah's government, which had obviously advanced the proposal for an enquiry in the hope that Pakistan would reject it and thus give it an excuse for acceding to India, did not nominate any representative and did not even reply to Pakistan's later reference to the matter.[64]

At midnight on 25 October, under cover of darkness, a caravan of a hundred cars and lorries left Srinagar. The Maharajah was quitting Kashmir. The Treaty of Amritsar had been torn to pieces. Dogra rule, foisted on Kashmiris by the British, had ended. Accompanying the Maharajah in his flight were such of his precious belongings as he could carry, his family, his family idol and, to make his decisions for him, the Indian government's official, V. P. Menon.[65] From Jammu, near the Indian border where he sought refuge, the Maharajah on 26 October addressed a letter to Lord Mountbatten, the Governor-General of India. This letter contained sundry allegations against the government of Pakistan, complained of the tribal raid, and asked for help from the Indian dominion. The Maharajah said:

> Naturally they [the Government of India] cannot send the help asked for by me without my State acceding to the Dominion of India. I have accordingly decided to do so and I attach the Instrument of Accession for acceptance by your Government.

The Maharajah concluded by saying:

> I may also inform Your Excellency's Government that it is my intention at once to set up an Interim Government and

---

[63] Telegram dated 18 Oct. 1947 from the Government of Kashmir, *ibid.*, p. 10.
[64] Telegram dated 19 Oct. 1947 from the Foreign Minister of Pakistan to the Prime Minister of Kashmir, *ibid.*, p. 12.
[65] Bazaz, *op. cit.*, p. 328.

h

ask Sheikh Abdulla to carry the responsibilities in this emergency with my Prime Minister.[66]

The very next morning, Mountbatten wrote back to the Maharajah:

In the special circumstances mentioned by Your Highness, my Government have decided to accept the accession of Kashmir State to the Dominion of India. Consistently with their policy that in the case of any State where the issue of accession has been the subject of dispute, the question of accession should be decided in accordance with the wishes of the people of the State, it is my Government's wish that, as soon as law and order have been restored in Kashmir and her soil cleared of the invader, the question of the State's accession should be settled by a reference to the people.

Mountbatten concluded the letter by saying:

My Government and I note with satisfaction that your Highness has decided to invite Sheikh Abdulla to form an Interim Government to work with your Prime Minister.[67]

This letter is dated 27 October. At 9 a.m. on 27 October, Indian airborne troops landed at Srinagar.

It is clear from Mountbatten's letter that he regarded the accession of Kashmir to India as not permissible and not proper and that the government of India was accepting it only because of what he described as "special circumstances." Further, there is an admission that the issue of the accession of Kashmir "has been the subject of dispute," *i.e.*, between the people of the state and its ruler. It is thus recognised that the people of Kashmir, or substantial numbers of them, did not approve of the Maharajah's act of accession to India. For that reason, the accession was accepted subject to the question being "settled by a reference to the people," so that it could be decided in accordance with their wishes. This further shows that the accession was improper and that those who accepted it regarded it as such and recognised that the question could be properly decided only by the people themselves.

[66] *White Paper on Jammu and Kashmir, op. cit.*, p. 47.
[67] *Ibid.*, pp. 47-48.

While telegrams were being exchanged by the governments of India and Kashmir with the government of Pakistan, the last named government, although Kashmir had a Standstill Agreement with it, was not informed of the accession transactions until they had been completed. The government of Pakistan told the Security Council that they "have not accepted and cannot accept the accession of Jammu and Kashmir State to India. In their view the accession is based upon violence and fraud." The fraud consisted in "deliberately creating a set of circumstances with the object of finding an excuse for staging the accession." The violence lay in the Maharajah's plan to liquidate the Muslim population of the state.[68] In any event the offer of accession was made by a ruler whose subjects had amply demonstrated that they were against it and who, because of this very issue of accession, had risen in revolt against him. Furthermore, the Maharajah's troops had either deserted him or had been defeated by the popular forces; he had fled his capital; and he exercised no authority over most of the territory of his state, within whose borders there had come into existence a rival government, commanding popular allegiance and functioning in the civil and military spheres.[69]

Pandit Nehru and Indian representatives in the Security Council have from time to time contended that the accession was valid since it had the support of what they had alleged to be the largest popular organization in Kashmir: the National Conference, headed by Sheikh Abdullah. As Bazaz points out, the National Conference could not be accepted as the sole representative body or even as the most popular party of the people of Kashmir. It had not at that time a single member in the Legislative Assembly. Though, as Bazaz remarks, the National Conference had boycotted the elections held in January 1947, this fact made it more doubtful that the Conference had any considerable following or that it would have been victorious at the polls.[70] The movement for Pakistan, and more so the decision

---

[68] S.C.O.R., 3rd Year, Supple. for Nov. 1948, Annex 6, p. 83.
[69] Bazaz, *op. cit.*, p. 326.
[70] *Ibid.*, p. 339.

to establish Pakistan, had destroyed whatever popularity the Congress party or parties allied to it had enjoyed amongst the Muslims of those areas in which they were in the majority. In the 1946 elections in the North-West Frontier Province, the Congress party had been returned in the majority; but in the referendum in 1947, the majority voted for Pakistan. Likewise in the referendum in Sylhet, where, too, the issue was supposed to be doubtful, people voted for Pakistan. Similarly, the National Conference in Kashmir lost whatever popularity it had. It must, however, be remembered that Sheikh Abdullah had supported accession to India subject to the condition that a plebiscite would be held to decide the issue. When he demanded the fulfillment of that condition, India refused and that "great leader,"[71] that "man of high integrity and patriotism,"[72] as Pandit Nehru then regarded him, was put into prison in 1953. Could it still be argued that the accession was valid because Abdullah had supported it?

The references to Sheikh Abdullah in the two letters described above are significant. Thus, in his letter of 26 October, the Maharajah informed Lord Mountbatten of his intention that Sheikh Abdullah "should carry the responsibilities in this emergency with my Prime Minister." He did not identify Sheikh Abdullah, nor explain why he should carry these responsibilities. Likewise, Mountbatten noted "with satisfaction that Your Highness has decided to invite Sheikh Abdullah"—and here is a little variation—"to form an Interim Government to work with your Prime Minister." These references clearly show that Sheikh Abdullah's role in Kashmir, after its accession to India, had been the subject of detailed discussion between the two governments which had reached an understanding about it quite some time before the accession. Indeed Sheikh Abdullah was in New Delhi for weeks before the date of the accession and even on the date of the incursion of the Pathans.

It will be recalled that in May 1946 Sheikh Abdullah had been jailed for having started the "Quit Kashmir" movement, the aim of

---

71 *White Paper on Jammu and Kashmir, op. cit.*, pp. 53-54.

72 *Ibid.*, p. 66.

which was to end the rule of the Maharajah and his dynasty over the state. On 29 September 1947 the Maharajah released the Sheikh. This happened after an emissary of the Maharajah had met Sheikh Abdullah in Badrawah jail, where he was serving a nine year sentence. Thereafter, Sheikh Abdullah was transferred to the military cantonment at Badami Bagh, a suburb of Srinagar, where, until his release some three weeks later, he was frequently visited by the Maharajah's emissaries.[73]

Why did the Maharajah release Sheikh Abdullah? Evidently well before the date of release the government of India, whose leaders had been friendly with Sheikh Abdullah, had proposed to the Maharajah that, in order that the accession of Kashmir to India should have some semblance of popular support, Sheikh Abdullah should be released from prison and associated with the government of Kashmir; and Abdullah had accepted this arrangement. There can be no other explanation, indeed there is none, for the Maharajah's release of Abdullah, the object of whose "Quit Kashmir" movement was the dethroning of the Maharajah and the abolition of his dynasty. It is significant that Sheikh Abdullah's release was no part of a general amnesty, for the leaders of the Muslim Conference, who were also in prison without trial but who would have undoubtedly demanded accession to Pakistan, were not released. Indeed, the Muslim Conference leaders (such as Ghulam Abbas), Muslim troops of the state forces, and all Muslim police were in custody, with machine guns trained on them to prevent their escape.[74]

Simultaneously with Abdullah's release, a campaign of ruthless repression was launched against all individuals, groups, and parties that were opposed to accession to India. A ban was imposed on all opposition meetings and processions, while those in support of accession to India were encouraged and even subsidised. Pro-Pakistan newspapers were either forced to close down or subjected to rigorous pre-censorship. Prominent leaders of the Muslim Con-

[73] Bazaz, *op. cit.*, p. 319.
[74] Birdwood, *India and Pakistan: A Continent Decides, op. cit.*, pp. 303-04.

ference, who had gone to Karachi, were refused re-entry into their homeland. On 15 October Mehr Chand Mahajan, a Hindu Punjabi lawyer and a declared antagonist of Pakistan, was appointed Prime Minister. Within a few hours of his taking office Mahajan issued a pro-Indian press statement in which he denounced Pakistan.[75] On 18 October the liberal-minded Bazaz and two of his colleagues asked for facilities to go to Delhi to plead with the Indian leaders for a policy of non-interference in Kashmir affairs. They were taken into custody.[76]

At the instance of Mr. Jinnah, the Governor-General of Pakistan, a conference of the Governors-General and Prime Ministers of the two countries was arranged to take place on 29 October. In the words of Ian Stephens,

> The conference was first postponed and then proved a tragic fiasco, owing to Pandit Nehru's "indisposition" and to Sardar Patel's "inability to leave Delhi"—though he soon afterwards managed relatively long trips to Srinagar and Junagadh.[77]

Sardar Patel, it will be remembered, was Deputy Prime Minister and also in charge of the affairs of Indian states. Mr. Jinnah, however, had a meeting with Lord Mountbatten on 1 November and put forward to him the following proposals for the consideration of the Government of India:

1. To put an immediate stop to fighting, the two Governors-General should be authorized and vested with full powers by both Dominion Governments to issue a proclamation forthwith, giving forty-eight hours' notice to the two opposing forces to cease fire. The Governor-General of Pakistan has no control over the forces of the Provisional Government of Kashmir or the tribesmen engaged in the fighting, but he will warn them in the clearest terms that if they do not obey the order to cease fire immediately, the forces of both Dominions will make war on them;

---

[75] Bazaz, *op. cit.*, p. 325.

[76] *Ibid.*, p. 326.

[77] Stephens, *op. cit.*, p. 114.

2. Both the forces of India Dominion and the tribesmen to withdraw simultaneously and with the utmost expedition from Jammu and Kashmir State territory;

3. With the sanction of the two Dominion Governments, the two Governors-General to be given full powers to restore peace, undertake the administration of Jammu and Kashmir State, and arrange for a plebiscite without delay under their joint control and supervision.[78]

These proposals were not accepted, Lord Mountbatten pointing out that "it would be constitutionally improper for him to undertake this duty." It might, however, be mentioned that throughout his subsequent tenure in India, Lord Mountbatten undertook and carried out with his usual efficiency a large number of duties that were clearly "improper" for a constitutional Governor-General, not the least of which had regard to the Indian invasion of Kashmir. Mountbatten was expressly entrusted by the Indian Cabinet with the entire responsibility for negotiating with the rulers on the question of accession and for dealing with Hyderabad.[79] He could have been entrusted with a similar responsibility in respect of Kashmir.

At this meeting, according to Pandit Nehru, Lord Mountbatten suggested to Mr. Jinnah that the plebiscite in Kashmir "should be conducted under the auspices of UNO."[80] This proposal was reiterated by Pandit Nehru on 8 November 1947: "The Governments of India and Pakistan should make a joint request to UNO to undertake a plebiscite in Kashmir at the earliest possible date."[81] Pakistan's view of a plebiscite was stated by Mr. Liaquat Ali Khan in the following words:

We are ready to request U.N.O. immediately to appoint its representatives in Jammu and Kashmir State in order to put

[78] Quoted by Sir Muhammad Zafrulla Khan in S.C.O.R., 3rd Year, 229th Mtg., 17 Jan. 1948, p. 90.

[79] Menon, *op. cit.*, p. 98.

[80] Telegram dated 8 Nov. 1947 from Foreign Minister, New Delhi, to Prime Minister, Pakistan, quoted in *White Paper on Jammu and Kashmir, op. cit.*, p. 61.

[81] *Ibid.*

> a stop to fighting and to the repression of Muslims in the State, to arrange the programme of withdrawal of outside forces, to set up an impartial administration of the State till a plebiscite is held and to undertake the plebiscite under its direction and control for the purpose of ascertaining the free and unfettered will of the people of the State on the question of accession.
>
> We are prepared to accept a similar solution of the dispute regarding Manavadar and Junagadh.[82]

Pandit Nehru objected to these proposals and insisted that the Indian troops should remain, that Sheikh Abdullah's administration should continue, and that the plebiscite should be held under Indian control with the representatives of the United Nations acting only as advisers.[83] How impartial Sheikh Abdullah's administration was may be judged from the fact that after coming into power he imprisoned or exiled almost all his political opponents.

Subsequent events have shown that Sheikh Abdullah always felt that Kashmir ought not to be a part of India, that in any event Kashmir should enjoy full internal autonomy, and that accession to India should be only in respect of defence, foreign affairs, and communications, as it originally had been. Further, there were the solemn assurances that accession to India would only be provisional and that after a plebiscite Kashmir would be entitled to withdraw from it and accede to Pakistan or remain independent with the right of seeking admission to the United Nations. These assurances must doubtless have weighed with Sheikh Abdullah. The alternative to co-operating with India was to let power pass into the hands of his political adversaries. For this the Sheikh was not at any time prepared. Little did he realise that his Indian "friends," when he had served the purpose for which they had befriended him, would cast him aside, throw him into prison without a trial, and destroy Kashmir's autonomy.

---

[82] Mr. Liaquat Ali Khan's statement dated 16 Nov. 1947, *ibid.*, p. 65.

[83] Telegram dated 21 Nov. 1947 from Prime Minister, India, to Prime Minister, Pakistan, *ibid.*, pp. 66-67.

Meanwhile, between Mr. Liaquat Ali Khan and Pandit Nehru there raged a battle of words, through press statements, radio addresses, and exchange of telegrams. The Indian Prime Minister accused the government of Pakistan of permitting the tribesmen to enter Kashmir and high Pakistani officials of assisting them. He asserted "that members of the Pakistan Army, whether on leave or deserters, have joined the raiders and that military equipment that could only have come from the Pakistan Army has been in possession of the raiders."[84]

The Prime Minister of Pakistan, on the other hand, charged:

> The stress has deliberately been shifted [by the Government of India] to the so-called raiders . . . . To present the rebellion of an enslaved people to the world as an invasion from the outside simply because some outsiders have shown active sympathy for it, is a dishonest rewriting of history.[85]

That the fighting in Kashmir was being done overwhelmingly by the Kashmiris and continued to be done by them, even after the Indian troops had entered, was recognised by all neutral observers. Robert Trumbull, Special Correspondent of *The New York Times*, in his report of 12 January 1948, from New Delhi, estimated that 65 per cent of the fighters on the side of *Azad* Kashmir were native Kashmiris, 30 per cent tribesmen and 5 per cent Pakistanis. According to Lord Birdwood, the *Azad* Kashmir government soon after its establishment on 24 October 1956 could muster an army of 30,000 villagers.[86]

> These were men who, returning from a world war, now rallied to a cause which, in the face of the military Dogra dictator-ship in their midst, rapidly turned to a fierce faith.[87]

The Gilgit area was liberated entirely by its people. Not even the Indians have ever suggested that any tribesmen or any Pakistanis,

---

[84] *Ibid.*, p. 67.

[85] Mr. Liaquat Ali Khan's broadcast on 4 Nov. 1947, *ibid.*, p. 58.

[86] Birdwood, *op. cit.*, p. 219.

[87] *Ibid.*

military men or others, ever took part in the action against the Maharajah's troops in Gilgit. "In regard to the modern military equipment that you allege to be in possession of the Azad Kashmir forces," Mr. Liaquat Ali Khan told Pandit Nehru, "our information is that these forces are poorly equipped and such few modern weapons as they might possess have either been captured from the Dogra and Indian troops, or have been in the possession of ex-soldiers of Poonch since the time of the British."[88]

Clearly, in the midst of mounting human misery, the situation in Kashmir demanded a conference where the representatives of the contending parties could work out a settlement. As we have seen, such a conference was avoided before Kashmir's accession to India by the Maharajah and after this by the government of India. On 16 November Mr. Liaquat Ali Khan declared:

> We have made repeated efforts to have a conference with the India Dominion to bring about a peaceful settlement, but, on one pretext or another, the India Government, with the might of military power behind them, have flouted the idea. The attitude of the India Government indicates that they were determined to force a military decision on Kashmir and to reduce the plebiscite to a farce by eliminating the Muslim population by the cruel methods which are now in operation.[89]

However, the Indian forces, their automatic weapons, artillery, aircraft, and bombs notwithstanding, met with determined opposition from the patriots. After six weeks of fighting, it became clear that in order to win, India would require a great new military build-up and fresh operations. Neither could be undertaken in the Kashmir mountains during winter. Faced with this situation, the Pandit agreed to meet Mr. Liaquat Ali Khan. They had two meetings after the first week of December. Mr. Liaquat Ali Khan tried to persuade Pandit Nehru that the United Nations should be requested

[88] Letter dated 30 Dec. 1947 from the Prime Minister of Pakistan to the Prime Minister of India, *White Paper on Jammu and Kashmir, op. cit.*, p. 81.

[89] Statement of the Prime Minister of Pakistan issued on 16 Nov. 1947, *ibid.*, p. 64.

to send out a commission with comprehensive powers to settle the dispute; but Pandit Nehru was not prepared to agree to more than inviting United Nations observers to the plebiscite. As the peak of winter approached, with the military situation showing no signs of improvement, India decided to refer the matter to the Security Council, which it did on the last day of 1947. This was welcomed by Pakistan.[90]

In its letter to the Security Council the government of India said:

> . . . But, in order to avoid any possible suggestion that India had utilized the State's immediate peril for her own political advantage, the Government of India made it clear that once the soil of the State had been cleared of the invader and normal conditions restored, its people would be free to decide their future by the recognised democratic method of plebiscite or referendum which, in order to ensure complete impartiality, might be held under international auspices.[91]

This was a formal reaffirmation of the pledge contained in Lord Mountbatten's letter to the Maharajah accepting the accession of Kashmir. This pledge had been repeated by Pandit Nehru on numerous occasions, some of which have already been referred to. In a telegram to Mr. Liaquat Ali Khan on 25 October 1947, the Pandit had stated:

> I should like to make it clear that the question of aiding Kashmir in this emergency is not designed in any way to influence the State to accede to India. Our view which we have repeatedly made public is that the question of accession in any disputed territory or State must be decided in accordance with wishes of the people and we adhere to this view.[92]

On 28 October 1947 the Pandit said:

> I wish to assure you that action Government of India has taken has been forced upon them by circumstances of imminent

90 See letter dated 30 Dec. 1947 from the Prime Minister of Pakistan to the Prime Minister of India, quoted in *ibid.*, p. 80.

91 S.C.O.R., 3rd Year, Supple. for Nov. 1948, Annex 28, p. 141.

92 *White Paper on Jammu and Kashmir, op. cit.*, pp. 45-46.

and grave danger to Srinagar. They have no desire to intervene in affairs of Kashmir State after raiders have been driven
away and law and order established.

In regard to accession also it has been made clear that this is
subject to reference to people of State and their decision.
Government of India have no desire to impose any decision
and will abide by people's wishes.[93]

On 31 October 1947, the Pandit reasserted that

. . . [the accession had been] accepted on the condition that
as soon as the invader has been driven from Kashmir soil,
and law and order restored, the people of Kashmir would
decide the question of accession. It is open to them to accede
to either Dominion then.

He added:

Our assurance that we shall withdraw our troops from
Kashmir as soon as peace and order are restored and leave
the decision about the future of the State to the people of the
State is not merely a pledge to your Government but also to
the people of Kashmir and to the world.[94]

In a broadcast from New Delhi on 2 November 1947, the Pandit
said:

And here let me make clear that it has been our policy all
along that where there is a dispute about the accession of a
State to either Dominion, the decision must be made by the
people of that State. It was in accordance with this policy that
we added a proviso to the Instrument of Accession of
Kashmir.[95]

In the same broadcast he said:

We have declared that the fate of Kashmir is ultimately to
be decided by the people. That pledge we have given, and the

93 Telegram from Mr. Liaquat Ali Khan to Mr. Jawaharlal Nehru, *ibid.*, p. 48.
94 Telegram from Mr. Jawaharlal Nehru to Mr. Liaquat Ali Khan, *ibid.*, p. 51.
95 *Ibid.*, p. 53.

Maharaja has supported it, not only to the people of Kashmir but to the world. We will not, and cannot back out of it. We are prepared when peace and law and order have been established to have a referendum held under international auspices like the United Nations. We want it to be a fair and just reference to the people, and we shall accept their verdict. I can imagine no fairer and juster offer.[96]

The same day Pandit Nehru telegraphed to Mr. Liaquat Ali Khan:

I have stated our Government's policy and made it clear that we have no desire to impose our will on Kashmir but to leave the final decision to the people of Kashmir. I further stated that we have agreed to an impartial international agency like the United Nations supervising any referendum. This principle we are prepared to apply to any State where there is a dispute about accession. If these principles are accepted by your Government there should be no difficulty in giving effect to them.[97]

On 21 November 1947 the Pandit telegraphed to Mr. Liaquat Ali Khan:

I have repeatedly stated that as soon as the raiders have been driven out of Kashmir or have withdrawn and peace and order have been established, the people of Kashmir should decide the question of accession by plebiscite or referendum under international auspices such as those of the United Nations.[98]

Speaking in the Constituent Assembly of India on 25 November 1947, the Pandit stated:

Further, we made it clear that as soon as law and order had been restored in Kashmir and her soil cleared of the invaders, the question of the State's accession should be settled by reference to the people.[99]

---

96 *Ibid.*, p. 55.
97 *Ibid.*
98 *Ibid.*, p. 67.
99 *Ibid.*, p. 69.

In the same statement the Pandit said:

> In order to establish our *bona fides* we have suggested that when the people are given the chance to decide their future this should be done under the supervision of an impartial tribunal such as the United Nations Organisation.[100]

In Pakistan, there was realistic appraisal of Pandit Nehru's pledge. In a telegram dated 24 November 1947 to the Prime Minister of the United Kingdom, Mr. Liaquat Ali Khan said: "The oft-repeated promise of the India Government and Pandit Nehru that they are willing to have a plebiscite in Kashmir is intended to mislead the world."[101] He pointed out:

> The India Government's insistence upon the retention of their troops in Kashmir until they have restored law and order to their own satisfaction can only mean that India troops will stay in the State until they have crushed by military force all opposition to their permanent occupation of Kashmir. The methods by which the maintenance of law and order is used to consolidate an alien rule are well known.[102]

Mr. Liaquat Ali Khan reiterated that "what the India Government is after is permanent occupation of Kashmir."[103]

In fact Mr. Liaquat Ali Khan told Pandit Nehru on 30 December 1947: "The plea that the accession is only temporary pending restoration of peaceful conditions is too flimsy to stand examination . . ."[104]

However, in presenting India's complaint to the Security Council, Mr. Gopalaswami Ayyangar said:

> . . . We desire only to see peace restored in Kashmir and to ensure that the people of Kashmir are left free to decide in an orderly and peaceful manner the future of their State. We

---

100 *Ibid.*, p. 71.

101 Quoted by Sir Muhammad Zafrulla Khan in S.C.O.R., 3rd Year, 229th Mtg., 17 Jan. 1948, p. 96.

102 *Ibid.*, p. 97.

103 *Ibid.*

104 *White Paper on Jammu and Kashmir, op. cit.*, p. 81.

have no further interest, and we have agreed that a plebiscite in Kashmir might take place under international auspices after peace and order have been established . . .[105]

A little later in the same speech Mr. Ayyangar went a step further and declared:

The question of the future status of Kashmir *vis-à-vis* her neighbours and the world at large, and a further question, namely, whether she should withdraw from her accession to India, and either accede to Pakistan or remain independent, with a right to claim admission as a Member of the United Nations—all this we have recognized to be a matter for unfettered decision by the people of Kashmir, after normal life is restored to them.[106]

---

[105] S.C.O.R., 3rd Year, 227th Mtg., 15 Jan. 1948, p. 28.
[106] *Ibid.*, p. 29.

chapter five

Kashmir Dispute: Failure of United Nations Mediation

It was under Article 35 of the United Nations Charter that India referred the Kashmir question to the Security Council as a "situation whose continuance is likely to endanger the maintenance of international peace and security." India complained:

> ... Such a situation now exists between India and Pakistan owing to the aid which invaders, consisting of nationals of Pakistan and of tribesmen from the territory immediately adjoining Pakistan on the north-west, are drawing from Pakistan for operations against Jammu and Kashmir, a State which has acceded to the Dominion of India and is part of India....[1]

In the Indian government's letter to the Security Council there was no mention of the revolt of the people of Kashmir against the

---

[1] Security Council, Official Records (S.C.O.R.): 3rd Year, Supple. for Nov. 1948, Annex 28, p. 139.

Maharajah, of his flight from Kashmir, or of the establishment of the *Azad* (Free) Kashmir government.

In reply, the government of Pakistan emphatically denied that they were:

> ... giving aid and assistance to the so-called invaders or have committed any act of aggression against India. On the contrary and solely with the object of maintaining friendly relations between the two Dominions the Pakistan government have continued to do all in their power to discourage the tribal movement by all means short of war.

That a certain number of independent tribesmen and persons from Pakistan may be "helping the Azad Kashmir Government in their struggle for liberty as volunteers" was not denied by the government of Pakistan.[2]

Pakistan, also under Article 35 of the Charter, brought to the notice of the Security Council all its disputes with India. Pakistan complained of India's attempts to paralyse Pakistan; of the genocide of Indian Muslims; of the forcible occupation by India of Junagadh and the adjoining states which had acceded to Pakistan; and of India's refusal to implement the partition agreements, a refusal that had led to the withholding of Pakistan's apportioned share of the cash balances and military stores so vital to its existence. India was accused by Pakistan of having obtained the accession of Kashmir by fraud and violence involving large-scale massacre and looting of Kashmiris by the armed forces and other subjects of the Maharajah and the government of India. Pakistan complained of repeated raids and incursions into its territory by Indian troops and bombings by the Indian Air Force. Finally, India was charged with openly threatening Pakistan with direct military attack.[3]

The government of Pakistan told the Security Council that the disputes to which it had drawn the attention of the Security Council

---

[2] *Ibid.*, Annex 6, Doc. I, p. 68.

[3] *Ibid.*, Doc. 2, pp. 68-75.

i

were "all inter-related" and pleaded for "a just and fair settlement of every one of these disputes being simultaneously achieved."[4] The Security Council was requested by Pakistan to take appropriate measures in respect of its various charges against India and

> . . . to arrange for the cessation of fighting in the State of Jammu and Kashmir; the withdrawal of all outsiders, whether belonging to Pakistan or the Indian Union, including members of the armed forces of the Indian Union; the restoration and rehabilitation of all Muslim residents of the Jammu and Kashmir State as on 15th August 1947, who have been compelled to leave the State as a result of the tragic events since that date, and the payment to them by the Indian Union of due compensation for the damage and injuries suffered by them; to take steps for the establishment of an impartial and independent administration in the State of Jammu and Kashmir, fully representative of the people of that State; and thereafter to hold a plebiscite to ascertain the free and unfettered will of the people of the Jammu and Kashmir State as to whether the State shall accede to Pakistan or India . . .[5]

Having heard the statements of the representatives of India and Pakistan, the Security Council on 17 January 1948 adopted a resolution calling upon the two governments "to take immediately all measures within their power (including public appeals to their people) calculated to improve the situation" and to refrain from saying or doing anything likely to aggravate it. Further the two governments were requested "to inform the Council immediately of any material change in the situation which occurs or appears to either of them to be about to occur."[6]

By a resolution adopted on 20 January 1948 the Council established the United Nations Commission for India and Pakistan, composed of three members, one to be nominated by India, the other

---

[4] *Ibid.*, p. 75.

[5] *Ibid.*, pp. 74-75.

[6] General Assembly, Official Records: 3rd Sess., Supple. No. 2 (A/620), p. 56.

by Pakistan, and the third by the two of them. This Commission was "to proceed to the spot as quickly as possible" and to keep the Council informed "of the development of the situation" and to submit regularly to the Council its conclusions and proposals. While the Commission was first to concern itself with the Kashmir situation, it was also to take up the other matters about which Pakistan had complained to the Security Council when it was directed by the Council to do so.[7] Following the adoption of this resolution, the description of the item on the agenda of the Security Council, hitherto "the Jammu and Kashmir question," was changed to the "India-Pakistan question" despite strong protests by the Indian representative.

If the Commission visualised in the resolution of 20 January 1948 had immediately proceeded to the spot, even though with imprecise instructions, it would have had a salutary effect on the Kashmir dispute. But no Commission was to come out for six months.

Mr. Gopalaswami Ayyangar, speaking for India, called upon the Security Council to persuade the government of Pakistan:

> (1) to prevent Pakistan Government personnel, military and civil, from participating in or assisting the invasion of Jammu and Kashmir State; (2) to call upon other Pakistani nationals to desist from taking any part in the fighting in Jammu and Kashmir State; (3) to deny to the invaders: (i) access to and use of its territory for operations against Kashmir; (ii) military and other supplies, and (iii) all other kinds of aid that might tend to prolong the present struggle.[8]

That the questions which Pakistan had raised in its counter-complaint were interlinked with the Kashmir question was generally recognised by the members of the Security Council. Thus Mr. José Arce (Argentina) said:

> ... I repeat, we cannot shut our eyes to these questions and ignore them; but supposing that, in order to conform to all

---

[7] S.C.O.R., 3rd Year, Supple. for Nov. 1948, Annex 28, pp. 64-65.

[8] S.C.O.R., 3rd Year, 227th Mtg., 15 Jan. 1948, p. 28.

the rules of procedure of a high court of justice, we were to take the question of Jammu and Kashmir first and the other questions afterwards, it is obvious that the Council could not deal with them separately but would be obliged to consider them as a whole.[9]

Mr. Arce referred to the Indian occupation of Junagadh and said:

> ... If that is not aggression, if that is not war, if anyone thinks that we should close our eyes to these things, I for my part cannot assent to such a procedure . . .[10]

However, all the members of the Council agreed that Kashmir should be dealt with first.

Sir Zafrulla Khan made the following demands, whose fulfillment, he said, was essential for a real settlement of the Kashmir question:

> ... Considering that it is mainly the population of Kashmir that is fighting, it must be completely assured, and effective guarantees must be given, that Muslims will not be persecuted and oppressed and that the people of the State shall decide their own constitution and the shape of their Government.

> Assurances must be given and fulfilled that Indian troops and all outsiders shall withdraw; this assurance must be given in order that law and order may be restored. If that assurance is given, it would go a very long way towards bringing about a cessation of the conditions that prevail today. All outsiders, that is to say, the Sikhs and Hindus who are coming from outside, the Muslims who may not be fighting but who come from outside for any sincere purpose, shall withdraw, and all those who have been compelled to leave the State of Kashmir and who are citizens of Kashmir shall be permitted to return. In order to enable a free choice to be made by the people of Kashmir in the matter of accession, that is, whether they will accede to Pakistan or whether they will accede to India, a neutral and impartial administration shall be set up. Assurance must be given to that effect.[11]

---

[9] S.C.O.R., 3rd Year, 231st Mtg., 22 Jan. 1948, p. 151.
[10] *Ibid.*, p. 152.
[11] S.C.O.R., 3rd Year, 235th Mtg., 24 Jan. 1948, p. 254.

Mr. Warren Austin (United States) called for "an interim Government that is free from the smell of brimstone" and for "the return of *émigrés*."[12] General Andrew McNaughton (Canada) advocated the establishment of an "authority which will be recognized by everyone concerned as strictly impartial."[13] Mr. Guy de la Tournelle (France) laid down three conditions:

1. The withdrawal of foreign troops from the State of Kashmir.

2. The return of the inhabitants, irrespective of their race —Hindu or Moslem—to their places of origin in that State.

3. The establishment of a free administration which would not exert pressure on the population and would give absolute guarantees of a free vote.[14]

On 28 January, the President of the Council, Mr. Fernand Van Langenhove (Belgium), submitted two draft resolutions: one concerned the plebiscite on the question of accession, which, it was proposed, was to be "organized, held and supervised under the authority of the Security Council" and the other related to "promoting the cessation of acts of hostility and violence."[15]

The President disclosed that he had received drafts of resolutions from the Pakistan and Indian Delegations. The Pakistan draft called upon the Commission to arrange for:

1. The establishment of an impartial interim administration in the State of Jammu and Kashmir;

2. The withdrawal from the territories of the State of Jammu and Kashmir of the armed forces of the Indian Union and the tribesmen; also all trespassers whether belonging to Pakistan or the Indian Union;

3. The return of all residents of the Jammu and Kashmir State who have left or have been compelled to leave the State as a result of the tragic events since 15 August 1947;

---

12 *Ibid.*, pp. 261-62.

13 *Ibid.*, p. 262.

14 *Ibid.*, p. 263.

15 S.C.O.R., 3rd Year, 236th Mtg., 28 Jan. 1948, p. 269.

4. The holding of a plebiscite to ascertain the free, fair, and
unfettered will of the people of the State as to whether the
State shall accede to Pakistan or to India . . .[16]

Hitherto India had given profuse promises about a plebiscite in
Kashmir. Faced with the necessity of reducing them to the language
of a resolution, it disclosed its real intentions. The Indian draft
resolution, while calling for the strictest measures for stopping the
fighting, made the plebiscite a remote and uncertain contingency.
After the stoppage of fighting, a period of six months was to be
allowed for the restoration of normal conditions. Indian troops were
to stay in Kashmir. An impartial administration was not to be
reconstituted and Sheikh Mohammad Abdullah, who was a partisan
of India, was to head the interim government under the Maharajah.
Even after the restoration of normal conditions the plebiscite was not
to be held at once. In fact there was no mandatory provision at all
for the holding of a plebiscite. It was one of the hopes expressed in
the Indian draft resolution. The other hopes were that steps would
be taken to convoke a national assembly based on adult suffrage and
that thereafter a national government would be constituted. In effect
the Indian resolution proposed that if a plebiscite were held at some
remote time, it should be in the presence of Indian troops and under
the supervision of a pro-Indian administration. Persons appointed
by the United Nations were to act merely as advisers and observers.[17]

The members of the Security Council, taken aback by the Indian
proposals, now spoke out their minds frankly. Mr. Philip Noel-Baker
(United Kingdom) said:

The cause which is now in dispute here, the cause of the
fighting in Kashmir, is the question: To which of the two
Governments, India or Pakistan, shall Kashmir accede?
In my conception, infinitely the best way to stop the fighting is
to assure those who are engaged in it that a fair settlement will
be arrived at under which their rights will be assured. In other

16 *Ibid.*, p. 268.
17 *Ibid.*, pp. 266-67.

words, as I remarked to the representative of India in our first talk after his arrival, in my profound conviction, a settlement arrived at quickly in the Security Council is the real way to stop the fighting. The whole thing from the preliminary measures as to the fighting, right up to the conduct of the plebiscite in the end, is all one problem. . . .[18]

Mr. Austin (United States) said:

I think that all members of the Security Council understand that a settlement would gain great strength if it had the approbation of good people all over the world. There is nothing, in my view of the matter, that will command that approbation as will a machinery that is free from suspicion and that gives to all the world the appearance of impartiality by actually being an impartial administration of the plebiscite.[19]

Mr. Tingfu F. Tsiang (China) said:

It is obvious that the key to the problem lies in the plebiscite. If the principle of a free and impartial plebiscite for deciding the all-important question of the accession of Kashmir to India or Pakistan should be accepted, much of the incentive to violence and the use of force would be removed.[20]

Mr. Arce (Argentina) said:

This matter having been referred to the Security Council, the Council is perfectly free to decide as it thinks fit, on the sole condition that it acts within the framework of the Charter. This is the legal point of view. But even from the factual point of view, there can be no other solution. Both the Maharajah, as absolute monarch of Kashmir, and the government or governments established by him, have already shown themselves biased in favour of one of the parties and cannot therefore preside over a free plebiscite. Even if they could, they should not do so, because the opposing party would not recognize the fairness of this plebiscite, even if it had been fairly conducted.

---

[18] *Ibid.*, p. 283.

[19] S.C.O.R., 3rd Year, 237th Mtg., 29 Jan. 1948, p. 287.

[20] *Ibid.*, p. 288.

Mr. Arce added:

> It is worth while remembering the Latin proverb, which says
> *sublata causa, tollitur effectus*, or, in other words remove the
> cause and the effects will disappear. In this case, the cause of
> all the disturbances, whether from India or Pakistan, or from
> the tribes, lies in the rebellion of the people of Kashmir
> against the absolute monarch who rules them as if he were
> running a farm and the 4 million inhabitants were so many
> heads of cattle and not human beings.[21]

Mr. Gopalaswami Ayyangar had objected to the establishment
of a reconstituted nonpartisan administration in Kashmir on the
ground that it would infringe the sovereignty of the Maharajah.[22]
Mr. Austin, commenting on that argument, said:

> ... Whenever a sovereign, whether it is a personal sovereign
> or a corporate sovereign, exercises his sovereignty in a specific
> manner which is found to be necessary to meet an emergency,
> he does not lose his sovereignty; he strengthens it. He may be
> saving it from destruction. He may exercise that sovereignty
> through an interim government, just as he is doing already,
> or he may exercise it in some other way. However, the mere
> exercise of sovereignty or the delegation of certain specific
> powers does not destroy or weaken his ultimate sovereignty.[23]

More pointedly, Sir Zafrulla Khan drew attention to the fact that
only a few days earlier the government of India had suppressed the
governments of the Maharajahs of Alwar and Bharatpur states and
appointed its own nominees to administer them, with a view to
facilitating the investigation of the murder of Mr. Gandhi. Said Sir
Zafrulla Khan:

> After having assumed in that manner the administration of
> these two States, it is the idlest pretence to contend that it
> would be against constitutional principles if the Government

---

21 S.C.O.R., 3rd Year, 240th Mtg., 4 Feb. 1948, pp. 366-67.
22 S.C.O.R., 3rd Year, 239th Mtg., 3 Feb. 1948, p. 329.
23 S.C.O.R., 240th Mtg., 4 Feb. 1948, pp. 372-73.

of India agreed to the establishment of conditions which alone could guarantee a free and fair plebiscite.[24]

In the words of Sir Zafrulla Khan, the government of India in refusing to agree to an impartial administration took up the position that: "A free and fair plebiscite we concede, but conditions under which alone a free and fair plebiscite can be held we do not concede."[25]

It will be recalled that in his broadcast of 2 November 1947 Pandit Nehru had categorically stated that his government had "added a proviso to the Instrument of accession of Kashmir" to the effect that "the decision must be made by the people."[26] This was contradicted by Mr. Ayyangar who said: "To the best of my memory, the Instrument, in the case of Kashmir, does not contain any conditions. It does not state that the accession is provisional."[27] However, Mr. Austin emphasised that in so far as Lord Mountbatten had accepted the accession of Kashmir to India subject to the proviso that it would be settled by reference to the people, the proviso "became an actual integral part of the terms of accession."[28]

On 10 February General McNaughton (Canada), who had become President of the Council, laid before the members a draft resolution[29] which called for ending all acts of violence and hostility; for the withdrawal of all irregular forces and armed individuals who had entered Kashmir; for the co-operation of the armed forces of the two governments in the establishment of order and security; for the withdrawal of regular armed forces on the re-establishment of law and order and for the return of refugees to their homes; for the removal of restrictions on legitimate political activity; for the release of political prisoners; for the establishment of an interim administration commanding general confidence; and for the holding

---

24 S.C.O.R., 3rd Year, 244th Mtg., 11 Feb. 1948, pp. 97-98.
25 *Ibid.*, p. 96.
26 *White Paper on Jammu and Kashmir* (Delhi: Govt. of India, n.d.), p. 53.
27 S.C.O.R., 3rd Year, 242nd Mtg., 6 Feb. 1948, p. 31.
28 S.C.O.R., 3rd Year, 240th Mtg., 4 Feb. 1948, p. 371.
29 S.C.O.R., 3rd Year, Supple. for Jan.-March 1948, Document S/667, pp. 24-25.

of a plebiscite to be organised and supervised under the authority of the Security Council at the earliest possible date.

The President also announced to the consternation of the members of the Security Council that India had asked for a postponement of the consideration by the Council of the Kashmir dispute.

Rejecting General McNaughton's draft resolution, Mr. Gopala-swami Ayyangar said:

> ... We are not prepared to agree to the existing Emergency Administration's being replaced by another, either at once or after being converted into a council of ministers with Sheikh Mohammad Abdullah as Prime Minister. That Administration has to be there till a national government, based upon a national assembly—for which our scheme provides—has come into existence. It is under that national government that we said the plebiscite should be taken. That is one point.
>
> The second suggestion that has been made in some of the speeches is that the Indian Army should withdraw as soon as the fighting ceases. That is a matter which we are not prepared to accept at the present moment.[30]

"As regards the plebiscite," the Indian representative said:

> ... our position has been made perfectly clear to the members of the Security Council on a previous occasion. We agree to a plebiscite; we agree to its being under international auspices, but the international auspices we are willing to agree to are only to the extent of having the Security Council give advice and guidance to the Kashmir Government in the organization and holding of that plebiscite and to having the Security Council send observers to see how that plebiscite is conducted. We are not prepared to go beyond that at the present moment.[31]

Explaining why he had asked for an adjournment, Mr. Ayyangar said:

---

[30] S.C.O.R., 3rd Year, 243rd Mtg., 10 Feb. 1948, pp. 67-68.

[31] *Ibid.*, p. 69.

> ... I am constrained to tell the Security Council that it is because I feel that the trend of opinion in the Security Council has not adequately appreciated the urgency and the immediacy of the solution of this problem, and that this trend has gone on to consider problems which, if not altogether irrelevant to the main issue, could certainly have waited for consideration for a considerable time.[32]

The Indian representative was now publicly confirming Mr. Liaquat Ali Khan's suspicions about the genuineness of the Indian promise of a plebiscite in Kashmir. Mr. Ayyangar asked for an adjournment to a date between 15 and 20 March.

Mr. Tsiang supported the request for an adjournment. But most of the other members of the Council were severely critical of the entire Indian attitude. According to Mr. Austin, what India desired was:

> ... that the Security Council should take up a position which would amount to that of an ally in a war, and should pull off Pakistan and allow India to finish the job by force against the tribesmen. That is the very last position which the Security Council ought to take.

He added:

> I hope that when the Indian delegation returns to its country it will make very plain the fact that the United Nations is not engaged in promoting war or taking sides in war, and that the Security Council's business is just the opposite—namely, trying to find a pacific solution of this problem.[33]

Mr. Alfonso López (Colombia) said:

> If I may be allowed to speak my mind rather frankly, I would say this situation worries me a great deal, because at a certain stage in our deliberations the Indian delegation made it distinctly clear that the suggestions they had advanced to the Security Council were the maximum they could accept.

---

[32] *Ibid.*, p. 66.
[33] *Ibid.*, pp. 75-76.

When they heard that we were continuing with our discussion, the representative of India went on to suggest that anything short of what he had advanced would place the Indian delegation in a difficult position. I should wish to know exactly what he meant. In the light of his letter to the President of the Security Council (document S-668), I believe I am warranted in saying that it is really surprising to find that after the Indian delegation had been invited to discuss this new draft resolution or suggestion, they should have notified the Security Council that the whole delegation had been instructed to return to India.

The members of the Security Council should bear in mind that we are discussing this question at the request of the delegation of India. We should bear in mind that we have been discussing the matter for six weeks, and that seems to give the representative of India good reason to say that the Security Council is fiddling while Jammu and Kashmir burns. Now they wish to leave. I therefore believe it would be more appropriate for us to say that after having insisted that this question is of a great urgency, they cannot wait any longer and want to drop the matter now. The delegation will then be travelling while Jammu and Kashmir burns. . . .

Before actually finishing discussion of their request for adjournment, we have also been informed that they already made arrangements to leave tomorrow.[34]

Speaking on the principle of the deferment, Mr. Noel-Baker (United Kingdom) said:

. . . It is a very serious matter that, while a war is going on, while men are being killed, the Security Council should suspend its work which is designed to bring the fighting to an end.[35]

Pleading with the Indian delegation to postpone its departure Mr. Noel-Baker said: "There is nothing irrevocable about an aircraft

---

[34] *Ibid.*, pp. 80-81.
[35] S.C.O.R., 3rd Year, 244th Mtg., 11 Feb. 1948, pp. 104-05.

ticket. There may be something irrevocable in the departure of the Indian delegation."[36] On the substance of the case he asked:

> ... Why does the Indian representative suggest that a plebiscite, which he admits is not irrelevant, is nevertheless a matter which could wait for a considerable time? Why does he call them, as he did, "long-range problems"? I think it would be a disaster both to India and to Pakistan if we so regard them. What is long-term about them? Why should it take long to make a settlement?[37]

Returning to the charge, Mr. López said:

> Then, another doubt arises in my mind. What is going to happen in Jammu and Kashmir in the meantime? Is the fighting to continue? Will the Indian Government be free to carry on its military operations? Does the Security Council expect, by any chance, that two, three, or four weeks from now, it is going to renew its discussions at the political or at the military level at which it discontinued them?[38]

Drawing attention to the record, the speaker pointed out that:

> ... from the moment that the Security Council did not agree to take the one action that the Indian delegation wanted— action to stop the fighting without taking action on the plebiscite—they have been gradually coming to the point at which they have arrived.[39]

Mr. López later said:

> ... When we did not agree with the members of the Indian delegation, they actually withdrew from the conversations with the President of the Security Council, and now they prepare to withdraw from the Security Council itself. That is putting it rather crudely, and in fact they do it more intelligently and in a very nice manner, but that is the net result of this suggestion in effect.[40]

---

36 *Ibid.*, p. 109.
37 *Ibid.*, p. 108.
38 S.C.O.R., 3rd Year, 245th Mtg., 11 Feb. 1948, pp. 111-12.
39 *Ibid.*, p. 114.
40 *Ibid.*, p. 123.

Mr. Arce (Argentina) declared that "Kashmir is not a territory of India—no Power will either propose or accept a plebiscite to surrender a part of its territory, as India's Government did." Stressing that "the cause of the present war is the rebellion of the Kashmir people against their Ruler," Mr. Arce said that the only remedy is to look to the will of these people and settle the matter of the plebiscite first of all, to which he added that the Security Council could not work as a tool for the applicants who came before it and was obliged to settle all the questions that divided India and Pakistan.[41]

Mr. Ayyangar, reminding the Security Council that he belonged to a "proud civilisation," said:

> Is this, I ask, the consideration that a great country like mine is entitled to expect from an international body? Are we really taking any steps for the purpose of sabotaging the consideration of this great problem by the Security Council?[42]

Mr. Ayyangar complained: "I have been too much twitted today by the unnecessary and very unjustified suspicion and reluctance with which this innocent request for an adjournment was made to you."[43]

The request, innocent or not, was acceded to. In the words of Sir Zafrulla Khan:

> ... Thereupon, if one might be forgiven for saying so, the matter went underground; that is to say, one was no longer conscious of what was happening. One had to depend upon scraps of information that appeared in the Press from time to time, to which one did not know how much value to attach. The Security Council will forgive me if I give expression to the feeling that subsequent events have shown that these indications in the Press were not so unfounded as one had, in one's innocence and simplicity, imagined at the time. They indeed gave a very accurate reflection of what was going on behind the scenes. If that is so, it would appear that at least some of the members of the Security Council seemed to have

---

41 *Ibid.*, p. 118.
42 *Ibid.*, p. 127.
43 *Ibid.*, p. 129.

realized during that interval, with a sense of sharp surprise, that the Security Council had for once let itself slip into a position of fairness and impartiality between two contending parties, which might help to restore to the United Nations a fraction of the prestige that it was so rapidly losing in the eyes of the world. . . .[44]

The full story of how the plan which was by consensus evolving in the Security Council was sabotaged has not yet been publicly told by those who know it. However, the Western powers abandoned in the Security Council the policy of "even-handed justice" which was supposedly producing "heavy-handed diplomacy."[45]

On Mr. Gopalaswami Ayyangar's return to New York, the Security Council resumed consideration of the Kashmir question on 10 March. But after the session on 18 March, the Council did not take up the question again until 17 April. Thus another month was lost. On 21 April the Council adopted a draft resolution[46] sponsored by Belgium, Canada, China, Colombia, the United Kingdom, and the United States.

This resolution differed in material particulars from General McNaughton's draft which, according to Mr. Noel-Baker, was a faithful translation of the broad principles which the Council held to be the basis of the settlement of the dangerous question of Kashmir.[47] Under the resolution adopted on 21 April, there was no provision for the unqualified and wholesale withdrawal of regular armed forces, but India was required to reduce them progressively to the minimum strength needed for the support of civil power. There was to be no joint responsibility of India and Pakistan for the maintenance of law and order, except with the agreement of the governments of the two countries. There was to be no interim administration to ensure the freedom of the plebiscite, but represen-

---

[44] S.C.O.R., 3rd Year, 285th Mtg., 19 April 1948, p. 26.

[45] Alan Campbell-Johnson, *Mission with Mountbatten* (London: Robert Hale, 1951), p. 287.

[46] S.C.O.R., 3rd Year, Supple. for April 1948, Document S/726, p. 8.

[47] S.C.O.R., 3rd Year, 243rd Mtg., 10 Feb. 1948, p. 64.

tatives of major political groups were to be asked by India to share in the conduct of the administration. The plebiscite was to be organised by a Plebiscite Administrator, nominated by the Secretary-General of the United Nations. The Plebiscite Administrator was to function as an officer of the state of Jammu and Kashmir. There were sundry provisions for ensuring the fairness of the plebiscite.

In vain did Sir Zafrulla Khan plead that the resolution violated every one of the principles that the members of the Security Council had repeatedly and emphatically advanced before the adjournment.[48] In vain did he protest that the resolution was unfair to Pakistan and would not assure a free and impartial plebiscite.[49] The representatives on the Security Council did not even bother to reply to Sir Zafrulla's arguments and adopted the resolution, the Soviet Union and the Ukraine abstaining.

India, having succeeded in coercing the Security Council into going back on the draft resolution of 10 February, was emboldened to embark on a series of defiances of that body. It served notice that it would not co-operate in the implementation of even the resolution of 21 April. However, it offered to confer with the United Nations Commission for India and Pakistan if it was sent out.[50] Pakistan, while criticising the resolution, did not reject it.[51] But the Commission, now consisting of five members, did not come out to the subcontinent until the first week of July.

It will have been observed that while in the earlier stages of the proceedings in the Security Council, the Indian representative was wont to emphasise the urgency of the matter and demand immediate action in Kashmir, in the later stages he adopted a totally different attitude. The case remained adjourned at his bidding for a month. Then, as we have noticed, there was another postponement for a month. The Commission did not start its work in the subcontinent

---

[48] S.C.O.R., 3rd Year, 285th Mtg., 19 April 1948, pp. 20-26.

[49] Ibid., pp. 28-29.

[50] S.C.O.R., 3rd Year, 290th Mtg., 7 May 1948, p. 37.

[51] S.C.O.R., 3rd Year, Supple. for May 1948, Document S/735, pp. 40-42.

until the second week of July. What was the reason for this loss of impatience on the part of India?

The London *Times* of 13 April 1948 carried a report from its special correspondent in Srinagar which said:

> The Indian Army has worked extremely hard during the winter months and its position has been much improved. In spite of snow-storms and rain and the resulting drifts, mud and landslips, it has doggedly moved up supplies and reinforcements, improved roads and airfields and intensified the training of its troops. Logistically, it has won a notable victory, but even now in April, traditionally the month for a spring offensive, this necessary phase has not been completed. . . .

The report added:

> . . . But the force has been considerably strengthened and it should be soon ready for a limited offensive. Already some units have advanced from Rajauri in Jammu and from Uri and some small successes have been reported. Fighting is bloody. . . .[52]

It was at this stage that the government of Pakistan received from its Commander-in-Chief his appreciation, dated 20 April 1948, of the general military situation:

> *General military situation:* (*a*) The build-up of the Indian Army for an all-out offensive in Kashmir started towards the end of February 1948 at a very rapid rate. Eight brigade groups, complete with supporting arms, artillery, armour, engineers etc. backed by a considerable air force of fighters, bombers and transport aircraft are at present deployed in Jammu and Kashmir and the process of building-up continues but appears to be almost complete now. On 15 March, 1948 the Indian Defence Minister announced in the Indian Constituent Assembly that the Indian Army will clear out the so-called raiders from Kashmir within the next two or three months. So far the main concentrations are in the south, i.e.,

---

[52] S.C.O.R., 5th Year, 464th Mtg., 8 Feb. 1950, pp. 26-27.

k

in the area Jammu-Naoshera; at least one additional brigade group is already reported to have moved into the Valley. . . .

The Commander-in-Chief added:

> . . . It is obvious that a general offensive is about to start very soon now. The present dispositions suggest that it will first start in the south with Bhimbar and Mirpur as the most likely objectives with a view to coming right up to the Pakistan border.

He recommended:

> . . . If Pakistan is not to face another serious refugee problem with about 2,750,000 people uprooted from their homes; if India is not to be allowed to sit on the doorsteps of Pakistan to the rear and on the flank at liberty to enter at its will and pleasure; if the civilian and military morale is not to be affected to a dangerous extent; and if subversive political forces are not to be encouraged and let loose within Pakistan itself, it is imperative that the Indian Army is not allowed to advance beyond the general line Uri-Poonch-Naoshera.[53]

The government of Pakistan accepted the recommendation of its Commander-in-Chief. To that there was no alternative, for the Security Council had clearly demonstrated its inability to halt Indian military activity in Kashmir and could not be relied upon to stop the new offensive. Pakistan with a clear perception of Indian intentions sent in limited forces to hold certain defensive positions. In the words of Sir Zafrulla Khan, "anyone responsible for the security of Pakistan who did not at least do that should have [been] impeached and executed."[54] He informed the Commission of these facts within a day of its arrival in Karachi. Answering the charge that the Security Council had not been notified, Sir Zafrulla had asked: "Did the Government of India, in mounting their offensive, notify the Security Council?"[55]

---

[53] *Ibid.*, pp. 27-29.
[54] S.C.O.R., 6th Year, 534th Mtg., 6 March 1951, p. 12.
[55] S.C.O.R., 5th Year, 464th Mtg., 8 Feb. 1950, p. 30.

Fighting in Kashmir was stopped on New Year's Day, 1949. In retrospect, it would appear that in agreeing to the cease-fire on that date, Pakistani officials committed a major blunder, their faith in the procedures of the United Nations being wholly misplaced. Knowing full well that India's aim was to maintain its hold on Kashmir, Pakistanis agreed to the cease-fire in the mistaken belief that the Commission would arrange a plebiscite. What is more regrettable, the cease-fire was agreed to after Pakistan had inflicted crushing losses on the Indian forces seeking to advance from Naoshera. Within a day the Pakistani forces could have advanced to Jammu and without opposition taken the road to Srinagar, with good chances of liquidating the Indian forces in the Valley and capturing their armour.[56] It is sometimes said that Pakistan agreed to the cease-fire because it was afraid of an outright attack on its borders by India. Such an attack was most unlikely, for while Pakistan's military resources were extremely limited, those of India at that time were also not disproportionately excessive. Pakistan ought at least to have occupied Jammu before agreeing to the cease-fire, in which case the cease-fire line would have been more favourable to Pakistan. Pakistan forces did none of these things. They adhered to the defensive line that they had been ordered to hold. There seems no doubt that but for the reverse at Naoshera, India would not have agreed to a cease-fire.

The efforts of the Commission resulted in its two resolutions of 13 August 1948 and 5 January 1949.[57] Accepted by both India and Pakistan, these resolutions together constituted an international agreement. These resolutions were not self-explanatory. The manner in which they were to be implemented was indicated in the various clarifications that the Commission gave to the two governments. The resolutions and the various clarifications were set out in the Com-

---

[56] *Cf.* Lord Birdwood, *Two Nations and Kashmir* (London: Robert Hale, 1956), pp. 72-73, 77.
[57] See, respectively, S.C.O.R., 3rd Year, Supple. for Nov. 1948, pp. 32-34 and S.C.O.R., 4th Year, Supple. for Jan. 1949, pp. 23-25.

mission's three reports to the Security Council.[58] Under the first resolution, Pakistan was to use its best endeavour to secure the withdrawal of the tribesmen and Pakistani nationals, who had entered the state for the purpose of fighting. Although this obligation did not arise until after the signing of the truce agreement, Pakistan fulfilled it without waiting for that agreement to be signed.[59] Next, the regular forces of India and Pakistan were to be withdrawn in such a way that after Pakistan had taken the first step, the bulk of the Indian forces were to begin withdrawing. The Commission assured the Pakistan government that this was to be a synchronised movement, arranged in consultation between the two High Commands.[60] Under Clause 4 of the resolution of 5 January 1949, the Plebiscite Administrator was to determine the final disposal of the residue of Indian and state forces, as well as the disposition of what were left of the *Azad* Kashmir forces, while having due regard for the security of Jammu and Kashmir and the freedom of plebiscite. Such was the scheme of demilitarisation embodied in the two resolutions.

The resolution of 5 January 1949 provided for the holding of the plebiscite after the demilitarisation of the state had been completed. The Plebiscite Administrator was to be appointed with wide powers for ensuring the fairness and impartiality of the plebiscite. It was because of these guarantees that the government of Pakistan acquiesced in the Commission's decision not to attempt to set up a nonpartisan or coalition government for the whole of Kashmir. This decision of the Commission, like several others, showed the extent to which it was, like its parent the Security Council, prone to succumb to Indian tactics. In fact it is to its lack of conviction and firmness that the Commission's failure must be attributed.

---

[58] S.C.O.R., 3rd Year, Supple. for Nov. 1948, Document S/1100, pp. 17-62; S.C.O.R., 4th Year, Supple. for Jan. 1949, Document S/1196, pp. 20-28; S.C.O.R., 4th Year, Special Supple. No. 7, n.d., Document S/1430, Add. 1 & 2, pp. 1-191.
[59] S.C.O.R., 4th Year, Special Supple. No. 7, n.d., Document S/1430, Add. 1, Annex 49, para. 9, pp. 179-80.
[60] S.C.O.R., 3rd Year, Supple. for Nov. 1948, Document S/1100, Annex 27, pp. 136-38.

Josef Korbel, a member of the Commission, records that it found Pakistan's suspicions of India frustrating. However, he admits that in the light of later developments these suspicions were well founded. According to Korbel:

> Pakistan obviously was of the opinion that once the fighting had stopped, India would be satisfied with a *de facto* division of Kashmir (the better part of which was in her possession), the situation would subsequently become stabilized, and India would then obstruct a free plebiscite.[61]

This is precisely what India did. The procedure adopted by India for obstructing the plebiscite consisted in what amounted to a refusal to withdraw its forces, to demand the disbandment of *Azad* Kashmir forces, and to ask for the possession of the Northern Areas. While the government of Pakistan put forward at a joint meeting a comprehensive scheme for the withdrawal of its forces, the government of India refused to present its proposals. When it at last communicated its scheme to the Commission, India did so subject to the condition that the scheme should not be disclosed to Pakistan until the truce agreement had been signed. India also forbade the Commission to reveal its own scheme to Pakistan.[62]

One of the new conditions of demilitarisation insisted upon by India was the disbandment of the *Azad* Kashmir forces. Of this there is no mention in the resolution of 13 August 1948 accepted by both India and Pakistan.[63] But the Indian representative in the Security Council said that, at the time when that resolution was formulated, the Commission did not have a complete picture of the strength of the *Azad* Kashmir forces and that they had since been augmented.[64] In reply Sir Zafrulla Khan read from the official minutes of the meeting between him and the Commission, held on 31 August 1948,

---

[61] Josef Korbel, *Danger in Kashmir* (Princeton: Princeton University Press, 1954), p. 144.

[62] S.C.O.R., 4th Year, Special Supple. No. 7, n.d., pp. 31, 49, and 52.

[63] *Ibid.*, Annex 22, p. 113.

[64] Sir Benegal Rau in S.C.O.R., 5th Year, 463rd Mtg., 7 Feb. 1950, pp. 7-8.

a statement by its Chairman to the effect that the Commission's plan aimed at assuring a military balance between the two sides and that "even after the withdrawal of the Pakistan army, the Azad forces would still muster 35 battalions of armed people who would not be asked to disarm or to withdraw."[65]

More specifically the Commission in its letter of 19 September 1948 had told the Foreign Minister of Pakistan ' that the resolution does not contemplate the disarmament or disbandment of the Azad Kashmir forces."[66] That position was admitted by the government of India in its letter to the Commission dated 18 February 1949.[67] In its letter of 10 March 1949, the government of India asked for preparations "for the ultimate disbanding and disarming of the Azad forces."[68] On 14 March 1949, the Commission wrote back to the government of India, restating its view of a "military balance" and reaffirming "that the Resolution of 13 August did not call for the disarming or disbanding of the Azad Kashmir forces."[69] The Commission reiterated this position in its letter to the government of India dated 28 April 1949.[70] But that government remained adamant.

Pakistan's position in respect of the Indian claim to the Northern Areas was summed up by Mr. Mushtaq Ahmad Gurmani, Minister for Kashmir Affairs, in his letter to the Commission, dated 1 October 1949:

> 9. As regards the Northern areas, the claim of the Government of India to post Indian garrisons in this area is not in accord with clause B. 2 of part II of the Commission's resolution of 13 August 1948, which permits the retention of Indian troops only "within the lines in existence at the moment of the cease-fire." The cease-fire line has since been

65 S.C.O.R., 5th Year, 465th Mtg., 9 Feb. 1950, p. 9.
66 S.C.O.R., 3rd Year, Supple. for Nov. 1948, p. 48.
67 S.C.O.R., 4th Year, Special Supple. No. 7, n.d., Annex 7, p. 81.
68 *Ibid.*, Annex 11, p. 93.
69 *Ibid.*, Annex 12, p. 95.
70 *Ibid.*, Annex 22, p. 113.

fixed and the "northern areas" do not fall on the Indian side of the line.

This claim also conflicts with the assurance given by the Commission on 31 August 1948 that neither the Government of India nor the Maharaja'[s] Government will be permitted to send any military or civil officials to the "evacuated territory". In its letter dated 3 September 1948, to the Foreign Minister of Pakistan, ... the Commission explained that the term "evacuated territory" used in paragraph A. 3 of part II of the resolution of 13 August 1948, "refers to those territories in the State of Jammu and Kashmir which are at present under the effective control of the Pakistan High Command". The area north of the cease-fire line has been as much under the effective control of the Pakistan High Command as the area west of the cease-fire line.

The assurance that no civil or military official of the Government of India or of the Maharaja's Government would be allowed to cross into the evacuated territory "for the purpose of administration or control" was reiterated in paragraph 4(d) of the Commission's letter dated 28 April 1949, to the Government of Pakistan....

It is thus clear from the analysis made above that the claim of the Government of India for administrative and military control of northern areas is in direct conflict with the provisions of the Commission's Resolution of 13 August 1948, and is, therefore, untenable.

10. I should further point out that the Government of India abandoned this untenable claim long before the settlement between India and Pakistan regarding Kashmir was reached. As stated by the Commission in paragraph 80 of its interim report dated 9th November 1948, ... Sir Girja Shankar Bajpai informed the Commission that India's acceptance of 13 August resolution was not conditional upon acceptance by the Commission of the contents of Prime Minister of India's letter dated 20 August 1948 laying claim to administrative and military control over the "northern areas". A claim of this nature which is inconsistent and incompatible with the settlement and which the Government of India had themselves

dropped before the settlement was reached cannot be entertained at this stage.[71]

On 6 September 1948 Sir Zafrulla had asked the Commission:

> ... [to] recognize that it is of the utmost importance that any agreement between the two Governments should be arrived at on the clearest possible basis, so that there is left no possibility of any misunderstanding of any of the matters agreed upon. In other words, it is essential that the two Governments should agree simultaneously to the same thing and in the same sense.[72]

But this was not to be. There were the two resolutions of the Commission to which both India and Pakistan had agreed. But these resolutions could not be implemented because there were differences regarding their meaning between the two governments. The government of India would not accept the interpretation given by the Commission, which was the author of those resolutions. The Commission thereupon proposed that these differences be submitted to arbitration. This proposal, which was backed by an earnest appeal from President Truman and Prime Minister Attlee, was accepted by Pakistan. It was rejected by India.[73]

The Commission, having come to the end of its resources, recommended that the Security Council should make other arrangements for settling the India-Pakistan dispute. In February 1950 the Canadian statesman, General McNaughton, after prolonged discussions with the parties, put forward his proposal for the demilitarisation of Kashmir and control of the Northern Areas.[74] Pakistan accepted the the proposal; India rejected it. Thereupon the Council appointed the Australian jurist, Sir Owen Dixon, as United Nations Representative with instructions to prepare and supervise a program for the de-

---

[71] *Ibid.*, Annex 42, p. 160.

[72] S.C.O.R., 3rd Year, Supple. for Nov. 1948, p. 44.

[73] S.C.O.R., 4th Year, Special Supple. No. 7, Annex 40, pp. 151-52.

[74] S.C.O.R., 5th Year, Supple. for Jan. through May 1950, Document S/1453, pp. 3-16.

militarisation of the state and to carry out the other responsibilities of the defunct Commission. Sir Owen spent some three months in Pakistan, India, and Kashmir. He too failed, for as he reported to the Security Council:

> ... In the end I became convinced that India's agreement would never be obtained to demilitarization in any such form, or to provisions governing the period of the plebiscite of any such character, as would in my opinion permit of the plebiscite being conducted in conditions sufficiently guarding against intimidation and other forms of influence and abuse by which the freedom and fairness of the plebiscite might be imperilled.[75]

Having come to that conclusion, Sir Owen Dixon suggested alternative solutions to the Prime Ministers of India and Pakistan. As a last possibility, he proposed the holding of the plebiscite in a limited area, including or consisting of the Valley of Kashmir, and for partitioning the rest of the state between India and Pakistan. The Prime Minister of India was agreeable to the plan, provided that Sir Owen did not insist upon measures to ensure the freedom and fairness of the plebiscite in the limited area. But these measures the United Nations Representative regarded as necessary, for reasons which he stated as follows:

> ... There were large numbers of regular soldiers of the Indian Army as well as of the State Militia and police and more often than not they were under arms. The State Government was exercising wide powers of arbitrary arrest. These are not matters that the Kashmiris inhabiting the Valley could be expected to disregard in choosing between voting as the Government of Kashmir asked them and voting for accession to Pakistan.[76]

Finally, Sir Owen abandoned the idea of partition and a partial plebiscite for, he said:

---

[75] S.C.O.R., 5th Year, Supple. for Sept. through Dec. 1950, p. 36.
[76] *Ibid.*, p. 42.

> ... I could not expose a plebiscite conducted under the authority of the United Nations to the dangers which I believed certainly to exist.[77]

He also abandoned his mission.

On the eve of the Commonwealth Prime Ministers' Conference in January 1951, Mr. Liaquat Ali Khan made it known that if it did not discuss the Kashmir question, he would not attend it. The Prime Ministers informally discussed the Kashmir problem for seven hours. To facilitate demilitarisation, the Australian Prime Minister, Mr. Robert Menzies, proposed three alternatives, namely, the stationing in Kashmir of (a) a Commonwealth force; or (b) a joint India-Pakistan force; or (c) a local force to be raised by the Plebiscite Administrator. Each one of these proposals was in turn accepted by Pakistan. All of them were rejected by India.[78]

When the Dixon Report came up for discussion by the Security Council in February 1951, demilitarisation was again the central issue. The government of India, while reaffirming its acceptance of the resolutions of the Commission, insisted on its own interpretation of those resolutions and on its own conditions for carrying them out. Said Sir Zafrulla:

> ... The Indian technique has been to go on affirming the acceptance of these obligations. Indeed it can do little else. They are there in black and white, endorsed by the Security Council. India refuses to carry them out. It either insists on some new condition which does not apply and has not been accepted by the parties, raises irrelevant issues or puts impossible constructions upon the language of the agreement, and in one manner or another it continues to evade its obligations.

He asked:

> Why does India go on insisting on these things which make demilitarization and, therefore, the holding of the plebiscite impossible? For the obvious reason that India's hold over

---

[77] *Ibid.*, pp. 42-43.
[78] *The Times* (London), as quoted in Korbel, *op. cit.*, p. 177.

Kashmir is only through its military forces. India does not want to let go and India knows that if a fair and impartial plebiscite were held, the plebiscite would go heavily against India.[79]

Replying to the Indian representative's accusations against Pakistan, Sir Zafrulla said:

> ... It has been said, on behalf of India, that India is a secular State, that it is democratic, that it is progressive and that it is non-violent. It is not my purpose to question India's greatness on the basis of these claims or, indeed, of many others which readily suggest themselves. It has been either alleged or insinuated that Pakistan has been guilty of aggression, that Pakistan is retrogressive, that Pakistan is a theocratic State. I do not know what that might mean, but somehow it is employed as a term of derogation.

> It is not my purpose, especially at this late stage, to enter into a discussion of the relative merits of India and Pakistan. Those who made these charges against Pakistan are well aware that the interim Constitution of Pakistan today is the same as the interim Constitution of India was before its new Constitution came into force. They are also aware that the proposed constitution of Pakistan which is being framed, to the extent to which the reports of the Committees have been received, guarantees the same or similar rights, privileges, and safeguards to minorities and groups. It safeguards the same freedoms as the Indian Constitution does. I have no desire to enter into a comparison on that basis. Let us assume for the moment, for the sake of argument, that Pakistan is guilty of all the crimes on the calendar—and I would repudiate any suggestion of that kind on the merits—but let us assume for the moment that Pakistan has been guilty of every crime, then does it follow that the people of Kashmir, because Pakistan has been guilty, should be denied the right of self-determination? What is the connexion between the two arguments? Should not their agony be terminated in some fair way?[80]

---

79 S.C.O.R., 6th Year, 534th Mtg., 6 March 1951, pp. 16 and 24.
80 S.C.O.R., 6th Year, 535th Mtg., 7 March 1951, pp. 14-15.

The Security Council next faced the situation that was then developing in Kashmir, where preparations were afoot to convene a constitutent assembly to decide the future of the state. The representative of India admitted that these preparations were being made but declared:

> ... My government's view is that, while the constituent assembly may, if it so desires, express an opinion on this question, it can take no decision on it.[81]

And again:

> ... The constituent assembly cannot be physically prevented from expressing its opinion on this question if it so chooses. But this opinion will not bind my government or prejudice the position of the Council ...[82]

On 30 March the Security Council adopted a resolution which, reaffirming the principle embodied in its previous resolutions and the two resolutions of the United Nations Commission that the final disposition of the State of Jammu and Kashmir would be made through the democratic method of a free and impartial plebiscite, declared:

> ... any action that Assembly might attempt to take to determine the future shape and affiliation of the entire State or any part thereof would not constitute a disposition of the State in accordance with the above principle.[83]

A new United Nations representative was to proceed to the subcontinent "to effect the demilitarisation of the State." The parties were called upon to co-operate with him and, in the event of failure to achieve agreement, to submit their difference to arbitration by an arbitrator or arbitrators, appointed by the President of the International Court of Justice, after consultation with the parties. This resolution was accepted by Pakistan. It was rejected by India.

[81] S.C.O.R., 6th Year, 536th Mtg., 9 March 1951, p. 8.

[82] S.C.O.R., 6th Year, 538th Mtg., 29 March 1951, p. 3.

[83] S.C.O.R., 6th Year, Supple. for Jan. through March 1951, Document S/2017/Rev./1, pp. 25-27.

Dr. Frank P. Graham was appointed United Nations Representative. As is clear from his reports for this period, between March 1951 and September 1952, he put forward a number of proposals for the demilitarisation of the state. Each one of these proposals, demanding new sacrifices by Pakistan, was accepted by Pakistan but rejected by India.

On 23 December 1952 the Security Council passed a resolution[84] urging the governments of India and Pakistan to enter into immediate negotiations, under the auspices of the United Nations Representative for India and Pakistan, in order to reach agreement on the specific number of forces to remain on either side of the cease-fire line at the end of the period of demilitarisation, this number to be between 3,000 and 6,000 armed men remaining on the Pakistani side of the cease-fire line and from 12,000 to 18,000 men in the armed forces on the side of the cease-fire line controlled by India. The government of Pakistan accepted this resolution but the government of India rejected it.

Dr. Graham once more visited the subcontinent in an effort to settle the dispute. After the failure of this effort, he recommended that the matter be left to the parties to decide between themselves. Dr. Graham submitted five reports to the Security Council.[85] A study of these reports reveals the extent of the concessions that Pakistan made to reach agreement and of the obduracy of India, which prevented a settlement.

In the meanwhile, the Constituent Assembly of Kashmir came into being. All its 75 members were elected unopposed, all of them Abdullah's men. As Korbel puts it: "No dictator could do better."[86] In November 1951 the Assembly adopted a constitution which

---

[84] S.C.O.R., 7th Year, Supple. for Oct. through Dec. 1952, Document S/2883, p. 66.

[85] S.C.O.R., 6th Year, Special Supple. No. 2, n.d., Document S/2375, Corr. 1 & 2; S.C.O.R., 7th Year, Supple. No. 1, n.d.; *ibid.*, Supple. No. 2, Document S/2611 & Corr. 1, pp. 1-19; *ibid.*, Document S/2783 & Corr. 1, pp. 19-48; S.C.O.R., 8th Year, Supple. No. 1, n.d.

[86] Korbel, *op. cit.*, p. 222.

safeguarded the autonomy of Kashmir, except in matters relating to defence, foreign affairs, and communications, which were to be the responsibility of India. This decision meant that in all internal matters the people of Kashmir, amongst whom Muslims were in the majority, would be masters of their destiny. This was resented in India and there was a demand for the full application of the Indian constitution to Kashmir. Speaking at Ranbirsinghpura on 10 April 1952, Abdullah described this attitude as "unrealistic, childish and savouring of lunacy." He charged: "No one can deny that communal spirit still exists in India."[87]

The speech was widely condemned in India and disapproved of by Pandit Nehru. But the Pandit knew how to go step by step. On 24 July 1952, he announced an agreement with Abdullah, recognising Kashmir's autonomous status, such as no other state in the Indian Union possessed: the Supreme Court of India was not to be the final court of appeal for Kashmir; Kashmir would continue to have its separate flag; the Indian President's power to declare a state of emergency in Kashmir would be exercised only with the consent of its government.[88]

One year was to elapse before the next decisive step was taken, namely, the imprisonment of Abdullah, which cleared the way for the complete merger of Kashmir with India. During this year a campaign was worked up against Abdullah, who was denounced as an anti-Hindu Muslim. Hindus started a movement of civil disobedience to bring about the full integration of Kashmir with India.

On 9 August Abdullah was arrested and put into prison, where he remained until his release on 8 January 1958. His place as Prime Minister was taken by Bakshi Ghulam Mohammed who was willing to do everything as bidden by India. Regarding Bakshi's character and antecedents, Korbel records:

> Bakshi was the chief organizer of the National Conference, and in the government he was Deputy Prime Minister and Home

[87] *Dawn* (Karachi), 12 April 1952.
[88] *The Statesman* (New Delhi), 26 July 1952.

Minister. In this latter capacity he was the chief of police
in Kashmir. Bakshi had embraced Christianity in his school
years but later returned to Islam, and since the nationalist
riots in 1931 he was closely associated with Sheikh Abdullah.
His brother is a wealthy military contractor, and other rel-
atives occupy important positions in the economic life of
Kashmir. Bakshi found it profitable to be in charge of state
supplies, public works, and transport. A popular wit has given
to his wide interests and associations a name—the Bakshi
Brothers Corporation. Paradoxically, he prided himself on
having once whipped a black marketeer on the streets of
Srinagar. His ambition has been power—if possible with com-
fort. The increasing rift between India and his superior,
Sheikh Abdullah, offered Bakshi the opportunity to realize
more of both than he had previously enjoyed.[89]

In a letter to the Security Council, written from his prison in
January 1957, Abdullah explained why he was arrested: for some
time he had been pressing the government of India for an early
settlement of the dispute with Pakistan, for "no peaceful progress
is possible in the State unless this dispute is amicably and finally
settled." But, he added: "India's reaction was averse to his approach
and her resentment towards me gradually culminated in positive
hostility." Abdullah continued:

> I was put under arrest along with another Minister of my
> cabinet and am now under continued detention nearly for the
> last three years without trial and without even a charge.

> Simultaneously with my arrest thousands of my followers and
> co-workers including Deputy Ministers, high-ranking gazetted
> officers, respectable businessmen, lawyers, members of the
> Assembly and public men of high position in life were clamped
> into prison. All manner of repressive measures were let loose
> in order to crush the spontaneous uprising of the people
> throughout the Valley. Indian Central Reserve Police and
> Army as well as the militia, and the special police were given

---

[89] Korbel, *op. cit.*,   p. 236.

a free licence to shoot at sight and commit all other possible
atrocities on the defenceless people.[90]

Obviously with the object of preventing the world from knowing
what was happening in Kashmir, the government of India threw an
iron curtain round the state. Foreign correspondents, such as Selig
S. Harrison of the Associated Press of America and Richard Williams
of the B.B.C., were refused permission to enter Kashmir. Foreigners
who were already there were externed.[91]

In a statement to the press in February 1958, Abdullah revealed
that in June 1953 he had proposed to Pandit Nehru the following
alternative solutions of the Kashmir question: (a) an overall plebiscite; (b) independence of the whole state; (c) independence of the
whole state, with joint control by India and Pakistan of foreign affairs and defence.[92] It will be noticed that Abdullah did not suggest,
as one of the alternatives, the maintenance of the *status quo*, *i.e.*,
accession to India without a plebiscite. This must have been sufficient
to infuriate the Pandit. According to a report in *The New York Times*:
"Abdullah said neither Bakshi nor Karan Singh had power to arrest
him and made clear he blamed most of all Nehru."[93]

Throughout Pakistan there were angry demonstrations against
the reign of terror that followed Abdullah's dismissal and arrest.
Prime Minister Mohammed Ali rushed to Delhi, hoping that in the
deplorable events that had taken place in Kashmir Pandit Nehru
would see the necessity of a speedy settlement of the dispute. The
two Prime Ministers issued a communiqué on 20 August 1953 in
which they declared "their firm opinion" that the dispute "should
be settled in accordance with the wishes of the people of that State,"
and "that the most feasible method of ascertaining the wishes of the
people was a fair and impartial plebiscite." They agreed that "the

---

[90] *Pakistan Times* (Lahore), 20 Jan. 1957.
[91] See A.P.A. reports in *Dawn* (Karachi), 12 and 13 Aug. 1953. See also *Dawn*,
21 Aug. 1953.
[92] *Pakistan Times* (Lahore), 26 Feb. 1958.
[93] *The New York Times*, 11 Jan. 1958.

plebiscite Administrator should be appointed by the end of April 1954." Previous to that date preliminary issues should be decided. "With this purpose in view Committees of Military and other experts should be appointed to advise the Prime Ministers."[94] The principal preliminary issue to be decided was, of course, that of demilitarisation, to be dealt with by the committee of military experts.

India was not prepared to go forward with the work of the experts' committee. Nor was India willing to appoint the Plebiscite Administrator, even though Pakistan had reluctantly agreed that another person be appointed instead of the American Admiral Chester W. Nimitz, whom Pandit Nehru, in spite of his previous commitment to appoint, was determined to discard. In Pakistan's proposed Mutual Security Pact with the United States, the Pandit found, as we have seen in an earlier chapter, an argument for not holding a plebiscite in Kashmir. He declared that the pact would affect the Kashmir question and especially the issue of demilitarisation. Said Mr. Firoz Khan Noon:

> The Government of India has put forward one pretext after another in an effort to justify its intransigent attitude. As the hollowness of one becomes apparent, another is thought up. I will refer now only to the latest. The latest pretext is that the acceptance by Pakistan of American military aid absolves India from its obligation to Pakistan, to the people of Kashmir and to the Security Council to honour its agreement to co-operate in a free and impartial plebiscite. India has not publicly withdrawn this contention, notwithstanding repeated assurances that any military aid may be and will be used exclusively for the purpose of self-defence.[95]

While demilitarisation and a plebiscite remained in abeyance, the process of integrating Kashmir with India went ahead. As a first step, according to Abdullah, "almost with a pistol on the necks of the Assembly members and with massacre and terrorism all over the

---

[94] *Dawn* (Karachi), 20 Aug. 1953.
[95] S.C.O.R., 12th Year, 761st Mtg., 16 Jan. 1957, p. 13.

1

valley, a vote of confidence for the Government, pitchforked into office with the help of Indian bayonets, was secured."[96] On 6 February 1954, the Assembly ratified the accession of Kashmir to India unanimously. Of its seventy-five members eleven were absent, six of them in prison.

These and subsequent steps taken by the Assembly to integrate Kashmir with India were, according to Abdullah, all illegal. He said that he was "prepared to prove to the hilt that most of the members of the Constitutent Assembly were forced to append their signatures to the document."[97] Abdullah made these statements during the period of his temporary release from prison in 1958.

In January 1957, after a lapse of five years, the Security Council once again discussed the Kashmir question. The debate occasioned Mr. V. K. Krishna Menon's speech of record-breaking length of eight hours, spread over three meetings. A filibuster, American newspapers called it, the first one ever to be attempted in the United Nations. On 24 January 1957 the Council adopted a draft resolution submitted by Australia, Colombia, Cuba, the United Kingdom, and the United States with ten votes in its favour and one abstention (USSR). This resolution,[98] after referring to the principle embodied in the earlier resolutions of the Council and to the resolutions of the United Nations Commission of 13 August 1948 and 5 January 1949 that the final disposition of the State of Jammu and Kashmir would be made in accordance with the will of the people, expressed through the democratic method of a free and impartial plebiscite conducted under the auspices of the United Nations, reaffirmed its resolution of 15 March 1951, and declared that any action taken by the Constituent Assembly of Jammu and Kashmir or by the parties concerned in support of such action, would not constitute a disposition of the State in accordance with that principle.

---

[96] Abdullah's letter to the Security Council, *Pakistan Times* (Lahore), 20 Jan. 1957.
[97] *Dawn* (Karachi), 24 Jan. 1958.
[98] S.C.O.R., 12th Year, Supple. for Jan. through March 1957, Document S/3779, p. 4.

On 14 February a draft resolution[99] was proposed by Australia, Cuba, the United Kingdom, and the United States which noted Pakistan's proposal for a temporary United Nations force for affecting demilitarisation in Kashmir and expressed the belief that the use of such a force deserved consideration. The resolution requested the President of the Security Council, the representative of Sweden, Mr. Gunnar Jarring, to proceed to the subcontinent to examine proposals for demilitarisation or otherwise achieving progress towards the settlement of the dispute.

The Soviet Union proposed amendments to this resolution which sought to omit references to demilitarisation and to a United Nations temporary force. Mr. Arkady Sobolev said that his government considered that "the Kashmir question has in actual fact already been settled in essence by the people of Kashmir themselves, who consider their territory an integral part of the Republic of India." But the Soviet representative did not stop at that. He denounced the idea of holding a plebiscite in Kashmir and declared that "the introduction of a United Nations force into Kashmir would be completely at variance with the principles of the United Nations Charter and would be an outright insult to the national sentiments of the people of Kashmir."[100]

The Soviet amendments were rejected by the Council. When it came to voting on the Four-Power resolution, it was defeated when the USSR exercised its 79th veto in the Security Council. Thereupon a new resolution[101] was submitted by Australia, the United Kingdom, and the United States, under which the Council, recalling its earlier resolutions and the resolutions of the United Nations Commission, requested Mr. Jarring to consider any proposal likely to lead to a settlement of the dispute and, for that purpose, to visit

---

[99] *Ibid.*, Document S/3787, pp. 7-8.
[100] S.C.O.R., 12th Year, 770th Mtg., 18 Feb. 1957, pp. 38-39.
[101] S.C.O.R., 12th Year, Supple. for Jan. through March 1957, Document S/3793, p. 9.

the subcontinent. This resolution was adopted by ten votes in favour and one abstention (USSR).

The debate in the Security Council from 16 January 1957 to 21 February 1957 led newspapers in far corners of the globe to express concern about Indian defiance of the United Nations over Kashmir. Thus, for example, the *Aftenposten* of Oslo in the course of an article on 28 January said:

> The Security Council resolution on a plebiscite holds good, and the United Nations has just as much right to demand that this resolution is respected as it has to the demand that Israel shall leave the Egyptian territory.
>
> If Nehru, certainly with no little justification, can claim that Kashmir has had great benefit of links with India, Ben Gurion can claim with at least as great justification that the resident Arab population in the Gaza area would preferably have links with Israel.
>
> If there is to be consistency in the United Nations policy, Secretary-General Hammarskjold must also intervene against India.
>
> The fact that the former Kashmiri Prime Minister, Sheikh Abdullah, has been in prison ever since 1953, when he opposed accession to India, and that his former Minister of Finance, Mirza Afzal Beg, was imprisoned in November 1955 because he led an action in favour of a plebiscite, in itself is a sign that everything is not as it should be.
>
> Now it is up to Nehru to show whether his high international ideals and respect for the United Nations also apply when his own immediate interests are at stake.
>
> At the moment, peace-apostle Nehru has one Indian soldier for every 39 inhabitants in Kashmir. If there is a plebiscite both Indian and Pakistani troops must withdraw and neutral United Nations forces march in.[102]

---

[102] *Pakistan Times* (Lahore), 6 Feb. 1957.

The Scotsman of Edinburgh of 26 January commented:

All her wrigglings and legalistic arguments cannot then disguise the fact that she [India] has deliberately flouted the Security Council, which has specifically stated that it does not recognise that the Constitutent Assembly has any authority to hand Kashmir over to India.

India would also be making it very plain that her reiterated statements that she was throughout willing to settle the Kashmir dispute by negotiation were in fact so much bluff.

She will indeed be saying in the bluntest way that she is going to have what she holds, and is prepared to defy world opinion and the United Nations to do anything about it.

She will be making it as difficult as possible for any but a partition solution to be applied to Kashmir.

Such action not only accords very ill with the high moral attitude adopted by Mr. Nehru in his interventions in the world's affairs but must lay India open to the sharpest rebuke from the United Nations, which on the evidence of her present attitude India will be bound to ignore.

That in its turn must have serious repercussions on the authority of the United Nations who would again be shown up as powerless to impose their authority on any issue in which the interests of a major Power are involved.

Such action would also be bound to have the most undesirable effect in Pakistan where action through the United Nations having been finally discredited, there would be increasing, perhaps overwhelming pressure, to attempt to settle the issue more equitably by force.[103]

The *Correio Paulistano* of São Paulo, writing under the caption "Kashmir: The Achilles Heel of India," on 27 January, said:

India assumed, notably under the influence of its present Prime Minister, the grandiose part of "defender of freedom" in the struggle against tyrannies, dictators and oppressors. "Free-

---

[103] *Ibid.*, 28 Jan. 1957.

156   *Pakistan and the United Nations*

dom and liberation of the people" is the motto used by India
in its policy of claiming the right to intervene in all international questions. This attitude is, however, nothing more
than cynical hypocrisy designed to disguise Nehru's imperialism.

Take the case of Hungary, where no one could deny that the
Russians dominated and terrorised that satellite against the
will of its people. But in the face of this, where honesty demanded condemnation of Soviet imperialism, New Delhi
looked for excuses and was incapable of assuming an energetic
attitude against Moscow.

Nehru could not claim the right of self-determination for the
Hungarians by means of general and free elections, because
this would serve as a precedent for the dispute over Kashmir.
The overwhelming majority of the people of Kashmir is
Muslim and it rebels against its oppressive and intolerant
occupation by India. It claims the right of its "anschluss" with
Pakistan.[104]

The Kashmir debate in the Security Council was editorially commented upon by *The New York Times* on 25 January and 5 February.
This newspaper stated that India's approach to the question had
gone far to justify some of Pakistan's fears and charges. What
Mr. Menon's speech boiled down to was simply that the case was
closed and that Kashmir was a part of India. The whole question
at issue was whether Kashmir was or was not "Indian soil." Kashmir
was not Indian soil or any other soil, until the Kashmiris themselves
had had a free chance to decide it.

The London *Times* of 28 January 1957, declaring that India had
no case "for maintaining the present oppressive regime in Kashmir,"
observed:

Sheikh Abdulla, the former Prime Minister was imprisoned
in 1953, because he showed separatist tendencies. He has remained under detention without a trial ever since. Similar
steps are taken from time to time against other members.
Apart, however, from such infringements of civil liberties,

---
[104] *Ibid.*, 6 Feb. 1957.

India has by her own action shown herself, even more clearly than before, as a defaulter from the resolutions of the United Nations.

Before Mr. Jarring's arrival in the subcontinent about the middle of March, an election took place in Kashmir, resulting in Bakshi Ghulam Mohammed's men being returned to all the seats. Warning Mr. Jarring not to be misled, *The New York Times* wrote editorially on 8 March:

What happened is no credit to India, no reflection of sentiment among the Kashmiris and no contribution to a solution of this thorny problem.

It was an "election" in which no votes were cast. The Indian-backed candidates for the Kashmir "Assembly" were declared elected, unopposed. Nine candidates who wished to run found their nomination papers thrown out on technicalities and their opponents declared elected. Forty-four leading Kashmiris who favor a plebiscite to determine the State's political future are in jail as political prisoners. Naturally, they did not run. This is not an "election" in any sense of the word. The term "election" means a choice. The Kashmiris had none.

Mr. Jarring in his report[105] noted that both governments adhered to the resolution of the United Nations Commission of 13 August 1948 and 5 January 1949. The government of India however confronted the United Nations Representative with the arguments that Mr. Menon had put forward in the Security Council. That government contended that Part I of the resolution of 13 August 1948, in particular its sections B and E, had not been implemented by the government of Pakistan. For that reason, it argued, there was no question of implementing Parts II and III of that resolution or of the resolution of 5 January 1949, which dealt with the plebiscite. The government of Pakistan, on the other hand, maintained that Part I of the first resolution had been implemented in full and that

---

[105] S.C.O.R., 12th Year, Supple. for April through June 1957, Document S/3821, pp. 13-16.

the time had come to proceed to the implementation of its Part II (preparatory to the implementation of the second resolution). Commenting on this point, Mr. Noon told the Security Council on 24 September 1957:

> ... The excuse that part I has not been implemented is now being put forward for the first time by India with a view to re-opening issues which have long been settled. The obvious object is to obstruct progress in the implementation of part II of the resolution, that is, demilitarization. The negotiations conducted by the Commission and the UN representatives were all directed towards finding a basis for the implementation of part II. At no stage did India refuse to enter into these negotiations on the plea that part I had not been implemented by Pakistan. The talks failed mainly because of India's obduracy to reach an agreement on the issue of demilitarization. India also did not raise any such question in the course of direct talks between the Prime Ministers of India and Pakistan in 1953. The experts committees, including Army representatives, set up by the two Governments, indeed covered considerable ground of part II of the resolution in their attempt to remove differences arising out of the character and quantum of forces which were to remain on both sides of the [cease-fire] line after demilitarization. . . .[106]

In support of his claim that Part I of the resolution of 13 August 1948 had been implemented, Mr. Noon cited the very clear statements made by Dr. Graham in paragraph 29 of his Third Report[107] and paragraph 44 of his Fifth Report.[108] Said Mr. Noon:

> This position was accepted by the Security Council, which, in the preamble of its resolution of 30 March 1951, says "*Observing* from Sir Owen Dixon's report that the main points of difference preventing agreement between the parties were:
>
> (a) The procedure for and the extent of demilitarization of the State preparatory to the holding of a plebiscite,

---

[106] S.C.O.R., 12th Year, 791st Mtg., 24 Sept. 1957, p. 7.

[107] S.C.O.R., 7th Year, Supple. No. 2, Document S/2611 & Corr. 1, pp. 1-19.

[108] S.C.O.R., 8th Year, Supple. No. 1.

(b) The degrees of control over the exercise of the functions of government in the State necessary to ensure a free and fair plebiscite."[109]

Emphasising that all that remained to be dealt with was demilitarisation, Mr. Noon drew attention to the Security Council's resolution[110] of 23 December 1952, which recommended that the two governments should

... enter into immediate negotiations under the auspices of the United Nations Representative for India and Pakistan in order to reach agreement on the specific number of forces to remain on each side of the cease-fire line at the end of the period of demilitarization. ...

Mr. Noon maintained:

The sole reason for India's now attempting to restart all controversies which have been set at rest and to re-open all the issues that have already been settled, abandoned or waived during the last ten years, is to create confusion, delay decisions and implementation of decisions, and to cloud the very simple issue of demilitarization. I regret to have to tell the Security Council that the *mala fides* of India is only too apparent.[111]

On the basis of the material before him, Mr. Jarring could well have rejected the Indian contention that Part I of the resolution of 13 August had not been implemented. He did not do so. Neither did he uphold that contention as well founded. He proposed that the matter be referred for determination by an arbitrator. The government of Pakistan accepted the proposal. The government of India refused to agree to it.

The government of India told Mr. Jarring that Pakistan had no

---

[109] S.C.O.R., 12th Year, 791st Mtg., 24 Sept. 1957, p. 9.
[110] S.C.O.R., 7th Year, Supple. for Oct. through Dec. 1952, Document S/2883, p. 66.
[111] S.C.O.R., 12th Year, 791st Mtg., 24 Sept. 1957, p. 10.

locus standi in the matter. This was another new argument. According to Mr. Noon:

> . . . If Pakistan had no *locus standi* in the matter, the logical course for India would have been to refuse to become involved in the whole structure of resolutions, commissions, reports and mediators. This India has never done, as indeed in the circumstances it could not do.[112]

In Part III of his report Mr. Jarring observed:

> In dealing with the problem under discussion as extensively as I have during the period just ended, I would not fail to take note of the concern expressed in connexion with the changing political, economic and strategic factors surrounding the whole of the Kashmir question, together with the changing pattern of power relations in West and South Asia.[113]

Mr. Jarring was obviously referring to what had been said to him by the government of India for, according to Mr. Noon, "nothing of the kind was ever mentioned by the Government of Pakistan." Mr. Noon told the Security Council:

> These extraneous matters have been raised by India for some time now in order to avoid its clear commitments and to bedevil the real issues involved in the Kashmir debate. But, even if for the sake of argument it is assumed that any political, economic or strategic factors have changed the pattern of power relations in West and South Asia, the changes that may have occurred have not even the remotest connexion with the plebiscite pledge to the people of Kashmir. What Pakistan or India may do or abstain from doing in the wider field of international relationship has no relevance at all to Kashmir. The recognized right of the people of Kashmir was to be exercised by them under the auspices of the United Nations, and the Plebiscite Administrator was to ensure that no outside influence would interfere with the free and unfettered

---

112 *Ibid.*, p. 11.
113 S.C.O.R., 12th Year, Supple. for April through June 1957, Document S/3821, p. 16.

exercise of this right. How in these circumstances Pakistan's membership of SEATO or of the Baghdad Pact has altered the situation to the prejudice of the people of Kashmir is beyond one's comprehension.[114]

The government of India tried to convince Mr. Jarring that it was incumbent on the Council to express itself on the question of "aggression committed by Pakistan on India" and that it was incumbent on Pakistan "to vacate the aggression." Says Mr. Jarring:

> It was argued that prior to the fulfilment of these requirements on the part of the Security Council, and on the part of Pakistan, the commitments of India under the resolution could not reach the operative stage.

But Mr. Jarring was not convinced:

> I explained to the Government of India that the Security Council had properly taken cognizance of their original complaint, and that it was not for me to express myself on the question whether its resolutions on the matter had been adequate or not. I pointed out that regardless of the merits of the present position taken by their Government, it could not be overlooked that they had accepted the two UNCIP resolutions.[115]

Speaking on this issue, Mr. Noon declared in the Security Council:

> Throughout the previous discussions in the Security Council, the representatives of all the Powers, great or small, who have considered this issue since January 1948, have all regarded the Indian allegation as unworthy of consideration. The scope of this unanimity is clear from a list of the countries which have participated in the Council's deliberations and none of which is on record as having given even the slightest credence to the Indian allegation. The countries concerned are: Argentina, Australia, Brazil, Canada, China, Chile, Colombia, Cuba, Egypt, Equador, France, Greece, Iraq,

---

[114] S.C.O.R., 12th Year, 791st Mtg., 24 Sept. 1957, p. 12.
[115] S.C.O.R., 12th Year, Supple. for April through June 1957, Document S/3821, paras. 13-14, p. 14.

Netherlands, Norway, Philippines, Sweden, Turkey, the U.S.S.R., the Ukrainian S.S.R., the United Kingdom, the United States and Yugoslavia.

In fact, the United Nations Commission for India and Pakistan was in possession of the full facts when it framed the resolutions of 13 August 1948 and 5 January 1949, which were accepted by both India and Pakistan and now constitute a valid international agreement. Nowhere has the Commission or any mediator called Pakistan an aggressor. Sir Owen Dixon himself did not make any "judicial investigation of the issue", as he put it, in spite of India's insistence that Pakistan should be declared as an aggressor, but only made a certain assumption in order to put a stop to Indian procrastination over the question of the demilitarization of the State.[116]

Mr. Noon finally dealt with the plea that because of the decision of the Kashmir "Constituent Assembly" and the action taken by India itself, Kashmir had become a part of India for good. "If that is so," said Mr. Noon,

India has acted in clear defiance of the Security Council directives and is guilty of aggression in that India has annexed that State, thereby breaking its own pledged word to the Security Council. It is also argued by India that, since it has annexed Kashmir, the State is a part of the Indian Union— and that this is final. This unilateral action of India, taken in flagrant disregard of the Security Council resolutions, is clearly invalid. India refuses to carry out the obligations under the resolutions of the United Nations Commission for India and Pakistan, knowing full well that the people will almost unanimously vote for Pakistan in a plebiscite. We, therefore, have the right to assume that the Indian annexation has taken place to prevent the Jammu and Kashmir State from acceding to Pakistan, and that thereby India has committed aggression a second time, by refusing to vacate the State—the first time being when the Indian army invaded the Jammu and Kashmir State and occupied it by force, as it occupied the Hyderabad State and the Junagadh State. India is defying not only the

---

[116] S.C.O.R., 12th Year, 791st Mtg., 24 Sept. 1957, pp. 5-6.

will of the people of Kashmir but also world opinion; and it is the duty of the Security Council now to make India vacate this blatant aggression.[117]

While it was in April 1957 that Mr. Jarring submitted his report to the Security Council, it was not considered by that body until September following. On 2 December 1957 the Council adopted a resolution[118] requesting the United Nations Representative for India and Pakistan, *i.e.*, Dr. Graham, to make recommendations for further appropriate action with a view to making progress towards the implementation of the resolutions of 13 August 1948 and 5 January 1949 and towards a peaceful settlement.

On the eve of Dr. Graham's arrival in the subcontinent, Abdullah was released from Kud jail on 8 January 1958. He had been under detention for four years and five months without a trial, notwithstanding the guarantees for freedom of person contained in the Indian constitution, which had been extended to Kashmir. Abdullah was received with widespread enthusiasm by the people of the Valley. They openly came out in their thousands to support his demand for a plebiscite. Abdullah asked also for the ouster of Indian forces from Kashmir and for the introduction of United Nations troops. The pro-Indian government in Srinagar resorted to mass arrests to suppress the people's enthusiasm for Abdullah. Finally on 30 April it rearrested Abdullah and sent him back to prison.

After spending a little over a month in the subcontinent Dr. Graham submitted his report[119] on 31 March 1958. He recorded that Pakistan accepted all the proposals made by him, namely, that it should: (a) make a renewed declaration undertaking to refrain from statements and actions that would aggravate the situation;

---

117 *Ibid.*, p. 15.
118 S.C.O.R., 12th Year, Supple. for Oct. through Dec. 1957, Document S/3922, pp. 21-22.
119 S.C.O.R., 13th Year, Supple. for Jan. through March 1958, Document S/3984, pp. 38-46.

(b) reaffirm respect for the cease-fire line; (c) withdraw Pakistan troops from the State simultaneously with the bulk of the Indian forces; (d) agree to the administration of the territory evacuated by Pakistan troops by local authorities in accordance with the provisions of the United Nations Commission's resolutions, pending a final solution; (e) consider the possibility of stationing in that area of a United Nations force on the Pakistan side of the border with the State; (f) abide by the terms of the Prime Ministers' communiqué of August 1953, in the matter of the interpretation of the 13 August 1948 resolution and those parts of the 5 January 1949 resolution which provide for a plebiscite; and (g) attend a conference at the Prime Ministers' level, under the auspices of Dr. Graham.[120]

Corresponding proposals made by Dr. Graham to the government of India were rejected by it, for in its view

> ... the sole onus of performance was on Pakistan and the United Nations, which had both the responsibility and the capacity for taking steps towards a peaceful approach to the situation and for making a contribution to resolving the difficulties between India and Pakistan.[121]

Other objections elaborated by the government of India against Dr. Graham's proposals are set out in paragraphs 28 to 33 of his Report. These objections are identical with those which have been dealt with above in considering the Jarring Report.

There the matter rests and what was described by Mr. Noel-Baker in 1948 as "the greatest and gravest single issue in international affairs"[122] is still unsettled.

---

[120] *Ibid.*, pp. 41-43.
[121] *Ibid.*, p. 43.
[122] S.C.O.R., 3rd Year, 284th Mtg., 17 April 1948, p. 11.

chapter six

Palestine and Suez

With the exception of the Kashmir question, no issue that has ever come up before the United Nations has so stirred the people of Pakistan, or has called forth such exertions from its representatives, as the question of Palestine. Even before the establishment of Pakistan, the Muslims of the subcontinent were deeply disturbed about developments in regard to the Holy Land. Palestine is sacred to Muslims, as it is to Christians and Jews. Muslims recognise as their own not only all the Jewish prophets but also Christ, and venerate the various places associated with them. Jerusalem was the first *Qibla* of the Muslims; that is, they said their prayers facing towards Jerusalem until the practice of facing towards Mecca was introduced. For these, and other religious and historical reasons, Muslims throughout the world attach the greatest sanctity to Palestine. However, in the question as it came up before the United Nations, Pakistanis were interested as believers in the Charter and the rights of peoples proclaimed by it.

The question of Palestine first came before the General Assembly at the request made in April 1947 by the United Kingdom, which had a League of Nations Mandate over Palestine. According to Noury As-Said (Iraq):

> ... It was not until the United Kingdom had settled over 500,000 foreign Jews in Palestine that it had been realized that it would be unable to carry out its fundamental duty in accordance with paragraph 4 of Article 22 of the Covenant, namely, to assist the people of Palestine to attain full independence. After the foreign Jewish community which the British had settled in Palestine had armed itself and had attacked them actively for two years, they had submitted the question to the United Nations.[1]

Briefly, the position taken up by Pakistan with regard to Palestine in the United Nations was that the Balfour Declaration and the Mandate of the League of Nations in which it was embodied, against the known wishes of the people of Palestine, and in disregard of the pledges of independence given to the Arabs, were invalid, and that the proposal to partition Palestine and to create in it a state for aliens in the face of the opposition of the indigenous population of the territory was contrary to the Charter. Pakistan's attitude, in the words of Professor Ahmed S. Bokhari, "was not motivated by anti-semitism, which was a phenomenon peculiar to Europe and practically unknown in the history of Islam."[2]

The *Ad Hoc* Committee, to which the Palestine question had been referred by the General Assembly, appointed two subcommittees to deal with it. These subcommittees were so constituted that all the members of each one of them belonged to one school of thought; that is, the members of subcommittee I were all in favour of the partition of Palestine and the creation of a Jewish state, while the members of subcommittee II were all opposed to partition and

[1] General Assembly, Official Records (G.A.O.R.): 2nd Sess., *Ad Hoc* Ctte. on the Palestinian Question, 6th Mtg., 6 Oct. 1947, p. 27.

[2] G.A.O.R., 6th Sess., *Ad Hoc* Political Ctte., 37th Mtg., 11 Jan. 1952, p. 204.

favoured the establishment of a unitary state for the whole of Palestine. There was, thus, no hope of a compromise solution emerging from either subcommittee. To redress this situation, the Chairman of subcommittee II, who was the representative of Colombia, requested the Chairman of the *Ad Hoc* Committee to nominate two states holding a neutral attitude in place of two Arab states who were members of the subcommittee and who were willing to resign from it. On the refusal of the Chairman of the *Ad Hoc* Committee, the representative of Colombia resigned his chairmanship of subcommittee II, and Sir Zafrulla Khan was elected in his place.

Subcommittee I in its report recommended the internationalisation of Jerusalem and the partition of the rest of Palestine into two states, one Arab and the other Jewish, with a common economic council.

Subcommittee II recommended a unitary state for the whole of Palestine, with constitutional safeguards for the rights of all its inhabitants. It further recommended for the approval of the General Assembly a resolution in these terms:

The General Assembly of the United Nations Resolves to request the International Court of Justice to give an advisory opinion under Article 96 of the Charter and Chapter IV of the Statute of the Court on the following questions:

(i) Whether the indigenous population of Palestine has not an inherent right to Palestine and to determine its future constitution and government;

(ii) Whether the pledges and assurances given by Great Britain to the Arabs during the first World War (including the Anglo-French Declaration of 1918) concerning the independence and future of Arab countries at the end of the war did not include Palestine;

(iii) Whether the Balfour Declaration, which was made without the knowledge or consent of the indigenous population of Palestine, was valid and binding on the people of Palestine, or consistent with the earlier and subsequent pledges and assurance given to the Arabs;

m

(iv) Whether the provisions of the Mandate for Palestine regarding the establishment of a Jewish National Home in Palestine are in conformity or consistent with the objectives and provisions of the Covenant of the League of Nations (in particular Article 22), or are compatible with the provisions of the Mandate relating to the development of self-government and the preservation of the rights and position of the Arabs of Palestine;

(v) Whether the legal basis for the Mandate for Palestine has not disappeared with the dissolution of the League of Nations, and whether it is not the duty of the Mandatory Power to hand over power and administration to a Government of Palestine representing the rightful people of Palestine;

(vi) Whether a plan to partition Palestine without the consent of the majority of its people is consistent with the objectives of the Covenant of the League of Nations, and with the provisions of the Mandate for Palestine;

(vii) Whether the United Nations is competent to recommend either of the two plans and recommendations of the majority or minority of the United Nations Special Committee on Palestine, or any other solution involving partition of the territory of Palestine, or a permanent trusteeship over any city or part of Palestine, without the consent of the majority of the people of Palestine;

(viii) Whether the United Nations, or any of its Member States, is competent to enforce or recommend the enforcement of any proposal concerning the constitution and future Government of Palestine, in particular, any plan of partition which is contrary to the wishes, or adopted without the consent of the inhabitants of Palestine.

The General Assembly instructs the Secretary-General to transmit this resolution to the International Court of Justice, accompanied by all documents likely to throw light upon the questions under reference.[3]

---

[3] See the text of the resolution given in the *Year Book of the United Nations 1947-48* (New York: United Nations, 1949), p. 241.

Both in the *Ad Hoc* Committee and in the General Assembly, the partition scheme was resolutely opposed by Pakistan. Sir Zafrulla Khan declared that "The Pakistan delegation was utterly and uncompromisingly opposed to partition."[4] The grounds on which he assailed the proposal were, first, that it was contrary to the principle of self-determination and beyond the competence of the United Nations; secondly, that as proposed it was unfair and impractical; and, thirdly, that if implemented it would lead to strife within Palestine and embitter the Arabs. So far as the juridical questions involved in the scheme were concerned, Pakistan urged that they should, as envisaged by subcommittee II, be referred to the International Court of Justice. With regard to the merits of the scheme, Sir Zafrulla Khan said:

> The first contention is this. There are 1,300,000 Arabs in Palestine and 650,000 Jews—with room wanted for more—and the problem has become insoluble. It is said: therefore, let us divide because it would be unjust and unfair that thirty-three per cent of the population—which is the Jewish population of Palestine today—should occupy a minority status in a unitary State. Let us have a fair solution, the Arabs to have their State and the Jews to have theirs.

> The boundaries were drawn accordingly. The Arab State will be an Arab State in the sense that there will be only 10,000 Jews in it and almost 1,000,000 Arabs. Very well, but what of the Jewish State? In the Jewish State there will be 498,000 Jews and 435,000 Arabs. Have you solved the problem? Jews are not to live as a minority under the Arabs, but the Arabs are to live as a minority under the Jews. If one of them is not fair then neither is the other; and if one is not a solution, the other is not.

> ... Of the cultivable area of Palestine the plains by and large, go to the Jewish State, the hills to the Arabs. There was a document circulated to the members of the Committees by

---

[4] G.A.O.R., 2nd Sess., *Ad Hoc* Ctte. on the Palestinian Question, 12th Mtg., 13 Oct. 1947, p. 73.

the United Kingdom representative showing that, of the irrigated, cultivable areas, 84 per cent would be in the Jewish State and 16 per cent in the Arab State. A very fair division for one-third of the population to receive 84 per cent, while two-thirds receive 16 per cent.

The United Nations Special Committee itself has observed that the largest export from Palestine is citrus produce, and that it is owned almost half and half by Arab and Jew, and that the citrus area will be almost entirely in the Jewish State. . . .[5]

The supporters of the scheme for carving out a Jewish state in Palestine put forward a number of arguments, the two most important of which were, first, that the Jews originally came from Palestine and were therefore entitled to return to it and, secondly, that to the problem of the persecuted and displaced Jews of Europe, there was no solution except that they should be settled in a Jewish state in Palestine. Amir Arslan (Syria), quoting at length from the *Jewish Encyclopaedia*, pointed out that the Jews of Eastern Europe were not in any way related to Israel, but that they were purely of Russian Khazar origin. Sir Zafrulla Khan deeply sympathised with the Jews in the misfortune that they had suffered in Europe. But the correct solution of their problem, he pleaded, was that they should be reabsorbed in the countries to which they belonged, and if that were not possible, that they should be offered facilities for settling down in the larger, newer countries, which had more space and greater resources than tiny Palestine.

Sir Zafrulla Khan argued that to adopt, in the face of the declared opposition of the people of Palestine, a scheme for partitioning it and for creating in it a new state for aliens, would be beyond the competence of the General Assembly for to do so would violate the principle of self-determination. To that argument, two kinds of replies were given. Mr. Herschel Johnson of the United States maintained in general terms that the Assembly had the necessary

---

[5] G.A.O.R., 2nd Sess., 126th Plenary Mtg., 28 Nov. 1947, p. 1374.

competence under Articles 10 and 14 of the Charter.[6] Mr. Jorge
García Granados (Guatemala) told the *Ad Hoc* Committee that:

> ... the inhabitants of any particular region had no say in
> international conferences at which their fate was decided.
> The Arab argument regarding self-determination of peoples
> constituted an ideal but not an axiom of international law.

Further, "Regarding the other basic argument put forward by the
Arabs, that of numerical superiority, Mr. García Granados' view
was that what characterized a nation was its culture and not the
number of its inhabitants."[7]

The representatives of the Jewish Agency and their supporters
endeavoured to justify the partition of Palestine by drawing a
parallel with the partition of the Indian subcontinent. Sir Zafrulla
Khan pointed out that there was no similarity between the two cases.
The area of the subcontinent was one hundred and eighty times that
of Palestine, while the population of the subcontinent was four
hundred million, against Palestine's less than two million. The new
state of Pakistan, resulting from the partition of the subcontinent,
consisted of two compact blocs, in which the community desiring
partition was in an overwhelming majority. Above all, the partition
of the subcontinent had been decided on with the explicit consent
of all the principal political parties in it.[8] In Palestine the majority
of its people, far from consenting to partition, were emphatically
opposed to it. Adverting to the matter in the First Committee in
November 1948, Sir Zafrulla Khan declared that:

> ... partition which had taken place in India had been based
> on the principle of ceding to the minority a number of areas
> in which they were in the majority. If that was what the Jews
> were asking for, Pakistan would be willing to grant their
> request. . . .

[6] G.A.O.R., 2nd Sess., 124th Plenary Mtg., 26 Nov. 1947, p. 1326.

[7] G.A.O.R., 2nd Sess., *Ad Hoc* Ctte. on the Palestinian Question, 10th Mtg.,
10 Oct. 1947, p. 56.

[8] *Ibid.*, pp. 72-73.

But he pointed out that "the Jews were in a minority everywhere, except in one out of fourteen sub-districts, that of Jaffa."[9]

The supporters of the partition scheme were determined to see it through at all costs. The vote was to be taken in the plenary session on 26 November 1947. But, according to Sir Zafrulla Khan, if it had been put to the vote on that day, partition would not have been carried. He said:

> That was Thanksgiving Eve, and word was passed about that the voting would be postponed until after Thanksgiving. Mr. Al-Jamali of Iraq and I went to the President and protested. We were told that the President was helpless because the Secretary-General had informed him that the staff could not be expected to work on Thanksgiving Eve or Thanksgiving Day and that therefore the matter must be postponed. So the adjournment took place. We found later that the staff quite cheerfully continued to work not only on Thanksgiving Eve but also on Thanksgiving Day.

> The matter was postponed. I will not dwell upon what happened in the meantime. But the result was that when the matter came to the actual voting after the adjournment, some of the States whose representatives had gone to the rostrum and announced in most indignant terms that the proposal before the General Assembly was a most inequitable one and that they would oppose it, tamely supported it, and the resolution was adopted.[10]

That is how, it would seem, the necessary two-thirds majority was obtained for the partition scheme, which was backed both by the United States and by the Soviet Union. Said Haj Amin Husseini of the Arab Higher Committee:

> The two great champions of freedom, the USSR and the United States, had joined hands—prompted, they said, by humanitarian motives—to support the monstrous perversion of the principle of self-determination in Palestine. They had

---

[9] G.A.O.R., 3rd Sess., Part I, 1st Ctte., 217th Mtg., 30 Nov. 1948, pp. 815-16.
[10] G.A.O.R., 7th Sess., 406th Plenary Mtg., 18 Dec. 1952, p. 412.

disagreed on everything constructive in the United Nations and had agreed on only one thing—the partition of Palestine. They had prepared for that destructive policy for divergent motives, the one to please Jewish voters in the United States, the other to permit tens of thousands of immigrants to inundate Palestine in order to propagate its theories and political aims.[11]

But since it was the influence of the United States that had led some of the delegations to change sides and to vote for partition, we find Sir Zafrulla Khan declaring "that the partition plan could be called a United States rather than a United Nations decision."[12]

This view received support from James Forrestal, at that time United States Defense Secretary, who was later to comment that "the methods that had been used by people outside the Executive branch of the government to bring coercion and duress on other nations in the General Assembly bordered closely onto scandal." Forrestal also records that he had been told by the National Democratic Chairman, Senator McGrath, that the party on account of "failure to go along with the Zionists might lose the states of New York, Pennsylvania and California."[13]

If today there are people in the Middle East who do not trust the Western powers, to a great extent it is because they believe that the United States government which was in office at that time, in order to advance its party's interests, made a most unfair use of its influence in the United Nations. They are no less bitter about it than they are about what they regard as the double dealing of Britain in promising after World War I in the McMahon letters that the Arab lands would be independent, then secretly entering into the Sykes-Picot agreement for the sharing of those very lands with the French and the Russians, then unilaterally issuing the Balfour

---

11 G.A.O.R., 2nd Sess., *Ad Hoc* Ctte. on the Palestinian Question, 31st Mtg., 24 Nov. 1947, pp. 199-200.
12 G.A.O.R., 2nd Special Sess., 1st Ctte., 122nd Mtg., Vol. II., 22 April 1948, p. 51.
13 Walter Millis, ed., *The Forrestal Diaries* (New York: The Viking Press, 1951), p. 363.

Declaration to create in Palestine a National Home for the Jews, and eventually paving the way for a Jewish state to come into existence.

To return to the General Assembly: speaking before the vote was taken, Sir Zafrulla Khan publicly condemned the manœuvres that were being resorted to by the supporters of the partition scheme:

> Those who have no access to what is going on behind the scenes have known enough from the Press to have fear in their hearts not only on this question—because this is one individual question—but that the deliberations on crucial questions of this great body, on which the hopes of the world for the future are centred, will not be left free.[14]

He pleaded:

> Let us pause and consider before we launch the United Nations upon a course which commits it to carrying through a scheme which lacks moral justification, is beyond the legal and juridical authority of the United Nations and is impossible of achievement. In making this futile, this fatal attempt, you set at nought the wishes of sixty-six per cent of the people of Palestine. You destroy the faith and trust of all the surrounding and neighbouring States in the fairness and impartiality of the United Nations, particularly having regard to what has been happening during the last three or four days—all the manœuvres, even with regard to the meetings of the General Assembly, that great and honourable nations are descending to.[15]

Giving a solemn warning to the Assembly—a warning amply justified by subsequent events—Sir Zafrulla said:

> It is said that if partition is not accepted, there would be no room left for a solution. On the contrary, if partition is accepted, the fatal step will have been taken. The Arabs and the Jews will have been set by the ears and never again will there be any chance of bringing them together. Far too many un-

---

[14] G.A.O.R., 2nd Sess., 126th Plenary Mtg., 28 Nov. 1947, p. 1366.
[15] *Ibid.*, p. 1376.

finished vendettas will then bar the way. If you delay and do not take the fatal step, you still leave open to the Arabs and the Jews the chance of a conciliatory solution through which they combine and work. . . .[16]

Foreseeing the disastrous consequences of the creation of Israel, Sir Zafrulla Khan said: "Remember, nations of the West, that you may need friends tomorrow, that you may need allies in the Middle East; I beg of you not to ruin and blast your credit in those lands."[17]

When the vote was taken, it was found that the supporters of the partition scheme were able to obtain for it the required two-thirds majority. Amongst the thirteen states that cast a negative vote were Afghanistan, Egypt, Iran, Iraq, Lebanon, Pakistan, Saudi Arabia, Syria, Turkey, and Yemen, that is, all the Muslim members of the United Nations. Commenting upon this fact, Mr. Alfonso López of Colombia said:

> From another angle, we cannot overlook or underestimate the fact that among the thirteen votes counted against the partition of Palestine, every one of the Moslem countries is included. If the Jewish problem is both religious and racial, we find that it does not forebode well for the execution of the plan that it should have been unanimously rejected by the whole Moslem world; not quietly rejected, but under strong protests; not by a small portion of mankind, but by the representatives of four hundred million people of one religious creed. No wonder that the plan has had to come across the Atlantic in search of the supporters that it failed to find in the countries adjoining Palestine, in the Eastern Mediterranean, in Western Europe or in the distant Asiatic mainland.[18]

After the vote was taken Mr. M. Ayub read Sir Zafrulla Khan's departing statement which observed:

> We much fear that the beneficence, if any, to which partition may lead will be small in comparison to the mischief which it

16 *Ibid.*, p. 1378.

17 *Ibid.*, p. 1367.

18 *Ibid.*, p. 1397.

might inaugurate. It totally lacks legal validity. We entertain no sense of grievance against those of our friends and fellow representatives who have been compelled, under heavy pressure, to change sides and to cast their votes in support of a proposal the justice and fairness of which do not commend themselves to them. Our feeling for them is one of sympathy that they should have been placed in a position of such embarrassment between their judgment and conscience, on the one side, and the pressure to which they and their Governments were being subjected, on the other.

Pakistan desires to wash its hands of all responsibility for the decision that has just now been taken. It will, therefore, take no part in the election of the United Nations Commission which will be set up to implement that decision.[19]

The partition scheme and the manner in which the General Assembly was led to adopt it were widely condemned in Pakistan, both on the political platform and in the press. *Dawn* of Karachi described it as an "impolitic, immoral and illegal move to partition a small country without reference to and against the declared will of the overwhelming majority of its people." It characterised the scheme as a "diabolical conspiracy to sow the seeds of war in the Middle East," and denounced "the questionable methods employed by the pro-partition Powers in their quest for votes" for it.[20] Sir Zafrulla Khan, a year later, declared in the First Committee, that:

... the Moslem world, which today may have to submit to the combined voting strength controlled by the great Powers, would be determined to wipe out this insult to its sacred sentiments no matter how long it might take.[21]

He expressed the same thought when he said that the setting up of the state of Israel in Palestine was tantamount to the introduction of a canker into the body politic of the Middle East, a canker "which would eventually either have to be ejected through a surgical

---

[19] *Ibid.*, p. 1426.

[20] *Dawn* (Karachi), 30 Nov. 1947.

[21] G.A.O.R., 3rd Sess., Part I, 1st Ctte., 210th Mtg., 24 Nov. 1948, p. 735.

operation or else would poison the culture, economic security and policy not only of the Middle East but of vast areas beyond that region." He reminded the assembled nations that:

> ... at no time and under no circumstances would the East ever assimilate or reconcile itself to a sovereign State of Israel. With Jewry as such the East had no quarrel; it had, indeed, deep sympathy with the sufferings of the Jewish race ...

According to Sir Zafrulla Khan,

> ... The so-called State of Israel was the culmination of a course of the most insidious aggression carried on and persisted in during the course of a third of a century, contrary to all the principles of the Charter of the United Nations, including the principle of equal rights and self-determination of peoples. ...

Sir Zafrulla Khan wondered,

> ... what would be the attitude of the representatives of the nations of the West both in Europe and in America if it were a case of the East seeking to set up in the heart of the West a sovereign independent State for the benefit of the East, however much the establishment of such a State might be supported by the kind of consideration which had been advanced in the case of the so-called State of Israel. ...[22]

Addressing the seventh session of the General Assembly, Sir Zafrulla Khan summed up the Pakistani view of the United Nations' decision to create and recognise the state of Israel, in the following words:

> ... It was an imposed decision to take away their country from a people who had inhabited a land for nearly 2,000 years and to hand it over to people who were coming from—and more of them expected to come—from outside. ...[23]

As was feared by Pakistan and some other member states, the General Assembly's resolution on Palestine, passed on 29 November

---

[22] G.A.O.R., 3rd Sess., Part I, 145th Plenary Mtg., 27 Sept. 1948, p. 212.
[23] G.A.O.R., 7th Sess., 406th Plenary Mtg., 18 Dec. 1952, p. 412.

1947, did not solve the problem of that unfortunate little country. In fact, in the wake of that resolution came a series of problems, some of them of a grave nature. 15 May 1948 had been set by the mandatory power as the date for the withdrawal of its forces from Palestine. Before that date, Jews in Palestine started military operations to take possession of the areas assigned by the General Assembly to the Jewish state, of areas reserved for the Arab state, of Jerusalem, and other Arab cities. On 14 May 1948 Israel proclaimed its independence, two months ahead of the date laid down by the General Assembly. On the following day the armies of the Arab states joined the fighting in Palestine. One of the consequences of these developments was that almost the entire Arab population of Palestine became refugees in the neighbouring Arab lands.

Pakistan's view was that Israel was the culmination of a course of aggression. Therefore, when it was proposed "to stamp that culmination with the approval of the United Nations," Pakistan demurred. "When that State had been created," said Sir Zafrulla Khan, "the United Nations had laid down three conditions, regarding the internationalization of Jerusalem, the Arab population of the Jewish state and the frontiers of the Jewish state. The problem, therefore, was one of ascertaining how well Israel had fulfilled those conditions."[24] Sir Zafrulla Khan observed:

> . . . According to Mr. Eban's statement, the State of Israel was not even ready to agree to the internationalization of the City of Jerusalem, to the resettlement of the Arab refugees in their homes or to the return of the areas occupied by Israel. . . .[25]

However, Israel was recognised to be a "peace-loving" state and admitted to the United Nations, Pakistan voting against it.

Armistice agreements negotiated under United Nations auspices were signed between the Arab states and Israel in 1949, United Nations observers keeping watch on the cease-fire lines. But a final

[24] G.A.O.R., 3rd Sess., Part II, *Ad Hoc* Political Ctte., 49th Mtg., 7 May 1949, p. 319.
[25] *Ibid.*, p. 321.

peace settlement between the parties, urged by the Security Council, has not yet been negotiated. Israel has repeatedly complained that the Arabs, because of their hostility, refuse to make peace and to have normal relations with it. The Arab attitude towards this question was examined by Sir Zafrulla Khan in the course of a speech in the Security Council in October 1953. He said:

> ... When the representative of Israel complains that the Arabs do not hasten to make peace with Israel, he wishes it forgotten that the Arabs regard Israel as an intruder which has, through guile, force and oppression, possessed itself of Arab lands and Arab homes, and has turned nearly a million Arabs loose in neighbouring Arab lands as homeless wanderers and derelicts.

> And what kind of peace does Israel invite the Arabs to make with it? Does it offer to negotiate on the basis of the rehabilitation of Arab refugees in their homes and the restoration of their lands and properties to them? No. It has persistently rejected that position. It offers to co-operate in their rehabilitation in Arab lands. It is argued that the Arabs have vast territories, that they have great undeveloped resources, that they can easily take in these refugees and make room for them. But these refugees are out of their own homes and lands. It is no consolation to them that other Arabs have vast lands and large areas. Besides, the economy of neighbouring Arab lands is already being disrupted through this influx of refugees from Palestine. That, again, is a pressing problem. Their appreciation of all these matters and questions and problems is coloured by these facts.

> Then, Israel bases itself on the Assembly resolutions. Has Israel itself kept to those resolutions? The Arabs do not accept them. But is Israel willing to revert to the Assembly resolutions in the matter of frontiers? With regard to frontiers, the authorized declaration on behalf of Israel, quoted to the Council the other day [639th meeting] by the representative of Lebanon, is: our frontiers were established by war; they will be changed only by war. Is that an invitation to peace or is that a challenge to war?

What is Israel's position with regard to Jerusalem, clearly required by the Assembly resolution to be internationalized? Israel has converted it into its capital.

The truth is that Israel talks peace and acts war. It steals marches and it confronts the Arabs and the United Nations with *faits accomplis*, and then insists that these *faits accomplis* should be confirmed as part of the peace settlement. And there is yet no end to its ambitions, designs and projects of expansion.

These are not the only factors blocking a peace settlement. There is no guarantee that Israel would keep a peace it might make. . . .[26]

As in the initial stages of the Palestine question, Pakistan continued to take an active interest in all subsequent developments resulting from it, as they came year after year before the General Assembly or the Security Council (during the years that Pakistan was a member of the latter body). While the idea of confining the state of Israel to the boundaries envisaged for it in the resolution of 29 November 1947 was as good as given up, an attempt was made to secure the internationalisation of Jerusalem, under the administering authority of the Trusteeship Council, which drew up a statute for it. But, on the reported refusal of the governments of Israel and Jordan to co-operate in carrying out the proposal, it was not pursued.

Some other offshoots of the Palestine question which have, on the complaint of the Israelis or the Arabs, come up before the Security Council, have related to incidents on either side of the cease-fire line. The most serious of these incidents were those of Qibya (1953) and Gaza (1955), for both of which the Security Council condemned Israel. Syria successfully objected in 1951 to Israel's drainage project in the Huleh marshes area, and in 1953 to what purported to be an Israeli attempt to divert the Jordan river into

---

[26] Security Council, Official Records: 8th Year, 640th Mtg., 20 Nov. 1953, pp. 8-9.

Israeli territory. In 1951, Israel complained against restrictions imposed by Egypt on the passage of Israeli ships through the Suez Canal, which restrictions, Israel reported in 1954, had been extended to the Gulf of Aqaba.

The problem of the Arab refugees from Palestine has been a hardy annual in the General Assembly. This question was the only one arising from the original Arab-Israeli dispute on which, in the eleventh regular session, a resolution was passed. Pakistan was one of its sponsors. Evidently the United Nations had been defeated on the question of the internationalisation of Jerusalem and the confining of Israel to the frontiers prescribed for it by the resolution of November 1947.

However, the new and dramatic developments represented by the invasion of Egypt in 1956 were not unconnected with the Arab-Israeli dispute. This was recognised in the resolution[27] of the First Emergency Special Session of 1956, which, *inter alia*, referred to the disregard by Israel of the Armistice Agreements of 1948, and urged that they be respected by the parties concerned.

It was in July 1956 that President Nasser announced the nationalisation of the Suez Canal Company and declared his intention of using the revenue from the Canal for the purpose of building the high Aswan dam. This was after the United States had withdrawn its offer of help in financing the construction of the dam. Nasser gave the assurance that nationalisation would affect neither the international commitments of Egypt with regard to the Canal nor the freedom of navigation in it. Pakistan's view from the beginning was that Egypt was within its rights in nationalising the Company. At the first Suez Conference, held in London in August, the Pakistan Foreign Minister, Mr. Hamidul Haq Choudhury, through a series of amendments to the resolution of Mr. John Foster Dulles, sought to make that resolution acceptable to Mr. Nasser. The aim of these amendments, which were accepted by Mr. Dulles, was to emphasise

---

[27] G.A.O.R., 1st Emergency Special Sess., 1-10 Nov. 1956, Supple. No. 1, Resolution 997 (ES-I), p. 2.

the sovereign rights of Egypt and to keep open the door of negotiations with it. Although seventeen out of the twenty-two nations
participating in the Conference accepted the resolution, it was unreal. It provided for an independent authority for the Canal (to
be created by treaty with Egypt) and as such it was rejected by
President Nasser. Egypt now exercises exclusive (and efficient) control over the Canal, which is recognised by the whole world.

There was talk of using force to bring the Canal under international control, and of the Western powers' forcing their way
through the Canal. Mr. Firoz Khan Noon, who had replaced Mr.
Hamidul Haq Choudhury as Foreign Minister in September 1956,
declared that Pakistan would "not associate itself in any way whatsoever with the use of force."[28] Asked about his government's
attitude towards the projected Canal Users' Association, he said:

> If any compromise could be arrived at with the willing co-
> operation of the Canal Users' Association and Egypt, no one
> will be more pleased than we, for that would be a peaceful
> solution.

He added:

> But, if the Canal Users' Association have any intention of
> enforcing their will, that, in our view, would be against the
> United Nations Charter and we, as a United Nations member,
> are pledged to resolve our disputes peacefully.[29]

He also said that nothing would be better than that the matter be
taken to the United Nations for a peaceful settlement. At the second
Suez Conference, held in London in September 1956, Mr. Noon
opposed the formation of the Suez Canal Users' Association and
announced that Pakistan would have nothing to do with it or with
anything else in the nature of an imposed settlement.[30]

---

[28] *Pakistan Times* (Lahore), 17 Sept. 1956.
[29] *Ibid.*, 19 Sept. 1956.
[30] *Ibid.*

The Anglo-French-Israeli invasion of Egypt came as no surprise to millions of people in Asia and Africa, who had always believed that Israel had expansionist aims and that it had been created for just the kind of part that it was playing in the invasion. In Pakistan there were spontaneous demonstrations and public meetings to condemn the invasion. This was in spite of the fact that in Egypt there had been public criticism of Pakistan for having taken, in the first Suez Conference, a stand considered unacceptable in Egypt. There was a widespread demand that Pakistan withdraw from the Commonwealth and the Baghdad Pact, in both of which it had Britain for a partner. There is no doubt that if the invasion had not been halted, this demand would have become irresistible.

On 29 October Israel invaded the Sinai Peninsula, a part of Egypt. On the same day the United States asked the Security Council to consider "steps for the immediate cessation of military activities of Israel against Egypt." On 30 October Britain and France issued their ultimatum preparatory to entering the fight on the side of Israel. On the same day these two permanent members of the Security Council vetoed the American resolution calling for an immediate cease-fire, withdrawal of Israeli troops behind the established armistice lines, and asking all members to refrain from introducing military goods into the area. The Council, however, adopted the Yugoslav resolution under the "Uniting for Peace" resolution for an Emergency Session of the General Assembly. On 31 October Britain and France started their air attack on Egypt.

Pakistan supported the resolutions in the Emergency Session of the General Assembly calling for a cease-fire in Suez, for the constitution of an international force "to secure and supervise the cessation of hostilities," and for the appointment of a Chief of the Command, and co-sponsored like resolutions in the regular session. Speaking in the General Assembly on the momentous character of the resolutions, Begum Ikramullah said:

> For the last few years a feeling of disillusion [ment] had been growing amongst the smaller nations of the world regarding

n

the United Nations. They had begun to feel that this Organization, that came into being with such high hopes and such
faith, born out of bitter suffering and great trial, was after all
nothing better than holy alliances for the unholy purposes of
the past and that it was almost futile to hope that justice
regardless of power politics could be had at the hands of the
United Nations; but, by taking at last bold and prompt action
in the case of Israel[i] and British-French aggression, the United
Nations has redeemed itself. It has restored the faith of the
small peoples of the world in its integrity. . . .[31]

True, nothing in the entire history of the United Nations had so
helped to build up its prestige as the resolutions calling upon Britain
and France to withdraw their forces from Egypt. In the same
speech Begum Ikramullah said:

The time has come when [we] must make clear that United
Nations resolutions are not mere pious declarations, but are
meant to be obeyed and applied without fear or favour.
My delegation has co-sponsored a draft resolution asking for
withdrawal of foreign troops from Egypt because we are
against all foreign troops and troops of occupation anywhere,
under any pretext, by anybody. We condemn aggression and
suppression of liberty equally in Egypt and in Hungary, and
in Algeria and in Kashmir. We are opposed to the last ditch
stand of the waning imperialism of Europe and are equally
determined to oppose the nascent rise of imperialism in Asia.
As I have said before from this rostrum [565th meeting],
we are against imperialism of all types and colours, white or
red, black or brown.[32]

The cease-fire in the Egyptian war was undoubtedly the most important achievement of the United Nations in its entire history. The
most striking aspect of the episode was that the United States had
boldly come out against Britain and France, its principal allies in
war and peace and against its protégé, Israel. Here was a good
opportunity for the United States to stand forth before the Arabs

---

[31] G.A.O.R., 11th Sess., 592nd Plenary Mtg., 23 Nov. 1956, p. 270.
[32] *Ibid.*, pp. 270-71.

as an impartial champion of peace, even if it meant condemning its friends. There was of course the threat of Marshal Bulganin to use rocket weapons against London and Paris. Yet there is no doubt that the one compelling force which brought about the cessation of hostilities and the withdrawal of the invading forces from the Canal Zone was world opinion, which asserted itself through the United Nations, with the United States and the Soviet Union acting in close co-operation. The division list on the resolution,[33] adopted by the Special Emergency Session, shows that the General Assembly was never nearer unanimity on a first class international issue. Sixty-four countries voted, Yes; five, No (United Kingdom, France, Israel, Australia, and New Zealand); and six abstained (Belgium, Canada, Laos, Netherlands, Portugal, and South Africa). It will be noticed that even many members of the aggressors' respective families did not vote against the resolution.

The United Nations Emergency Force which entered the Suez Canal Zone was created by another Emergency Session resolution.[34] That resolution also established a committee to advise the Secretary-General on plans and developments regarding problems relating to UNEF, the Suez, and canal clearance. Of this committee Pakistan was elected a member, the other members being Brazil, Canada, Ceylon, Colombia, India, and Norway.

---

[33] G.A.O.R., 1st Emergency Special Sess., 562nd Plenary Mtg., 1 Nov. 1956, pp. 34-35.
[34] G.A.O.R., 1st Emergency Special Sess., 1-10 Nov. 1956, Supple. No. 1, Resolution 998 (ES-I), p. 2.

chapter seven

Self-Determination and Other Rights

Pakistan has been particularly concerned in the United Nations about questions in which the principle of self-determination or self-government was involved. Having recently attained its independence, Pakistan has been anxious that other countries still under colonial rule should also become independent. Until that happened, declared Sir Zafrulla Khan in the General Assembly, "they would not be able either to enjoy or to appreciate to the fullest extent their own recently achieved freedom and sovereignty."[1]

The Kashmir question, to which Pakistan is a party, is, as has been recognised by the United Nations, essentially one of the right of self-determination. Again, it was out of respect for that right that Pakistan fought hard to prevent the partition of Palestine and the creation of the state of Israel. Pakistan has supported the claim

---

[1] General Assembly, Official Records (G.A.O.R.): 4th Sess., 227th Plenary Mtg., 24 Sept. 1949, p. 59.

to independence of Indonesia, the former Italian colonies in Africa, Tunisia, Morocco, and Algeria. Further, Pakistan has advocated the acceleration of the pace of self-government in trust territories and non-self-governing territories.

INDONESIA

The Indonesian question was dealt with in the United Nations by the Security Council, an organ on which Pakistan was not serving at that time. However, Pakistan was throughout a strong supporter of independence for Indonesia and spoke vigorously for it in the Conference of Asian and Australasian countries convened in Delhi in January 1949. Pakistan supported the proposal for the inclusion of the Indonesian question in the agenda of the fourth session of the General Assembly. When the Dutch started their so-called "police action" against Indonesia, Pakistan reacted to it by denying the use of Karachi airport to Dutch aircraft. The fact that Dutch aircraft could not use the landing and refueling facilities at Karachi, on their way to Indonesia, effectively hindered the delivery of supplies to the Dutch forces in Indonesia and correspondingly helped the Indonesians. Eventually, with the help of the United Nations Commission for Indonesia, an agreement was arrived at between the Indonesians and the Dutch and sovereignty transferred in December 1949 to the government of the Republic of Indonesia. This was welcomed in Pakistan. To celebrate that event the government of Pakistan declared a nation-wide holiday.

The Indonesian struggle for independence was referred to by Sir Zafrulla Khan in his address to the 1950 session of the General Assembly. He described it as a United Nations-sponsored struggle and the attainment of independence by Indonesia as the coming of age of the principle of self-determination.[2]

An important offshoot of the Indonesian question has come before the United Nations, namely, the West Irian issue. The Charter

2 G.A.O.R., 5th Sess., 289th Plenary Mtg., 28 Sept. 1950, p. 179.

of the Transfer of Sovereignty to the Republic of Indonesia had provided that this issue should be settled through negotiations between Indonesia and the Netherlands. Negotiations were under-taken but yielded no solution and in July 1954 the Netherlands declared that it would break off the talks.

Pakistan was a party to the Bogor Communiqué of December 1954 and the Bandung Communiqué of April 1955. These declarations expressed the hope that the Netherlands would resume negotiations with Indonesia and that the United Nations would assist the two countries in finding a solution to the dispute.

Pakistan was one of the countries that asked for the inclusion of the West Irian question in the agenda of the tenth session of the General Assembly.[3] On 16 December 1955, the Assembly adopted a resolution[4] calling for the early resumption of negotiations and expressing the hope that they would be fruitful. A similar resolution,[5] with Pakistan co-sponsor, was passed by the First Committee in its eleventh session; but for lack of a two-thirds majority, it was not adopted by the General Assembly. In the twelfth session a resolution[6] calling for resumption of negotiations was again passed by the First Committee, Pakistan voting for it. But this resolution too was not adopted by the General Assembly for lack of the required majority.

FORMER ITALIAN COLONIES IN AFRICA

As a result of its defeat in World War II, Italy had to forego its possessions in Africa. Italian aggression against Ethiopia had been a factor in destroying the prestige of the League of Nations. After

---

[3] Letter dated 10 Aug. 1955 addressed to the Secretary-General by the per-manent representatives of Afghanistan, Burma, Egypt, India, Indonesia, Iran, Iraq, Lebanon, Liberia, Pakistan, Philippines, Saudi Arabia, Syria, Thailand, and Yemen to the UN (A/2932).

[4] General Assembly Resolution 915(X), 16 Dec. 1955.

[5] G.A.O.R., 11th Sess., Annexes: Agenda item 63, p. 2.

[6] G.A.O.R., 12th Sess., Annexes: Agenda item 62, p. 2.

World War II Ethiopia regained its independence. After that war, Libya (barring the Fezzan), Eritrea, and Italian Somaliland were under the military occupation of the British. The Fezzan, a part of Libya, was held by the French. The four powers having failed to agree on the disposal of these colonies, the question went to the third session of the General Assembly in 1949. The First Committee, during the second half of the session, advanced a solution identical with that previously agreed upon between Britain, France, and Italy, the so-called Bevin-Sforza agreement. This solution contemplated that Libya should be independent after ten years; in the meantime Cyrenaica should be under British trusteeship, the Fezzan under French trusteeship, and Italy (which was not even a member of the United Nations) should assume trusteeship for Tripolitania. Italy was, in addition, to have trusteeship over Italian Somaliland. It was also proposed that the western provinces of Eritrea should be merged with the Sudan and the rest of Eritrea with Ethiopia.

Pakistan, along with several other smaller powers, including all the states of the Middle East, opposed these proposals. Sir Zafrulla Khan was against the reimposition of colonial rule under a new name and urged that independence should be given to a united Libya, comprising Tripolitania, Cyrenaica, and the Fezzan. If it was considered that immediate independence was not feasible, Sir Zafrulla Khan asked that the region be placed under United Nations trusteeship, under the Trusteeship Council.[7]

Pakistan resisted the proposal for an Italian trusteeship over former Italian Somaliland. In the First Committee, Sir Zafrulla Khan advocated a greater Somaliland, comprising Italian Somaliland, French Somaliland, British Somaliland, and the Somali areas of Ethiopia. He said: "If the principle of ending colonial exploitation was accepted, it should be applied not only in the former Italian colonies but in neighbouring areas as well."[8]

---

[7] G.A.O.R., 3rd Sess., Part II, 216th Plenary Mtg., 17 May 1949, p. 536.
[8] G.A.O.R., 3rd Sess., Part II, 1st Ctte., 243rd Mtg., 18 Apr. 1949, p. 54.

However, in the General Assembly, while that part of the First Committee's resolution[9] which related to Cyrenaica and the Fezzan was adopted, the other, concerning Italian trusteeship over Tripolitania, failed to secure the required two-thirds majority. Thereafter the Latin American countries, which were primarily interested in an Italian trusteeship over Tripolitania, joined the opposition and voted against the resolution, which was defeated. Thus the way was opened to a reconsideration of the entire question, which was done in the fourth regular session of the Assembly.

Pakistan, playing a full part in the discussions, had the satisfaction of seeing its labours, and the labours of the member states that had collaborated with it, rewarded when on 21 November 1949 the General Assembly[10] decided that Libya, comprising Tripolitania, Cyrenaica, and the Fezzan, should become independent by January 1952. To prepare for that consummation, the Assembly appointed a Commission of which Pakistan was elected a member.

On Eritrea, too, a start had to be made all over again. It will be recalled that under the plan, contemplated in the draft resolution rejected in 1949 by the General Assembly in the second part of its third session, certain portions of Eritrea were to go to Ethiopia. The justification advanced for this arrangement was that Ethiopia needed an outlet to the sea, that the Christian population of Eritrea desired union with Ethiopia and that, as compensation for what Ethiopia had suffered at the hands of Italy, Eritrea should be handed over to Ethiopia. With regard to this last argument, Sir Zafrulla Khan condemned the mentality of those who looked upon Eritrea as "a bundle of chattels which had been taken away from Italy and the question was whether it should be given as a reward or a prize to Ethiopia."[11]

The General Assembly appointed a five-member commission to ascertain the wishes of the people of Eritrea and to make recom-

---

[9] G.A.O.R., 3rd Sess., Part II, Annexes: Agenda item 13[66], pp. 98-99.

[10] General Assembly Resolution 289(IV), 21 Nov. 1947.

[11] Speech in Karachi, *Pakistan Horizon*, Vol. II, No. 3, p. 126.

mendations regarding its future. Pakistan was named a member of this commission, its other members being Guatemala, Burma, Norway, and South Africa. The members of the commission were divided in their findings, the majority favouring the original plan of partitioning Eritrea between Ethiopia and the Sudan. When the question came back to the General Assembly, Pakistan proposed in the *Ad Hoc* Political Committee in 1950 that Eritrea should be constituted a sovereign independent state by 1 January 1953, and that a national assembly be convened to draft a constitution.[12] This proposal was supported by all the Communist governments, by most Muslim states, and by some South American ones; but it failed to obtain a majority.

Eventually, on 2 December 1950, the General Assembly adopted a resolution[13] to the effect that Eritrea, as an autonomous unit, should federate with Ethiopia under the sovereignty of its Emperor. The resolution provided that an Eritrean government was to be established under a constitution to be prepared by 6 August 1952. In August 1952 the constitution received the approval of the United Nations Commissioner, appointed for the purpose, and the assent of the Emperor of Ethiopia.

As regards Italian Somaliland, it will be recalled that Pakistan had put forward a rather radical solution, namely, that it should be amalgamated with other Somali areas to form an independent Somalia, which would be ethnically and culturally homogeneous. The demand of the Western powers was that Italian Somaliland be placed under Italian trusteeship. To this, public opinion in Pakistan was opposed. *Dawn* of Karachi editorially warned against the dangers of entrusting colonial territories to individual powers. It said: "Colonial rule, whether with or without the blessings of the United Nations, remains the same and that is why Pakistan opposes trusteeship under individual countries."[14] Sir Zafrulla Khan strongly

---

[12] G.A.O.R., 5th Sess., Annexes: Agenda item 21, pp. 126-27.

[13] General Assembly Resolution 390(V), 2 Dec. 1950.

[14] *Dawn* (Karachi), 8 Oct. 1949.

opposed Italian trusteeship. Fifty years of Italian rule over the area, he said, had not prepared its people for independence. Nor was a single newspaper published in their language.[15] Finally, the General Assembly decided that Italian Somaliland be placed under United Nations trusteeship, with Italy as the administering power, aided by an advisory council, consisting of Colombia, Egypt, and the Philippines.[16] This arrangement was to last for ten years, with Italian Somaliland becoming independent in 1960.

The manner of the disposal of the former Italian colonies was unprecedented. As territorial possessions of a vanquished party to a war, they would have, under the old order, gone to the victors by outright annexation or, under the post-World War I arrangements, in the guise of mandates. In the words of an American writer, the United Nations decisions regarding these African colonies constituted "an uncommon event in the annals of international diplomacy," perhaps the first instance of a territorial settlement in which the great powers had bowed before "an international organization acting with binding authority."[17]

Newly independent countries, with their limited resources and small populations, have to face serious problems of finance and technology. This is particularly true when the people of such a country have had no opportunities for education or development. Libya had problems of this nature, to which the representative of Pakistan drew attention when the Annual Report of the United Nations Commissioner came up for discussion in January 1952. Colonel Abdur Rahim Khan said:

> The responsibility of the United Nations in the matter had not ended with the transfer of power and authority from the administering Powers to the Libyan people. Economic stability was almost as important as political freedom. Pakistan

---

[15] G.A.O.R., 3rd Sess., 1st Ctte., 270th Mtg., 12 May 1949, p. 350.

[16] General Assembly Resolution 289(IVB), 21 Nov. 1949.

[17] Benjamin Rivlin, *The United Nations and the Italian Colonies* (New York: Carnegie Endowment for International Peace, 1950), p. 79.

would welcome any proposal that would enable the United Nations to render assistance to Libya in the economic field....

Believing that the financial arrangements which had been entered into by Libya with certain powers were not, from the Libyan point of view, the best possible, Pakistan

> ... would have liked that assistance to be obtained from international bodies such as the International Bank for Reconstruction and Development, the International Monetary Fund, but the regulations governing the activities of those organizations were an obstacle. The difficulties might be overcome, but the time for that would be when Libya had become a Member of the United Nations and could raise the issue itself. At the present stage, Pakistan would only draw the Committee's attention to the importance and urgency of continuing and improving the technical assistance which the United Nations and the specialized agencies had been rendering to Libya.[18]

TUNISIA

The freedom movements of the three countries of the "Maghreb" evoked a great deal of sympathy in Pakistan. Their leaders, Habib Bourguiba, head of the Neo-Destour party of Tunisia, Allal El-Fassi of the Istiqlal party of Morocco, and Mohammed Yazid of the National Liberation Movement of Algeria, and several others, repeatedly visited Pakistan to explain their respective causes and were enthusiastically received. For some time a branch of the Maghreb Office of Cairo functioned in Karachi, as did also an influential local Maghreb Committee. For its part, the government of Pakistan gave all possible support in the United Nations to the aspirations of the Arabs of North Africa. This was in consonance with a cardinal principle of Pakistan's foreign policy, namely, that all colonial people struggling to be free should be helped. The people of Tunisia, Morocco, and Algeria also happened to be Muslims.

---

[18] G.A.O.R., 6th Sess., *Ad Hoc* Political Ctte., 48th Mtg., 23 Jan. 1952, p. 266.

The struggle against the French and the Spanish in the Maghreb has been going on for many a long year. In the twenties there was in Morocco a widespread revolt, which the ruling powers were able to suppress because of their superior modern arms. However, agitation continued. The three countries, like their neighbour, Libya, experienced a tremendous upheaval as a result of becoming involved in World War II. The achievement of independence by Libya, through the United Nations, no doubt encouraged the people next door in Tunisia to step up their struggle. The French replied by jailing the leaders, gagging the press, and proclaiming martial law, and generally putting an end to all civil liberties. The Tunisian government complained to the United Nations. In April 1952 it asked the Security Council urgently to consider the "grave situation in Tunisia."

Pakistan was one of the eleven Asian and African governments which in April 1952 requested the Security Council to consider the Tunisian situation, under Article 34 of the Charter, as one likely to endanger international peace and security. Pakistan was then a member of the Security Council and the Pakistani representative, Professor Ahmed S. Bokhari, was President for the month.

While the Tunisian question was put on the provisional agenda of the Security Council, its adoption was vigorously opposed. Indeed, as Dr. Tingfu F. Tsiang, the representative of China, pointed out, never before in the history of the United Nations had such opposition been offered to the mere adoption of the agenda.[19] This opposition was, of course, led by France itself. Professor Bokhari gave a quotation from a speech made by the representative of France on 3 September 1946, at the 59th meeting of the Security Council, when that body was considering the Ukrainian SSR's complaint against Greece. Mr. Alexandre Parodi had then said: "In my view, to adopt the method of declining to place a question on

---

[19] Security Council, Official Records (S.C.O.R.): 7th Year, 575th Mtg., 10 Apr. 1952, p. 7.

the agenda involves serious disadvantages and risks."[20] Bokhari quoted also from Mr. Ernest Bevin's statement to the second meeting of the Security Council on 25 January 1946, when the British Foreign Minister had said:

> ... I am very anxious, in all these cases, that complainants should be heard by the Council, whoever they may be. I think it is a mistake if a Government feels that having a complaint against another Power, whether it be great or small, it cannot come to this Council and state its case. ...[21]

The legal answer to the objection against the competence of the Security Council was to be given later in the year by Sir Zafrulla Khan. However, Professor Bokhari, who was not a lawyer, gave a telling non-legal reply. He asked:

> ... What is the United Nations for if a situation like this cannot be aired here? What are we to understand to be our functions around this table if a suppressed people cannot raise its voice here, through eleven responsible nations representing, as my colleagues well know, the whole of Asia with a few exceptions and barring those which are not Member States. ...[22]

The French delegate opposed the inclusion of the item in the agenda, contending that it related to a matter essentially within the domestic jurisdiction of a member state and was, as such, barred by Article 2(7) of the Charter. This viewpoint was upheld by the British delegate, who argued that the dispute was like one between the Soviet Union and Uzbekistan.[23] There being only five members (Brazil, Chile, China, Pakistan, and the Soviet Union) in favour of it, the item was not included in the agenda.

---

[20] S.C.O.R., 1st Year, 2nd Series, No. 7, 59th Mtg., 3 Sept. 1946, pp. 190-91; as quoted by Mr. Bokhari in S.C.O.R., 7th Year, 575th Mtg., 10 April 1952, p. 17.

[21] S.C.O.R., 1st Year, 1st Series, No. 1, 2nd Mtg., 25 Jan. 1946, pp. 16-17; as quoted by Mr. Bokhari in S.C.O.R., 7th Year, 575th Mtg., 10 April 1952, p. 18.

[22] S.C.O.R., 7th Year, 574th Mtg., 4 Apr. 1952, pp. 22-23.

[23] S.C.O.R., 7th Year, 575th Mtg., 10 Apr. 1952, p. 5.

Having met with frustration in the Security Council, the Asian-African nations brought the Tunisian question before the General Assembly in 1952. The resolution, which was introduced by Pakistan, asked for the restoration of civil liberties in Tunisia and for negotiations with a view to enabling its people to exercise their right of self-determination. Speaking in the First Committee, after the French delegation had decided to withdraw from the Assembly and to take no part in its proceedings, Sir Zafrulla Khan pointed out that:

> . . . While the Tunisian and the Moroccan questions presented almost as many aspects as were embraced within the Charter—political, economic and humanitarian aspects, as well as those relating to peace and security and the self-determination of peoples—he preferred to view them principally as human problems since he was persuaded that the aspect of the dignity and worth of the person overshadowed all other aspects.[24]

He referred to articles on the right of self-determination, drafted in identical terms, in the Draft Covenant on Economic, Social and Cultural Rights and the Draft Covenant on Civil and Political Rights. The articles read: "All peoples and all nations shall have the right of self-determination, namely, the right to freely determine their political, economic, social and cultural status."[25]

Coming specifically to the issue of jurisdiction, Sir Zafrulla Khan observed that:

> . . . Although the French Government had often repeated its accord with the spirit of the Charter, including Article 73 b, it had suggested that Article 2 (7) barred discussion of those matters and any intervention by the United Nations. That paragraph read: "Nothing contained in the present Charter shall authorize the United Nations to intervene in matters which are essentially within the domestic jurisdiction of any State. . . ." France accepted as "a sacred trust," under Article 73, the obligation to develop self-government in Tunisia,

---

[24] G.A.O.R., 7th Sess., 1st Ctte., 537th Mtg., 4 Dec. 1952, p. 187.
[25] *Ibid.*, p. 191.

and he did not believe that anything arising out of that obligation could be treated as a matter essentially within France's domestic jurisdiction.[26]

Sir Zafrulla Khan recalled that the question of the interpretation of Article 2(7) had arisen during the discussion on the trial of high church dignitaries in certain East European countries and the discussion on the treatment of persons of Indian origin in South Africa. In both cases, the competence of the United Nations was in question; in both the General Assembly had exercised its competence.

The Foreign Minister of Pakistan referred to the Treaty of Bardo and the Convention of La Marsa, which, he said, undoubtedly committed certain specific matters to the government of France. All other matters remained under the sovereignty of the Bey. The specific complaint was that through interference with the Bey's sovereignty, France had in effect set it aside and substituted its own direct rule in the place of the indigenous authority. "Certainly such interference by France could not be a matter essentially within the jurisdiction of France." Sir Zafrulla Khan also observed that:

> ... it could scarcely be contended that a matter arising out of a treaty between two States was essentially within the domestic jurisdiction of one of those States. It was certainly at least within the domestic jurisdiction of two States.[27]

It will be recalled that Libya had already become independent. Sir Zafrulla asked what distinguished the case of Tunisia from that of Libya:

> ... Had the members of the French delegation been present, he was sure they would have been the first to repudiate any suggestion that Tunisia was in any respect more backward than Libya. The truth was that the benefits, if they were such, that Tunisia had received from France disentitled her from enjoying the incomparable boon, the honour and dignity of independence.[28]

---

[26] *Ibid.*

[27] *Ibid.*

[28] *Ibid.*, p. 192.

The resolution was supported by most Asian and African states, by all Communist governments, and by Guatemala and Yugoslavia, making a total of twenty-one. Against it were twenty-four votes, including those of the United Kingdom and the United States, whose representatives had spoken against it. There were seven abstentions. Thus the resolution was rejected.[29] On 17 December 1952 the General Assembly adopted a Latin American resolution expressing the hope that, in conformity with the principles of the Charter, France would develop free institutions in Tunisia.[30]

Pakistan was one of the fourteen Asian and African states at whose request the Tunisian question was included in the agenda of the 1953 session of the General Assembly which referred it to the First Committee. France again declined to participate in the debate, claiming that, without contravening Article 2(7) of the Charter, the Assembly could not interfere in the relations of France and its North African protectorate.

Pakistan was one of the thirteen states which, on 22 October 1953, submitted a draft resolution, recommending that necessary steps be taken to ensure the realisation by the people of Tunisia of their sovereignty and independence, for the restoration of civil liberties, and for negotiations with a Tunisian government established through free elections.[31] Though passed by the First Committee in a modified form, the resolution failed to obtain the required two-thirds majority and was not adopted by the Assembly.

The last time the Tunisian question came up before the General Assembly was in 1954, Pakistan again being one of the sponsors. The request for the inclusion of the question in the agenda of the ninth session was sent by letter in July. When it was considered by the First Committee on 16 December, the representative of France was not present. However, negotiations were then in progress between France and Tunisia. A long debate was avoided and an agreed

---

29 G.A.O.R., 7th Sess., Annexes: Vol. II, Agenda item 60, pp. 4-5.
30 General Assembly Resolution 611(VII), 17 Dec. 1952.
31 G.A.O.R., 8th Sess., Annexes: Agenda item 56, p. 3.

resolution, "expressing confidence" that the negotiations would bring about a satisfactory solution, was passed by fifty-four votes to none, with three abstentions. One of the countries which abstained was the United Kingdom, whose representative explained that while he sympathised with the spirit of the resolution, he felt that the substance of it was beyond the competence of the United Nations. In 1956 Tunisia was admitted as a member of the United Nations.

MOROCCO

The case of Morocco was analogous to that of Tunisia. In Morocco there was the Sultan, as in Tunisia there was the Bey. Morocco too was bound to France by treaty, that of Fez. This treaty permitted France to conduct the foreign relations of Morocco. Therefore, said France, the United Nations was debarred from considering the Moroccan question. The French delegation consequently took no part in the discussions on it.

The question was first debated in the General Assembly in 1952, at the instance of thirteen Asian and African states, Pakistan being one of them. Their draft resolution failed to obtain the required two-thirds majority in the Assembly, which on 19 December 1952 adopted a Latin American resolution expressing the hope that France would further the fundamental liberties of the people of Morocco, in conformity with the principles of the Charter, and continue negotiations towards developing free institutions.[32]

The same Asian and African states in a letter dated 21 August 1953 requested the President of the Security Council to call an urgent meeting for considering the situation in Morocco, whose sultan had been deposed and jailed by the French who had, they said, converted it into a colony. Despite every effort by the Pakistani representative on the Security Council (and by his Lebanese colleague)

---

[32] General Assembly Resolution 612(VII), 19 Dec. 1952.

o

the Moroccan question was not inscribed on the Council's agenda. However, it was included in that of the General Assembly.

Speaking in the First Committee, Sir Zafrulla Khan stated that his sole purpose was to seek

> ... a satisfactory and rapid solution based on friendly co-operation between France on the one hand and Tunisia and Morocco on the other and ensuring to the latter their right of self-determination and of directing their own affairs. It had never been his intention to create difficulties for France. . . .

Sir Zafrulla Khan observed that:

> ... Inspired by the principle that the United Nations was a centre for harmonizing the action of nations in the attainment of a common goal, Pakistan had always staunchly upheld the principles of freedom, independence and law within the United Nations. It was unfortunate that France had not recognized the sincerity of his delegation's motives. France itself, which considered no sacrifice too great when the triumph of its ideals was at stake, would appreciate that those ideals must be applied to all mankind and not merely to a privileged few.[33]

Sir Zafrulla Khan referred to the Treaty of Fez, which, it had been argued, barred the discussion of the question in the United Nations. He held that:

> ... Those using that argument would do well to reflect on the circumstances in which such instruments were normally imposed . . . . the people of Morocco would be quite entitled to plead that it was null and void today. . . .[34]

Referring to the disillusionment of the peoples of Asia and Africa, Sir Zafrulla said:

> ... After the Second World War, when the Charter had been adopted, they had believed that a great organization had been created to defend the fundamental rights of man. . . . They had felt that the world could not survive half free and half

---

[33] G.A.O.R., 8th Sess., 1st Ctte., 637th Mtg., 15 Oct. 1953, p. 65.
[34] *Ibid.*, p. 66.

enslaved. In several cases, including that of Pakistan, that hope had become a reality. But today it seemed that the great Powers were ashamed of the ideals that they had proclaimed and were ready in certain cases to repudiate them deliberately. The peoples of Tunisia and Morocco who had, through difficult times, lent their support to what was proclaimed to be the cause of freedom had firmly believed that the days of their bondage were drawing to a close. Today they were disillusioned. Even if the French régime were the most benevolent possible, it would be no substitute for freedom.[35]

In the course of the discussion on the competence of the United Nations in the matter, Sir Zafrulla Khan made no reference to the Act of Algeciras of 1906, under which, it had been determined by the International Court of Justice, France was not competent to legislate for Morocco. He felt that "it was enough to recall that the General Assembly, by placing the item twice on its agenda, had declared itself in favour of its own competence."[36]

The draft resolution of the thirteen Asian and African states, recommending that martial law be terminated and civil liberties restored in Morocco and that steps be taken to make it independent within five years,[37] was defeated in the First Committee, which adopted a mild Bolivian draft resolution asking for the "reduction of tension in relation to the question of Morocco."[38] This resolution failed to obtain a two-thirds majority in the General Assembly and was consequently not adopted.

At the request of fourteen Asian and African states, of whom Pakistan was again one, the Moroccan question was included in the agenda of the ninth General Assembly. France did not participate in the discussion. The matter was debated in the First Committee and then in the Assembly, where, eventually, on 27 December 1954, a resolution was passed taking note of the impending negotiations

---

[35] *Ibid.*

[36] *Ibid.*

[37] G.A.O.R., 8th Sess., Annexes: Agenda item 57, p. 4.

[38] *Ibid.*, p. 5.

between France and Morocco and deciding to postpone further consideration of the item. In 1956 Morocco was admitted as a member of the United Nations.

ALGERIA

Pakistan was one of the fourteen Asian and African states which, in July 1955, asked for a consideration of the question of Algeria by the tenth General Assembly. Since November 1954, a war had been going on between the Algerian nationalists and the French authorities. The Bandung Conference in April 1955 had urged the French government to seek a peaceful solution of the issue. The matter was one of international concern.

Tunisia and Morocco were French protectorates. Algeria had been conquered by the French. Without consultation with the Algerian people, Algeria had been "integrated" with metropolitan France. The French delegate pleaded in the General Committee that in view of the status of Algeria the item related to a matter that fell within the domestic jurisdiction of France. As such, the United Nations was barred by Article 2(7) from discussing it. The General Committee decided not to recommend the inclusion of the item in the agenda. This decision was overruled by the Assembly. The representative of France protested and declared that his government would not accept the intervention of the United Nations in the matter which he declared to be beyond its competence. He gave the warning that the decision of the General Assembly to consider the Algerian question might influence the relations of France with the United Nations.[39] The entire French delegation then withdrew and ceased to attend the meetings of the General Assembly and its Standing Committee. On 25 November 1955, on a procedural motion by India, the First Committee decided not to consider further the Algerian question in the tenth session. This was reaf-

---

[39] G.A.O.R., 10th Sess., 530th Plenary Mtg., 30 Sept. 1955, pp. 194, 196.

firmed in the General Assembly on the same day, without a debate or objection.[40]

Meanwhile, the war in Algeria raged fast and furiously. Speaking in the general debate in the eleventh session, Mr. Firoz Khan Noon referred to this unhappy fact and said:

> We are deeply concerned about the tragic happenings in Algeria, of whose claim to freedom Pakistan is a staunch supporter. If wiser counsels do not prevail and the forces of repression that have been let loose in North Africa are not checked, the whole of that area will be submerged under chaos and anarchy. In respect of several of these grave situations, this Organization has stood aside helplessly and watched the situation grow worse. My delegation feels that in addition to giving clear directives to the parties concerned in such situations, the United Nations should bring into play its resources of reconciliation, clearly enunciated in its Charter.[41]

The Algerian question was debated at length in the First Committee where Pakistan co-sponsored a resolution which, recognising the right of the people of Algeria to self-determination, invited France and the Algerian people to enter into immediate negotiations for cessation of hostilities and a peaceful settlement, in accordance with the principles of the Charter.[42] The representative of France participated in the discussion with a view to elucidating the position of his country. He, however, made it clear that in his view the General Assembly had no competence in the matter and no recommending powers with regard to the right of self-determination. The principle of self-determination, he said, was so vague that it should not be laid down in a provision governing competence.[43]

Speaking for Pakistan, Begum Ikramullah declared her country's support for the Algerian cause. She held that:

---

40 General Assembly Resolution 909(X), 25 Nov. 1955.

41 G.A.O.R., 11th Sess., 601st Plenary Mtg., 29 Nov. 1956, p. 415.

42 G.A.O.R., 11th Sess., Annexes: Agenda item 62, p. 2.

43 G.A.O.R., 11th Sess., 1st Ctte., 830th Mtg., 4 Feb. 1957, p. 99.

... Pakistan's attitude was not anti-Western, but her country stood for the right of peoples to self-determination.

Moreover, she added that:

> The Pakistan delegation understood perfectly that the national aspirations of a non-self-governing people could be fulfilled by the free association of the territory with the metropolitan country: but no such association would be fully valid without the consent of the population concerned. . . .[44]

The resolution, of which Pakistan was one of the co-sponsors, was not adopted. The counsel that moderation was the best means of securing a satisfactory solution in Algeria, as it had been in Tunisia and Morocco, prevailed and the General Assembly adopted a resolution in 1957, which took note of the statements of the various delegations and of the suffering and loss of human lives in Algeria, and expressed the hope that a peaceful, just, and democratic solution would be found.[45]

When the Algerian question came up for discussion in the First Committee in 1957, Mr. G. Ahmed, speaking for Pakistan, declared that his country shared the apprehensions expressed by the critics of the *loi-cadre*, that, because it was a unilateral measure and lacked the element of consent, it would lead to a permanent division of Algeria: furthermore, it transferred only limited power to the people, and ruled out, apparently indefinitely, what had been called "Algeria's vocation for independence." As regards the interests of the *colons*, Mr. Ahmed thought that they could be durably guaranteed only through a generous understanding with the majority of the Algerian people.[46] The General Assembly, in its resolution adopted on 10 December 1957, expressed concern over the situation in Algeria and took note of the offer of good offices made by the King of

---

[44] *Ibid.*, p. 173.

[45] General Assembly Resolution 1012(XI), 15 Feb. 1957.

[46] G.A.O.R., 12th Sess., 1st Ctte., 920th Mtg., 4 Dec. 1957, p. 301.

Morocco and the President of Tunisia and expressed the wish that *pourparlers* would lead to a solution in conformity with the United Nations Charter.[47]

PROBLEMS OF NON-SELF-GOVERNING AND TRUST TERRITORIES

Under Article 73 of the Charter, members of the United Nations who are responsible for the administration of territories that are not fully self-governing are required, with due regard to the culture of their peoples, to ensure their political and social advancement, to take account of their political aspirations, and to develop in those territories self-government based upon free institutions. The administering powers are also required to transmit information regarding economic, social, and educational conditions in the territories for which they are responsible. The question soon arose if the administering powers should not furnish information on political conditions as well. The attitude of those powers was that under the Charter they were not required to and that they would not furnish such information. Pakistan has always held and advocated the contrary view.[48]

In 1947 Pakistan voted in favour of the resolution through which the Assembly had expressed the hope that the administering powers would propose trusteeship agreements regarding some or all territories, not yet ready for self-government.[49]

At the third session of the General Assembly in 1948 there arose the question of administrative unions affecting trust territories. Pakistan voted in favour of a resolution which, while recognising that certain trusteeship agreements authorised customs, fiscal, or administrative unions between trust territories and adjacent colonies,

---

[47] General Assembly Resolution 1184(XII), 10 Dec. 1957.

[48] G.A.O.R., 2nd Sess., 108th Plenary Mtg., 3 Nov. 1947, p. 706; G.A.O.R., 4th Sess., 4th Ctte., 114th Mtg., 3 Nov. 1949, pp. 126-27.

[49] G.A.O.R., 2nd Sess., 4th Ctte., 44th Mtg., 14 Oct. 1947, p. 92.

endorsed the view of the Trusteeship Council that administrative unions must remain purely administrative.[50]

At the fourth session, the extension of the life of the Special Committee on Information on Non-Self-Governing Territories was opposed by the colonial powers in the Fourth Committee. The representative of France said that such a committee was not warranted by the Charter and that if it had been the intention of the framers of the Charter to create a body of that character, parallel to the Trusteeship Committee, the Charter would have indicated it.[51] Pakistan took the contrary view and at the fifth session was elected a member of the Special Committee.

In 1950 we find the Pakistan delegate in the Fourth Committee declaring that his country "was eagerly awaiting the time when all the Trust Territories would become free nations and Members of the United Nations."[52] Pakistan and Indonesia co-sponsored a resolution which, "considering that the promotion of educational advancement of the inhabitants of the Trust Territories is essential for their progressive development as early as possible towards self-government or independence," recommended that the Trusteeship Council devote particular attention to long-range programmes of educational development.[53]

In the same session, the representative of Pakistan told the Fourth Committee that his government did not recognise that the administrative powers had any legal rights in relation to non-self-governing territories, as these had been acquired by might. The United Nations should not protect rights based on might.[54]

As the years went by, under pressure from the Asian and African member states, helped by other smaller countries, the trusteeship

---

[50] General Assembly Resolution 224(III), 18 Nov. 1948.

[51] G.A.O.R., 4th Sess., 4th Ctte., 116th Mtg., 4 Nov. 1949, p. 134.

[52] G.A.O.R., 5th Sess., 4th Ctte., 146th Mtg., 4 Oct. 1950, p. 17.

[53] General Assembly Resolution 437(V), 2 Dec. 1950; G.A.O.R., 5th Sess., 4th Ctte., 160th Mtg., 30 Oct. 1950, p. 107.

[54] G.A.O.R., 5th Sess., 4th Ctte., 185th Mtg., 22 Nov. 1950, pp. 265-66.

system of the United Nations developed into an instrument for assuring that the administration of the trust territories was in the interest of the peoples of those territories. Periodic missions went out to those territories and petitions from their people were received. The principle was firmly established that the administering powers were accountable to the United Nations for their conduct of the affairs of the communities committed to their charge and that these communities should eventually be led to self-government or independence. The most outstanding example of the consummation of this process is to be seen in the case of Togoland under British administration.

In December 1955, the Assembly endorsed the recommendation that a plebiscite be held in that territory under United Nations supervision. Eduardo Espinosa Prieto of Mexico was appointed United Nations Plebiscite Commissioner. He reported to the eleventh General Assembly that the plebiscite had been held and that the people of British Togoland had voted in favour of attaining independence, with their territory becoming amalgamated with Ghana, which was to become an independent unit of the British Commonwealth in 1957. The Fourth Committee's recommendation that the result of the plebiscite be accepted was adopted by the General Assembly. Pakistan was one of the co-sponsors of this resolution. Speaking in the General Assembly, Mr. K. Sarwar Hasan expressed the gratification of his country at the development. There were, he had observed, several reasons for that gratification:

> First, a colonial territory emerges to the status of independence. This is a matter of the utmost satisfaction to Pakistan, which, since its establishment in 1947, has in this Organization and outside, firmly and consistently maintained that all peoples have the right to rule themselves and advocated that colonialism should end as speedily as possible.

> Secondly, the transaction which is now taking place is of importance in so far as it demonstrates the fulfilment of the objectives of the Trusteeship System. It establishes that the

Trusteeship System is not bogus. Here we have a colonial territory emerging to independence or self-government through the decision of the United Nations.

Thirdly, our decision is an historic one in so far as we are giving recognition to the principle of ascertaining the will of the people through a plebiscite. Earlier in history there have been plebiscites under international auspices, but this is the first one that has been carried through at the behest and under the supervision of the United Nations.

We regard, and I think anyone who has respect for democracy would regard, a plebiscite as the safest, the soundest, the most reliable and most unerring method of ascertaining the wishes of a people with regard to their political future.[55]

In the course of the Fourth Committee discussion on the proposal to transform British Togoland into a self-governing territory as a part of Ghana, the representative of Pakistan called attention to the fact that territorial boundaries in Africa did not coincide with cultural frontiers. That, unfortunately, he said, would apply to British Togoland also after its merger with Ghana, but nothing could be done about it for the present. When the various states affected became independent, the necessary adjustment might be made under United Nations auspices.[56]

In the case of South-West Africa Pakistan has taken a consistent interest. As far back as its first session in 1946 the General Assembly had adopted a resolution recommending that South-West Africa, which had been held by South Africa under a League of Nations mandate, be placed under the United Nations trusteeship system. It thereupon invited the South African government to propose a trusteeship agreement. In 1947 Pakistan, which had by then become a member of the United Nations, voted in favour of reaffirming the recommendation of the first session.[57]

---

[55] G.A.O.R., 11th Sess., 619th Plenary Mtg., 13 Dec. 1956, p. 687.

[56] G.A.O.R., 11th Sess., 4th Ctte., 564th Mtg., 4 Dec. 1956, p. 69.

[57] G.A.O.R., 2nd Sess., 4th Ctte., 45th Mtg., 15 Oct. 1947, p. 98.

At the 1948 session in the Fourth Committee Pakistan again supported the demand that South Africa submit a trusteeship agreement regarding South-West Africa. Resisting this demand Mr. Eric Louw quoted Field Marshal Jan C. Smuts' view that geographically, strategically, and ethnologically, South-West Africa was a part of South Africa. This view, replied the Pakistan representative, was irrelevant to the consideration of the matter, unless the governments of South Africa and South-West Africa were in the hands of their respective indigenous people, and in any case it was for them to decide whether the two countries should integrate.[58]

In 1949 the South African government discontinued submitting reports on its administration of South-West Africa and proceeded virtually to annex it. On this situation the International Court of Justice was asked to give its advisory opinion. The Court held that the South African government continued to have international obligations in respect of South-West Africa and that it was not competent to modify the territory's international status without the consent of the United Nations. Efforts to negotiate with the South African government were all unfruitful.

In the meantime, South-West Africa had been amalgamated with South Africa to the extent of the former sending representatives to the Union Parliament. Speaking in 1956 before the Fourth Committee of the eleventh General Assembly, Mr. K. Sarwar Hasan noted that:

> ... The extension to the Territory of representation in the Union Parliament was tantamount to the establishment of Union sovereignty over it. The subsequent transfer of the administration of Native Affairs to the Union and the motion passed by the Legislative Assembly declaring the Union of South Africa and South West Africa to be one nation, which was mentioned in paragraph 13 of Annex II of the Committee's report, were further examples of the way in which the Union Government was seeking to modify the international status of

---

[58] G.A.O.R., 3rd Sess., Part I, 4th Ctte., 78th Mtg., 11 Nov. 1948, p. 316.

the Territory in defiance of the International Court of Justice. It was the view of his delegation that in no circumstances should defiance of the United Nations, violation of the right of self-determination or annexation of territory be tolerated. . . .[59]

The General Assembly adopted two resolutions, one asking the Secretary-General to explore ways and means of satisfactorily solving the question of South-West Africa, and the other requesting the Committee on South-West Africa to report on what legal action was open to ensure that South Africa fulfills its obligations under the mandate.[60]

HUMAN RIGHTS

Pakistan has taken a sustained interest in the question of human rights in the United Nations. When in 1948 the Universal Declaration of Human Rights came before the General Assembly, the Pakistan delegation supported its adoption because, in the words of Begum Ikramullah, Pakistan believed in the dignity and worth of man. She said:

> . . . It was imperative that the peoples of the world should recognize the existence of a code of civilized behaviour which would apply not only in international relations but also in domestic affairs. . . .[61]

In the Third Committee, with regard to Article 14, which declared that all men and women of full age have the right to marry, to found a family, and to have equal rights in marriage, Begum Ikramullah said that she understood it to be designed to prevent child marriages and marriages without the consent of the parties. As such she supported it and added that the laws of Pakistan already recognised all the rights referred to in the article. But she made it

---

[59] G.A.O.R., 11th Sess., 4th Ctte., 577th Mtg., 18 Dec. 1956, p. 139.

[60] General Assembly Resolutions 1059(XI) and 1060(XI), 26 Feb. 1957.

[61] G.A.O.R., 3rd Sess., Part I, 3rd Ctte., 90th Mtg., 1 Oct. 1948, p. 37.

clear that equal rights did not mean identical rights.[62] The Pakistan delegation opposed a Mexican amendment to the article, because it disregarded the religious factor in marriage.[63] However, it was adopted, Pakistan voting against it. In the Third Committee in 1948 Pakistan supported the Yugoslav proposal[64] that rights proclaimed in the Declaration of Human Rights should apply also to the people of non-self-governing and trust territories.[65]

The 1948 session was also notable for the adoption of the Genocide Convention. Pakistan voted for it both in the Sixth Committee and in the plenary session of the General Assembly. In the Sixth Committee Pakistan made an effort to have the crime of cultural genocide specifically mentioned in the Convention.[66] Cultural genocide was to be defined in terms of two specific crimes, namely, forcible mass conversion and the destruction of religious edifices.[67] This effort did not meet with success. However, in the plenary meeting Begum Ikramullah elaborated her conception of cultural genocide. She said:

> ... It must be realized that very often a people did not differ from its neighbours by its racial characteristics but by its spiritual heritage. To deprive a human group of its separate culture could thus destroy its individuality as completely as physical annihilation. Moreover, those guilty of the crime of mass extermination committed that crime because the existence of a community endowed with a separate cultural life was intolerable to them. In other words, physical genocide was only the means; the end was the destruction of a people's spiritual individuality.[68]

Pakistan, already a member of the Commission on Human Rights, was, at the fifth session, elected a member of the Commission to prepare a draft convention on Freedom of Information.

---

[62] *Ibid.*, 125th Mtg., 8 Nov. 1948, p. 374.
[63] G.A.O.R., 3rd Sess., Part I, 3rd Ctte., Annexes: Agenda item 58, p. 27.
[64] *Ibid.*, p. 46.
[65] G.A.O.R., 3rd Sess., Part I, 3rd Ctte., 163rd Mtg., 29 Nov. 1948, p. 745.
[66] G.A.O.R., 3rd Sess., Part I, 6th Ctte., 83rd Mtg., 25 Oct. 1948, pp. 193-95.
[67] G.A.O.R., 3rd Sess., Part I, 6th Ctte., Annexes: Agenda item 32, p. 23.
[68] G.A.O.R., 3rd Sess., Part I, 178th Plenary Mtg., 9 Dec. 1948, p. 817.

In the General Assembly's session in 1951 Pakistan co-sponsored a resolution in the Third Committee that the two covenants on human rights should include an article in the following terms: "All people shall have the right to self-determination."[69] This resolution was carried. It was further provided that the right to self-determination was to be promoted in the non-self-governing and trust territories by the respective administering powers.[70] In the 1954 session Pakistan urged in the Third Committee the recognition of the permanent sovereignty of peoples and nations over their national wealth and resources. This principle was included in a resolution adopted by the Committee.[71]

Pakistan was one of twenty countries that asked the Third Committee in 1954 that the right of self-determination be mentioned in the first article and all other relevant articles of the two covenants that were under preparation, respectively, on the civil and political rights and economic and social rights.[72]

Pakistan took its part in the discussions on the draft covenants in 1955 and 1956, and at the General Assembly's eleventh session in 1956 supported the draft Covenant on the Nationality of Married Women, which was adopted.

RACE RELATIONS IN SOUTH AFRICA

The racial issue in South Africa is not a colonial question, nor is South Africa a colonial country. But, as Professor Bokhari pointed out:

> . . . inasmuch as it [is] a country where people of one race in their own native land [are] being subjected to indignities and relegated to a lower stage of civilization to the advantage of a minority representing the early conquerors of the country, it was practising a form of colonialism. The colonial Powers

---

[69] G.A.O.R., 6th Sess., 3rd Ctte., Annexes: Agenda item 29, p. 22.

[70] *Ibid.*, p. 31.

[71] G.A.O.R., 9th Sess., 3rd Ctte., 595th Mtg., 26 Nov. 1954, p. 273.

[72] G.A.O.R., 9th Sess., Annexes: Agenda item 58, pp. 11-12.

in their respective colonial areas had acquired the best lands
and were exploiting the raw materials therein for the benefit
of the home economy. . . .[73]

The question of the treatment by the Union of South Africa of
its citizens of Indian and Pakistani origin is by no means a new
one. For quite half a century before the partition of the subcontinent,
all sections of political opinion in it as well as the government of
India, then controlled by British officials, had felt deep anxiety
about this question. The people involved were descendants of settlers
who had gone to South Africa in the last quarter of the nineteenth
century from various parts of the subcontinent that is now comprised
by India and Pakistan. Their status is, therefore, a matter of concern
not only for the present government of India, but also that of
Pakistan.

It was in the first session of the General Assembly in December
1946 that the pre-partition government of India brought up the
question. The Indian complaint referred, in particular, to discriminatory measures such as the Asiatic Land Tenure Act and the
Indian Representation Act of 1946. These measures segregated
Indian settlers both commercially and residentially. The government of India charged South Africa with violating the human rights
provisions of the Charter and the agreement entered into between
India and South Africa at Cape Town in 1927 and renewed in 1932,
which defined the status of South Africans of Indian origin. The
Indian government asked the General Assembly to call upon the
South African government to revise its policy and its laws affecting
its Asiatic citizens and to bring them into conformity with the
principles and purposes of the Charter of the United Nations.

The case for the Union of South Africa was put before the Assembly by no less a person than Field Marshal Smuts, regarded in
the West as a great apostle of internationalism. Smuts argued that
the Assembly was debarred under Article 2(7) of the Charter from

---

[73] G.A.O.R., 7th Sess., *Ad Hoc* Political Ctte., 15th Mtg., 13 Nov. 1952, p. 76.

taking cognizance of the matter, which fell within the domestic jurisdiction of South Africa. It was also denied that the Cape Town Agreement was an international instrument giving rise to treaty obligations. South Africa asked that the question as to whether the matter was essentially within its domestic jurisdiction or not should be referred to the International Court of Justice for its advisory opinion.[74] This proposal was rejected by the Assembly, which took the view that the matter affected friendly relations between two member nations of the United Nations and that the treatment of South African citizens of Asiatic origin should be in conformity with the obligations imposed by agreements concluded between the governments of South Africa and India and the principles and purposes of the Charter. The two governments were asked to report to the next session of the General Assembly.[75]

South Africa expressed its willingness to negotiate, but not on the basis of the Assembly's resolution, which it regarded as unconstitutional. Consequently, no talks took place. South Africa was unwilling to admit that it had broken agreements or violated the principles of the Charter.

When the question came up for discussion again at the General Assembly in 1947, Pakistan had come into existence and had been admitted as a member of the United Nations. Mr. Mirza Ispahani, speaking for Pakistan, listed the following as the most serious violations of the fundamental rights of Indian and Pakistani settlers in South Africa:

(a) They had no right to vote, nor any right to be represented in local, provincial and central administrative bodies of the country;

(b) they had not the right to move from one Province to another;

---

[74] G.A.O.R., 1st Sess., 2nd Part, Joint Ctte. of the 1st and 6th Cttes., 21 Nov. 1946, pp. 3-4.

[75] General Assembly Resolution 44(I), 8 Dec. 1946.

(c) their right to engage in commerce and their property rights were severely restricted;

(d) since 1912 Indians had been prevented from acquiring arable land, and the 1946 Asiatic Land Tenure Law confined them within certain urban areas of limited extent;

(e) finally, there was complete segregation of Indians in schools, hospitals, railway stations, public parks, etc.[76]

Mr. Ispahani disputed the validity of the contention of the South African government that these measures of discrimination did not proceed from any intention to suppress those against whom they were applied and its further contention that fundamental human rights of all races could not be safeguarded unless a distinction was made with regard to rights which were not fundamental. Mr. Ispahani said further:

> ... The right to vote, the right of ownership, the right to take part freely in commercial activities, the right to participate in public administration, were, without any possible doubt, fundamental human rights.[77]

South Africa again challenged the competence of the Assembly and again denied that it had violated any international agreements, the agreements of 1927 and 1932 carrying, in its view, no international obligations. South Africa also asserted that it had not violated any fundamental human rights and repeated its request that the Assembly should ask for the advisory opinion of the International Court of Justice. Replying to these arguments, Sir Zafrulla Khan said:

> A study of the history of the question showed that the treatment of the Indians in the Union of South Africa could not be regarded as exclusively a domestic affair. The labour conditions of Indians in the Union of South Africa had been settled at the beginning of immigration into that country, and formed the subject of agreements between the Govern-

---

[76] G.A.O.R., 2nd Sess., 1st Ctte., 108th Mtg., 14 Nov. 1947, p. 441.
[77] *Ibid.*, p. 442.

P

ments of India and Natal, and later of the Union. The Governments of India and Pakistan were in duty bound to take an
interest in the fate of the Indians until they acquired full
liberty. . . .[78]

He then went on to propound the thesis that a purely domestic
question could at a certain time and in certain circumstances assume
an international character. The case of the Sudeten Germans in
Czechoslovakia was an example. He said:

... If it was remembered that the treatment of Indians in
South Africa had been regarded in England as one of the
causes of the Boer War, it must be admitted that the international character of the question was beyond dispute.[79]

Sir Zafrulla Khan then went on to ask:

What had the South African representative in mind when he
had stated that the Cape Agreements were not binding but
were merely an honorable statement of principles? Had he
meant that a word of honor did not involve any obligations?[80]

Replying to the South African demand that the matter should be
referred to the International Court of Justice, Sir Zafrulla said that
it would be useless to do so, for even if the Court pronounced it
to be a purely domestic question that would not in the smallest
degree hasten its solution; and it had to be solved. A remedy had
to be found in order to improve relations between the Union of
South Africa on the one hand, and India and Pakistan on the other.
"The United Nations must play its part in finding such a solution."[81]

At the 1947 session of the Assembly, however, no resolution
could be passed for the reason that of the two proposals before it,
neither could secure the necessary two-thirds majority. In 1949
India, Pakistan, and South Africa were asked to hold a Round
Table discussion, taking into consideration the purposes and prin-

[78] G.A.O.R., 2nd Sess., 1st Ctte., 109th Mtg., 15 Nov. 1947, p. 451.

[79] *Ibid.*

[80] *Ibid.*

[81] *Ibid.*

ciples of the Charter and the Universal Declaration of Human Rights. Preliminary talks were held in Cape Town in February 1950 and an agenda for the talks was agreed upon. In the meanwhile, however, the South African government had introduced further discriminatory laws, in the form of the Group Areas Act. As a protest against this, Pakistan and India withdrew from the Conference.

In the *Ad Hoc* Political Committee in 1950 the Pakistani delegate refuted the South African contention that the Universal Declaration of Human Rights imposed no obligations on member states of the United Nations to observe human rights. He stated that:

> ... The terms of Articles 13, 55 and 56 clearly implied the existence of mandatory obligations. The legal duty to promote respect for human rights included the duty to respect them. The General Assembly had taken that view when it had recommended to the Government of the USSR, in resolution 285 (III), the withdrawal of certain measures taken with regard to USSR citizens who were the wives of foreign nationals. Moreover, the absence of a definition of human rights did not destroy the obligation to respect them. Although aggression had not yet been defined, action had been taken against the invaders in Korea.[82]

With regard to the argument that the matter was one of domestic jurisdiction for the Union of South Africa, the Pakistan delegate held that:

> ... An unduly rigid interpretation of Article 2, paragraph 7, could lead to the virtual annulment of most of the provisions of the Charter. Although that Article was important, it had to be considered in relation with other provisions. A violation of human rights was a matter of international concern and ceased to be a question of domestic jurisdiction. When the Union of South Africa recognized the Pakistanis and Indians in its territory as nationals in the full sense of that word, Pakistan and India would withdraw their complaint.[83]

---

[82] G.A.O.R., 5th Sess., *Ad Hoc* Political Ctte., 43rd Mtg., 15 Nov. 1950, p. 265.
[83] *Ibid.*

The Assembly adopted a resolution calling upon the parties to hold a conference on the basis of their agreed agenda, bearing in mind the provisions of the Charter and those of the Universal Declaration of Human Rights and in the meanwhile to refrain from taking any steps which would prejudice the success of the negotiations, particularly by enforcing the Group Areas Act.[84]

South Africa refused to hold a conference on the basis of the resolution and the matter again came up in the General Assembly in 1951, when a resolution was passed providing for the establishment of a Special Commission to assist India, Pakistan, and the Union in conducting negotiations. One of the members of the Commission was to be nominated by India and Pakistan, one by South Africa and the two nominees were to nominate the third member or, on their failure to do so, he was to be nominated by the Secretary-General.[85] However, no action was taken on these provisions.

When the matter came up again before the General Assembly in 1952, the Pakistani permanent representative, Professor Bokhari, declared in the *Ad Hoc* Political Committee that:

> ... The laws enacted and recently strengthened by the South African Government were avowedly designed to keep the native and coloured inhabitants at the lowest possible level of civilization. They were denied land, forced to live in segregated areas, prevented from earning more than a specific wage, and deprived of educational, trade-union and political rights. Their dignity as human beings was being degraded by the discriminatory practices which refused them access to common public facilities and placed them in economic subservience to the white population.[86]

The only place in the world, said Professor Bokhari, where the representatives of the South African government sat side by side with others not of their colour was at the United Nations. He referred to

---

[84] General Assembly Resolution 395(V), 2 Dec. 1950.
[85] General Assembly Resolution 511(VI), 12 Jan. 1952.
[86] G.A.O.R., 7th Sess., *Ad Hoc* Political Ctte., 15th Mtg., 13 Nov. 1952, p. 76.

a statement by a leader of the South African white community that racial inequalities had been divinely ordained and should be perpetuated.

> ... If such was the racial doctrine of the National[ist] Party of South Africa, the people of Pakistan repudiated it with all their force, for it was a blasphemy according to their religion and to the principles on which their country had been founded. . . .[87]

Professor Bokhari thought that the situation in South Africa was explosive and warned the colonial powers about it. These powers, according to him, did not seem to realise that there were in Africa only four million whites—more than half of whom were in South Africa—in a continent of 150 to 200 million non-whites. The lives of the white minority were being placed in the gravest jeopardy. To leave the question alone was to sanction a struggle to the death between the Africans and their white masters. For so long as the latter continued to enforce their position by brute force and in-human laws, a final bloody clash was inevitable. Pakistan and the countries sharing its views did not wish to see the blood of Europeans or Africans shed in such a holocaust. Moreover, a violent bloody revolution in the continent of Africa would not necessarily be inevitable if the United Nations exercised one of its basic functions properly. Professor Bokhari went on to say that:

> ... The United Nations could not prevent war by closing its eyes to the perpetuation of circumstances which must lead to war. The possibility that the conflict between the whites and non-whites throughout the world might take precedence over the prevailing struggle between communism and anti-communism must compel all nations to pause to think and to act rightly. The heritage of European culture and its liberal tradition was a justifiable cause for pride. But the small nations had joined with Pakistan to call a halt to the European process of civilizing with the whip and the gun and the enforcement of white superiority in the colonial parts of the world. The

---

[87] *Ibid.*

United Nations should not be deterred from abolishing that
process by the short-sightedness of some who failed to realise
that the problem of racial inequality and persecution was
clearly a threat to international security and to the security
of white and non-white alike. . . .[88]

The General Assembly passed a resolution constituting a Good
Offices Commission, with Cuba, Syria, and Yugoslavia as its
members. The Commission reported to the 1953 session that it
had been unable to carry out its task, South Africa having refused
to recognise it or the constitutionality of the resolution on which it
was based. The General Assembly in 1953 resolved to continue the
Good Offices Commission. Then, in 1954, the Assembly, after considering the report of the Commission, called upon the governments of India, Pakistan, and the Union of South Africa to negotiate directly. Under the terms of the Assembly's resolution, the
Secretary-General in June 1955 appointed Ambassador Luis de
Faro Jr. (Brazil) to assist the parties in settling the dispute. Pakistan
and India offered their full co-operation to him but the South
African government declined to collaborate. In 1955 the Union
government withdrew its delegation from the General Assembly,
which, nevertheless, adopted a resolution urging the parties to
pursue negotiations with a view to the settlement of the question.
Again in 1956 and 1957 like resolutions were passed, but in vain.

Thus the situation in respect to discrimination practised in the
Union of South Africa against its citizens of Asian origin remains
unresolved. The resolutions passed by the General Assembly and its
appeals to the Union government have been of no avail. That
government has with impunity defied the United Nations.

No condemnation can be strong enough against the policy of
apartheid, which is legally enforced by such measures as the Group
Areas Act which divides the country into racial zones, the Populations Registration Act which compels all inhabitants to register
themselves by race, and the Bantu Education Act which aims at

---

[88] *Ibid.*, p. 77.

training Africans as servants or unskilled workers for the whites. Under other laws, the movement of Africans is controlled; they may not move out of their reserve areas without permission, travel without identity cards, mingle with whites on trains or buses or park benches, or own property except in the reservations. Of course, Africans may not marry whites or go to the same schools as whites or hold public office or belong to a union or go on strike.

Speaking on *apartheid* the representative of Pakistan in the Special Political Committee of the 1956 session of the General Assembly observed:

> ... If the United Nations did not stand for the dignity of man, and for peace and progress in the world, it would be nothing more than a sounding board for rival ideologies and a battleground for national rivalries. He hoped he would not be misunderstood by his friends in the West if he appealed to them to readjust their ideas and recognize the passion for equality which dominated the thinking of the people of Asia and Africa. If due respect was not shown to those peoples, economic, social or political assistance would fail to win them.
>
> . . . .
>
> His delegation was convinced that human rights were the concern of the whole human race, and that the solution of the Union of South Africa's racial problem lay not in the domination of one race by another but in a partnership of races on the bases of equality and freedom. . . .[89]

After a long discussion, a resolution was passed by the Assembly calling upon the Union of South Africa "to reconsider its position and revise its policies in the light of its obligations and responsibilities under the Charter and in the light of the principles subscribed to and the progress achieved in other contemporary multi-racial societies."[90] In 1957 the Assembly passed a resolution appealing to the government of the Union of South Africa to revise its policy in the light of

---

[89] G.A.O.R., 11th Sess., Special Political Ctte., 12th Mtg., 14 Jan. 1957, p. 54.
[90] General Assembly Resolution 1016(XI), 30 Jan. 1957.

the principles and purposes of the United Nations Charter and of world opinion.[91]

The question naturally arises, where will *apartheid* take South Africa? It is, of course, clear that the South African negroes will not forever remain subservient or accept their present situation as a final settlement of their status. Unless the situation is rectified, as Bokhari pointed out, there is bound to be an upheaval in South Africa. If the South African whites are determined not to accept the negroes as their equal, the logical result of *apartheid* must be a separation. It is interesting to note that the United Nations Commission on the Racial Situation in South Africa in its second report, presented to the 1954 session of the General Assembly, examined various possible solutions, one of which is separation, as in the case of India and Pakistan.[92] Such a solution has also been put forward by certain organisations and individuals in South Africa.

It is noteworthy that when the West European and South American countries have supported South Africa in the General Assembly, they have done so on the ground of the jurisdictional competence of the United Nations. They all condemned racial discrimination. Most of the South American countries, however, have voted against South Africa. The United States of America has either abstained or voted in support of South Africa, depending upon the nature of the resolution.

---

[91] General Assembly Resolution 1178(XII), 26 Nov. 1957.

[92] G.A.O.R., 9th Sess., 2nd Report of the United Nations Commission on the Racial Situation in the Union of South Africa, Supple. No. 16 (A/2719), p. 70.

chapter eight

Economic Assistance Programs

The Preamble of the United Nations Charter speaks of social progress and better standards of life. Amongst the purposes of the Charter is listed international co-operation in economic, social, cultural, and humanitarian matters. Article 55 recognises that the creation of conditions of stability and well-being is necessary for peaceful and friendly relations among nations. It sets down as objectives the achievement of higher living standards; full employment and economic and social progress; the solution of international economic, social, health, and related problems; the promotion of cultural and educational co-operation; and the inculcation of universal respect for human rights and fundamental freedoms. These are truly revolutionary provisions and, in their comprehensiveness, unprecedented in any international statute. It is fortunate that these provisions were embodied in the Charter, for the activities that have resulted from them, though still of a very restricted character, serve as a needed counterpoise to the many failures of the United Nations in the political sphere.

Pakistan has taken a keen interest in the activities of the Economic and Social Council (ECOSOC) which was established to carry out the objectives stated in Article 55. Pakistan has already been elected to ECOSOC for three terms, namely, 1950-52, 1954-56 and 1957-59. Twice Pakistan has been elected its President, once its Vice-President, and once Chairman of its Technical Assistance Committee. It might even be claimed that Pakistan has influenced thinking in the United Nations on economic and social questions. In this sphere Pakistan has played a part that has been more sustained, more constructive, and more decisive than its part in the political sphere.

How economically backward certain parts of the world are, and how deficient in worldly goods certain peoples are, as compared with others, can easily be judged from a few simple figures. Out of an estimated total world income of $548 billion in 1948,[1] the United States, with less than 6 per cent of the world population, had in 1948 a national income of $223.5 billion, accounting for 40 per cent of the world total. On the other hand, Asia, with about 55 per cent of the world population, has only $90 billion, or less than 17 per cent of the total world money income. The per capita income in the United States is over $2,000 a year, in the United Kingdom $900, and in countries like Pakistan the money income is only $50, although the corrected real income would yield a somewhat higher figure. As a consequence, the mass of the people of these economically backward countries ekes out a miserable existence, with poor housing, poor food, few schools, and few facilities for medical treatment.

At the 1952 summer session of ECOSOC, Mr. Chaudhri Salah-ud-din, the Pakistan representative, pointed out that this state of general poverty was due to two facts, namely, overpopulation and the inability of the countries concerned to plan their economies

---

[1] W. S. Woytinsky and E. S. Woytinsky, *World Population and Production: Trends and Outlook* (New York: The Twentieth Century Fund, 1953), p. 394.

during the period of colonial rule.[2] However, Mr. Salah-ud-din did not give the whole explanation. Even until the end of the seventeenth century the West was no more "advanced" than Asia. Thereafter the people of Asia, a good many of whom had come under the rule of the West, lost all intellectual initiative and became stagnant. There was little encouragement for them to develop their talents for progressive purposes. Clinging to the tradition of their past glories, they began to look upon it as a virtue. The West, on the other hand, breaking away from its tradition, embarked on a new adventurous age of exploration, discovery, and conquest. This age gave it vast empires in America, Africa, Asia, and Australia. There followed the invention of the steam engine and a succession of other inventions, which were applied to industry and transport. Raw materials were cheaply bought in the colonial countries and, after being mechanically processed, were sold back to them. By the middle of the nineteenth century the West had become far richer and the fabulous East far poorer than they had been a century earlier. The West also utilized effective measures for birth control.

The representative of Pakistan also observed that "there had spread among the people of the underdeveloped countries an awareness that they, too, could attain the standard of living of the people of the highly developed countries." But he warned that:

> ... when they [the people of underdeveloped countries] compared their standard of living with that of the people of other countries, they were inclined to jump to baseless and irresponsible conclusions. ...

Significantly, he noted that:

> ... The problem of over-population in South and South East Asia was acute. In the circumstances prevailing, birth control could not be successfully advocated. Apart from the solution of the problem through the development of more and more resources in the countries concerned, the United Nations

---

[2] Economic and Social Council, Official Records (ECOSOC, O.R.): 14th Sess., 645th Mtg., 16 July 1952, p. 583.

might take up the question of migration on a global basis. Any discrimination on racial or territorial grounds would be against the purposes and principles of the United Nations as set forth in the Charter. There were certain areas in the world which were under-populated and in need of man power.[3]

If the desideratum was that the living standard of the economically underdeveloped countries should approach that of the more developed ones, certain complicated problems must be faced. In the summer of 1952 Mr. S. Amjad Ali pointed out before the Economic and Social Council that:

> ... the gap between the standards of living in the developed and in the under-developed areas was increasing. The position in some under-developed regions represented a vicious circle. In order to achieve economic and social progress and even political stability, those countries had to use their resources in direct improvement of standards of living. Nevertheless, the level of their national income in relation to that of the necessary investments did not enable them to do so. In most cases the circle could only be broken by external help added to internal effort. Although the external help essential to prevent the gap from widening might seem considerable, it was comparatively modest when set against the level of current expenditure on armaments. It was in any case well beyond what private investors could provide in the existing circumstances; although that did not mean that private investment, which had hitherto been lacking, could not make an important contribution.

> ... the technical assistance programmes of the United Nations and the specialized agencies, and other extensive technical assistance programmes that had been undertaken, could greatly increase the technical capacity of the under-developed countries to solve their own problems. ...[4]

That technical assistance was not enough was argued by Pakistan in 1954 at the eighteenth session:

---

[3] *Ibid.*
[4] ECOSOC, O.R., 14th Sess., 570th Mtg., 20 May 1952, p. 3.

The problems facing the under-developed countries were an inadequate flow of capital and an insufficient and uncertain return for their raw materials in relation to their import requirements. The problem of the stabilization of commodity prices was not one for the under-developed countries alone but could seriously affect the industrialized countries as well. A fall in foreign exchange receipts inevitably led to a tightening of import restrictions and the balancing of world trade at a lower level. A vicious circle could thus be created and lead to a depression affecting production and employment everywhere. Such a situation could be mastered only by international co-operation based on the realization that peace and prosperity were interdependent, and that the world could not remain permanently divided into prosperous and needy nations.[5]

The needs of the economically underdeveloped countries in the financing of their economic development led Pakistan to strive for the establishment of the International Finance Corporation (IFC) and the Special United Nations Fund for Economic Development (SUNFED). Pakistan sponsored a resolution for the establishment of IFC and urged member governments to extend their co-operation in giving it a concrete shape so as to facilitate the flow of international capital for financing economic development in the economically backward countries.[6] The IFC is an international institution, closely linked with the World Bank, with a capital of 92 million dollars subscribed by 52 member states.

The idea of SUNFED took shape in March-April 1949. In 1951 a group of experts was appointed by the Secretary-General to study measures for the economic growth of the underdeveloped countries. This group recommended the establishment of an International Development Authority for the purpose of assisting economically underdeveloped countries. After this proposal had been examined in 1951 at the thirteenth session of the ECOSOC, the plan for SUNFED was evolved. By the summer of 1952 the Council set up

---

[5] ECOSOC, O.R., 18th Sess., 798th Mtg., 6 July 1954, p. 35.

[6] ECOSOC, O.R., 18th Sess., Resolutions, Supple. No. 1, 5 Aug. 1954 [532 (XVIII)B], p. 3.

a Committee of Nine (Experts), which included Mr. S. Amjad Ali, to prepare a detailed plan for a Special Fund. The plan envisaged grants-in-aid and low-interest long-term loans to economically less-developed countries, designed to accelerate their economic development by financing non-self-liquidating projects basic to their economic growth. According to Mr. Said Hasan: "In spite of its statements to the contrary, the International Bank for Reconstruction and Development (IBRD) seldom financed projects that were non-self-liquidating."[7]

The report of the Committee of Nine was presented to the Council, which decided that the member states should be asked to furnish their views on the scope, nature, and structure of SUNFED. At the summer session of the Council in 1955, Pakistan co-sponsored a resolution to keep the subject alive.[8] Pakistan's thinking with regard to SUNFED is to some extent reflected in the following report of Mr. Said Hasan's speech to the 1956 summer session of ECOSOC:

> ... In its reply to the questionnaire, Pakistan had expressed the view that SUNFED should be primarily concerned with long-term, low-interest-bearing loans, in order to avoid becoming a charitable organization and also in order to ensure that the recipient country would have given high priority to the project in respect of which assistance was requested. Pakistan had also emphasized that the repayment of interest should be permitted in local currency for such time as its repayment in foreign exchange would strain the balance-of-payments position of the recipient country. As he had informed the Council at the eighteenth session (812th meeting), the long-term loan agreement between the United States of America and Pakistan provided that the loans should be repayable in local currency and that payments would not be convertible without the consent of Pakistan or without taking Pakistan's currency situation into account. In the view of his delegation, repayment of SUNFED loans should be on a

---

[7] ECOSOC, O.R., 18th Sess., 812th Mtg., 21 July 1954, p. 143.

[8] ECOSOC, O.R., 20th Sess., Resolutions, Supple. No. 1, 5 Aug. 1955 [583(XX)A], p. 3.

similar basis. Once the conditions of a loan had been agreed upon between SUNFED and the recipient country, however, they should not be subject to change. The sanctity of contract should be ensured.

So far as concerns the minimum amount necessary before SUNFED could start operations, he would like to repeat what he had said at the twentieth session (885th meeting)— that $250 million would be only a drop in the ocean in view of the fact that $1,900 million would be needed to raise per capita income in the under-developed countries by a mere 2 per cent. The amounts suggested in the replies to the questionnaire ranged from $62.5 million to $2,000 million, thus revealing considerable differences of opinion on the subject. Perhaps it would be appropriate to keep the estimate of the minimum amount necessary to start operations at the figure of $250 million suggested by the Committee of Nine.[9]

At this session, it became clear that the principal Western powers, who would be the chief contributors to the Fund, were not in favour of its immediate establishment. They felt that unless a general agreement on disarmament was reached and resources released from armaments, they would not be able substantially to contribute to SUNFED. Speaking on this critical point, Mr. Said Hasan raised the question of:

... whether the establishment of SUNFED should be conditional upon agreement being reached on internationally-supervised disarmament under the auspices of the United Nations, or whether, as had been affirmed by the Government of Denmark (A/2646, p. 36), it was "neither necessary nor desirable" to hold the establishment of SUNFED in abeyance pending such agreement. While the underdeveloped countries almost universally adhered to the latter view, the major contributing countries seemed to favour the establishment of SUNFED only after they had succeeded in making some budgetary economies as the result of the institution of an internationally supervised system of disarmament. Only Canada, Denmark, France and the Netherlands, among the

---

[9] ECOSOC, O.R., 22nd Sess., 947th Mtg., 2 Aug. 1956, p. 206.

prospective contributing countries, did not seem to stipulate such a condition. It therefore seemed that SUNFED might have to wait until such time as international tension was sufficiently relaxed to allow for the agreement envisaged. As suggested by the French Government, however, it would be worth while to take steps to draw up a draft statute for SUNFED.[10]

Despite these reservations, Pakistan supported a resolution recommending that the General Assembly establish a preparatory commission which would set up SUNFED and select a limited number of projects.[11] At the 1958 session of the General Assembly, a compromise resolution was adopted providing for the establishment of a Special Project Fund, which would be an expansion of the technical assistance and development activities of the United Nations. According to that resolution the level of the United Nations Technical Assistance Programme would be raised from $31 million to $100 million and its scope widened. To define the projects to which the resources of this Fund would be applied, a preparatory committee was appointed, Pakistan being one of its members. It might, however, be noted that the Special Projects Fund and SUNFED are two different things and the former is not to be a substitute for the latter. SUNFED has been shelved, at least for the time being.

Industrialisation, which is an essential element in the over-all economic development of a country, involves economic, social, fiscal, technical, and organisational problems regarding which ECOSOC has been promoting studies. Through a resolution sponsored by Pakistan at the Council's 1956 summer session, the need for industrialisation of underdeveloped countries was emphasised and the Secretary-General was requested to consider what further steps and facilities were needed for that purpose.[12] That a separate

---

10 *Ibid.*, p. 207.
11 ECOSOC, O.R., 24th Sess., Resolutions, Supple. No. 1, 31 July 1957 [662(XXIV)B], p. 7.
12 ECOSOC, O.R., 22nd Sess., Resolutions, Supple. No. 1, 6 Aug. 1956 [618(XXII)], p. 6.

specialised agency was called for was the view of the Pakistan delegation. This view had been first put forward by Mr. Said Hasan
at the spring session in 1956 when he had urged as primary requirement the establishment of:

> ... a body within the United Nations responsible for assist-
> ing the underdeveloped countries on industrial questions;
> manpower training was not the only problem involved in
> industrialization. The body in question might undertake to
> collect and disseminate information on industrial principles
> and techniques. . . .[13]

That the United Nations should furnish more than technical
assistance had also been urged by Pakistan in the Second Committee in 1952:

> ... Pakistan was grateful for the assistance received under the
> programme. When the programme had first been launched,
> Pakistan had been confronted with a serious shortage of
> technical and trained personnel, following the greatest pop-
> ulation movement in history across national frontiers. Under
> the expanded Programme scores of experts had been supplied
> and personnel from Pakistan had been trained abroad. His
> [the Pakistan] Government had at times felt somewhat dis-
> satisfied with the quality of some of the experts provided. . . .
>
> Emphasis [had been] laid on supplying experts and fellow-
> ships. Its facilities were primarily of value to countries at the
> initial stage of surveying their resources or of drafting plans
> for their development. Countries which had evolved beyond
> that stage urgently required training facilities and institutions
> within their own territory. The technical assistance programme
> should include provision for establishing such institutions and
> for supplying them with staff and equipment. It should also
> lay increasing emphasis on demonstration projects and on
> supplying equipment, machinery and personnel for them. . . .[14]

So far as Pakistan is concerned, this position has not altered. It

[13] ECOSOC, O.R., 21st Sess., 909th Mtg., 24 Apr. 1956, p. 52.
[14] General Assembly, Official Records (G.A.O.R.): 7th Sess., 2nd Ctte., 203rd
Mtg., 4 Nov. 1952, p. 65.

q

has been ascertained that the experts that have been supplied to Pakistan are not always such as are required. This feeling exists not only about experts furnished by the United Nations, but also about those that have come under other programmes.

With regard to "the chronic problem of under-employment in the rural areas of the under-developed countries," the representative of Pakistan in 1952 declared in the Committee on Economic and Financial Questions that it "could be solved only by establishing a network of cottage and small-scale industries. . . . There was need for a new large-scale experiment in rural rehabilitation."[15]

As a country whose economy is dependent upon the export of a few primary commodities, Pakistan is vitally interested in the stability of the prices of such commodities. ECOSOC reviews annually the reports presented by such bodies as the Interim Co-ordinating Committee for International Commodity Agreements (ICCICA) and the Commission on International Commodity Trade (CICT). The main function of the former is to facilitate through appropriate means intergovernmental consultation or action with respect to international commodity problems. The task of the latter is to examine measures designed to avoid excessive fluctuations in the prices and volume of trade in primary commodities. This includes measures aimed at the maintenance of an equitable relationship between the prices of primary commodities and the prices of manufactured goods in international trade as well as making recommendations for that purpose.

Pakistan was not a member of ECOSOC when the proposal for the setting up of ICCICA was approved. The government did not join ICCICA because it felt that the demand for Pakistan's exports, particularly jute and cotton, was stable and that there would be no advantage to the nation from commodity agreements. Pakistan also felt that the pegging of maximum prices would deprive it of gains resulting from upward trends in the prices of raw materials.

---

15 *Ibid.*

At the 1954 spring and summer meetings of the Economic and Social Council, Pakistan supported the creation of the Commission on International Commodity Trade, and has been a member of that Commission since its inception in 1954. The stabilisation of prices and of the volume of trade in primary commodities is of considerable importance to a country like Pakistan, whose main source of foreign exchange earnings is the export of primary commodities. At the summer session of the Council in 1957, Pakistan expressed the view that CICT had not justified the hopes that had been entertained about it and indicated a willingness to support any proposal for the merger of CICT with ICCICA.

The idea of the establishment of a world food reserve emanated during the 1954 session of the United Nations General Assembly at which a resolution was adopted requesting the Secretary-General to invite the Food and Agriculture Organization (FAO) to prepare a factual and comprehensive report on the feasibility of establishing a world food reserve. This reserve would relieve emergency situations, prevent extreme short-term fluctuations in the prices of agricultural commodities, and promote rational disposal of intermittent agricultural surpluses.[16]

When the report of FAO was considered by ECOSOC at its summer session in 1956, the delegation of Pakistan stressed the need for a food reserve for combating unforeseen food shortages and short-term balance of payment difficulties. The Council adopted a resolution sponsored by Pakistan, recognising the need for such a reserve to stabilise prices and assist less-developed countries to resist strains on their foreign exchange position caused by unexpected food shortages. At the summer sessions of the Council in 1956 and 1957, it was pointed out by Pakistan that a single world food reserve would not serve all the various requirements and it was suggested that a world food capital fund, complementary to the proposed SUNFED, should be established.

---

[16] G.A.O.R., 9th Sess., Resolutions, Supple. No. 21, 14 Dec. 1954, p. 14.

The need for a world food reserve was stressed by Mr. Firoz Khan Noon in the course of his address to the General Assembly in 1956. He said:

> My delegation is convinced that the establishment of a food reserve is urgently needed to provide assurance, in time of emergency, of an adequate stock of food to prevent distress as well as shortage caused by scarcity. In our opinion, it is necessary to devise a method by which a country may procure food grains to meet a shortage in any one year, without upsetting for that year or the following years its programme of economic development, which would be upset if it had to use its limited foreign exchange resources for importing food. Asian countries could be helped to become self-supporting in food if some of the foreign aid were given in the shape of modern aids to agriculture—for example, tractors. Part of the cultivable land—already much partitioned into small holdings—which at present is given to raising fodder for the oxen would, with the help of tractors, be able to produce much needed foodgrains. The tractors could be worked on a co-operative basis. Each cultivator could easily afford to pay the hire. Thousands could be purchased privately if we had the foreign exchange. There is no doubt that the position would be the same in many Asian countries.[17]

However urgent the need for a world food reserve and whatever the extent of its utility, it is of the highest importance that each country should take steps to meet threats to its food production and indeed to augment that production. So far as Pakistan is concerned, three primary problems to be faced are: the development of arid zones, the rational utilisation of water resources, and land reforms. At various times Pakistan has drawn the attention of ECOSOC to these problems. Speaking at a 1952 Council meeting, the representative of Pakistan reported that:

> Almost all of West Pakistan lay in an arid zone, where crops could only grow by irrigation. In addition, Pakistan must now face the problem caused by the increases of population. Since

17 G.A.O.R., 11th Sess., 601st Plenary Mtg., 29 Nov. 1956, p. 416.

partition in 1947, Pakistan had had to take in a very large number of refugees. . . . That influx raised many problems of rehabilitation, housing and food in a country where the economy was predominantly agricultural. . . .

In its efforts to cope with the situation, his Government had made use of new agricultural techniques and was attempting to bring arid land under cultivation. To do so it would have to develop their irrigation system considerably. . . . Pakistan had therefore undertaken multi-purpose irrigation programs, and projects for the exploitation of hydro-power resources, which were scheduled to be carried out under the six year national development plan. Under this plan there was a Lower Sind barrage project which aimed at bringing 2,800,000 acres of arid land under irrigation. . . .

A second project known as the Thal project was based on the utilization of the waters of the Indus: 250,000 acres of land had already been brought under the plough. . . .

The third project in the multi-purpose programme for the exploitation of water resources was the dam on the Kabul River, a tributary of the Indus. That installation, with a capacity of 180,000 kilowatts, would also make possible the irrigation of 100,000 acres of land. On the Kurram River, similar work would make possible the irrigation of 150,000 acres of arid land and the construction of a 4,000-kilowatt power station.[18]

The representative of Pakistan also referred to the problem of waterlogging and accumulation of salts, which had rendered waste 236,000 acres of land in Pakistan. Such waste areas were increasing at the rate of 40,000 acres annually, of which the government was able to reclaim 25,000 acres annually. The representative of Pakistan said that:

The carrying out of such schemes had imposed a very heavy burden, and if Pakistan did not receive technical, material and financial help from abroad, it would be difficult to finish the programme according to schedule. . . . Australia, Canada and

---

[18] ECOSOC, O.R., 14th Sess., 585th Mtg., 29 May 1952, p. 92.

New Zealand gave Pakistan valuable financial assistance under the Colombo Plan.[19]

At the 1956 spring session of ECOSOC, Pakistan sponsored a resolution proposing the drafting of a covenant to define the rights and duties of states with respect to the utilization and development of international water resources.[20] In support of the resolution, the representative of Pakistan observed that:

> ... If the Council really wished to ensure the development of those resources, it would have to begin precisely by establishing rules for the utilization of the waters of international rivers. If it took no step in that direction, progress was hardly to be expected. In making his proposal he had been motivated not by the special interests of Pakistan, but simply by the great importance of the question to millions of human beings. He had cited examples of certain disputes regarding the utilization of river waters, not with any desire to cast aspersions on the countries concerned, but merely in order to bolster up his arguments and bring out the real importance of the question and the need to take it up without further delay. He cited figures to show that the water resources wasted each year were considerable. The economy of many countries, including Pakistan, depended mainly on agriculture, which in turn depended on irrigation; in most of those countries, irrigation techniques were quite advanced and active research was being pursued.
>
> He therefore saw little to recommend the draft resolution submitted by France and the United States (E/L. 721), which merely requested the Secretary-General to make a preliminary study of hydrological data despite the fact that the United Nations had been working on the question for eight years. The study would not represent any progress over what had been done in some countries, in whose case irrigation was a vital necessity. It was not desirable to give the impression that adequate international action was being taken in that regard when, in fact, that was not the case.[21]

---

19 *Ibid.*
20 ECOSOC, O.R., 21st Sess., Annexes: Agenda item 7, p. 14.
21 ECOSOC, O.R., 21st Sess., 924th Mtg., 3 May 1956, p. 140.

It will be recalled that in view of its dispute with India over the waters of the Indus basin, Pakistan had a direct interest in the matter. However, the Pakistani draft resolution did not find favour with the Council.

On the problems of land reforms, which the representative of Pakistan described as "basic," he reported that:

> ... In East Pakistan a great new venture in land ownership had been launched. The Provincial Government was buying up all proprietary and intermediary holdings of land above a certain minimum with a view to eliminating all intermediary interests between the State on the one hand and the tiller of the soil on the other. In West Pakistan, where there were vast numbers of peasant proprietors owning the land they cultivated, the problem was largely one of better technique, better finance and better marketing. . . .

> In that context, he drew the Committee's attention to one aspect of the land reform question which had not received adequate attention in the past. Land reform was not merely a matter of willingness to initiate a certain process; it was also a question of finance. His Government did not believe in expropriation without adequate and reasonable compensation. The total value of all the landed interests to be acquired would however be so great as to leave practically nothing for other development projects. The will to initiate reforms was therefore limited by the availability of funds.

> In order to facilitate thorough consideration of the subject, he was submitting a draft resolution . . . requesting, first, that the Secretary-General include in his questionnaire to governments a question on the financial implications of their projected programmes of land reform and in his report to the Economic and Social Council consolidate and analyse the replies received and secondly, that a study of the financial aspects of land reform should be undertaken by the Committee of nine. . . .[22]

So many and so varied are the activities of the United Nations in the economic and social sphere that it is obviously not possible to

---

[22] G.A.O.R., 7th Sess., 2nd Ctte., 203rd Mtg., 4 Nov. 1952, p. 65.

take account of all of them in this study. We might, however, note
one more, *viz.*, the United Nations Children's Fund (UNICEF).
Speaking about it in a plenary meeting of the 1957 session of the
General Assembly, Mr. Noon said:

> ... This organization, which is financed by voluntary con-
> tributions from different countries and organizations, has this
> year a budget of $24,000,000, a considerable increase over
> last year's budget. It hopes, through continuous efforts, to
> abolish malaria throughout the world in about ten years'
> time, having made considerable progress in this direction
> already. What this means to the poorer nations living in un-
> favourable climates can be imagined only by us who live there.
> In Pakistan, the UNICEF has set up a DDT factory which
> is already in production. It is also setting up a penicillin
> factory which will soon go into production. This antibiotic
> is in very short supply in the eastern countries. In fact, it is
> almost unobtainable because of the shortage of foreign ex-
> change. . . .[23]

At the 1956 session of the General Assembly Pakistan drew attention to an important new fact relative to the economic programme
of the United Nations, namely, that the financial resources of the
world organization would be subjected to a further strain as a result
of its enlarged membership. Mr. M. Ahmed observed:

> ... that the percentage of total assistance allocated to Africa
> in 1957 was 10.7 as compared with 9.3 in 1956, an increase
> which had inevitably reduced the amount of assistance avail-
> able to Asia and the Far East. Pakistan willingly accepted the
> sacrifice in favour of the newly independent countries, among
> them Tunisia and Morocco. However, past experience had
> shown that the extension of the geographical range of coun-
> tries and territories covered by the Programme, however
> desirable in itself, did not always prove effective. It meant
> spreading the limited resources even thinner than before.
> Attention must therefore be directed towards increasing the
> total resources of the Programme. The Programme for 1957,

---

[23] G.A.O.R., 12th Sess., 694th Plenary Mtg., 30 Sept. 1957, p. 216.

the financial resources for which amounted to over $31 million, was inadequate when measured in terms of the area to be covered. A target of $50 million should be set.

So far as currency utilization was concerned, in many cases when the contributions were not large the problem of utilization was not difficult, particularly when those currencies were used for meeting the local costs. Special problems had arisen in connection with large contributions in inconvertible currencies. It was a disadvantage in the present system that countries like Pakistan, which had been unable to use some of those inconvertible currencies, had found their proportionate share of the funds reduced. If the available resources could be treated as a pool from which their shares could be apportioned to the various countries irrespective of their ability to use any particular currency, the disadvantages of the existing system would be partly overcome. The draft resolution on currency utilization, co-sponsored by Pakistan, went a long way towards securing the principles his delegation had in view. . . .[24]

The United Nations is not the only source of foreign aid for Pakistan, nor by any means the most important. In fact the United Nations provides only technical assistance, *i.e.*, experts, training facilities abroad, and demonstration equipment. It provides no capital assistance. Pakistan has received aid of a varied kind and on a very large scale from the United States. Pakistan has also received substantial aid under the Colombo plan from Australia, Canada, and New Zealand. Technical assistance has come also from the Ford Foundation and from Sweden, West Germany, Japan, and other countries, including a large measure of such aid from the United Kingdom.

Foreign economic assistance has played a vital part in the development of Pakistan. Beginning with a relatively small amount in 1950, given by a few countries, the scope and volume of this assistance had by the end of 1959 increased to $1,541.68 million, serving a variety of needs in a wide range of fields, such as agriculture, industries,

---
[24] G.A.O.R., 11th Sess., 2nd Ctte., 392nd Mtg., 3 Dec. 1956, pp. 26-27.

mining, transport, health services, trade, commerce, labour, and public administration.

By far the largest amount of aid to Pakistan has come from the United States. It began coming in 1950, after President Truman had announced his Point Four programme. Until the end of December 1959 the United States had given as economic aid to Pakistan $1,118.97 million.

The total allocations from Colombo plan countries until the end of 1959 were as follows:

1. Canada	$(c)109.56	million
2. Australia	$ 27.55	,,
3. New Zealand	$ 5.71	,,
4. United Kingdom	$ 3.80	,,

The assistance received from the United Nations and its specialised agencies since the inception of their programme in Pakistan in 1950 has been as follows:

Year	*Total* (in US dollars)
1950-51	268,000
1952	1,042,000
1953	946,000
1954	756,000
1955	929,000
1956	1,076,000
1957	1,025,019
1958	993,060
1959	{ 981,390 { 2,283,100
Total	10,299,569

The World Bank has so far allocated to Pakistan twelve loans of the value of $151.35 million and the International Finance Corporation has given two loans totalling $1.38 million. The Ford Foundation had until 1959 allocated grants of the value of $15.02 million.[25]

The Pakistan Institute of International Affairs Study Group on

25 Govt. of Pakistan, Press Information Dept. Release for 23 March 1960.

the United Nations examined the working of the aid programmes, particularly those relating to technical assistance. With regard to the expanded technical assistance programme of the United Nations, the Group expressed the view that the programme lacked the flexibility to take account of the varying needs of the recipient countries. That was due to the rigid programming procedures of the United Nations. There is the Technical Assistance Committee of ECOSOC and under it the Technical Assistance Board, on which are represented all the specialised agencies as well as the United Nations Technical Assistance Administration. The Board prepares its programmes for aid about two years in advance. However, when the time comes for using the aid, it is often found that the programme is no longer relevant, conditions and attitudes in the recipient country having in the meanwhile changed. For situations like this, Pakistani officials are sometimes themselves to blame. The Group thought that most of the difficulties resulting from procedures of the agencies giving or administering aid and discrepancies between what is offered by them and desired by the recipient countries are bound to be resolved, if the latter take up definite attitudes, backed by adequate advance planning.

The shelving of SUNFED, whose creation had been urged by Pakistan and recommended by ECOSOC, was due mainly to political considerations of the more powerful countries. This was a great blow to the underdeveloped countries. There are specialised agencies like UNESCO, FAO, and WHO for education, agriculture, and health; but there was none for the industrial development of the underdeveloped countries. Proposals for creating such an agency had on one ground or the other been opposed and put off. The International Finance Corporation had, however, been established and started functioning in 1956. But it was taking too long in deciding on the applications made to it and no funds had been received from it in Pakistan (at any rate until April 1958). In any case, the scope of the Corporation was confined to private industry of a very profitable type.

The United Nations provides technical assistance in the form of experts but makes little provision for supplying equipment. The experts that came out under the various aid programmes, the Group felt, were far too expensive and their utility was not commensurate with their cost to Pakistan. In several instances, experts came and wrote reports that called for still more experts to advise on the same problem. Thus, to deal with the problem of waterlogging, which is an extremely serious one in Pakistan, four groups of experts submitted four reports. How much better it would have been if the problem had been attacked in the field. More often than not, the experts that came out to Pakistan under the aid programmes, it had been found, did not give practical advice. In any case advice was not what was wanted most. The country needed equipment, training centres, and results above all.

The Group thought that a most important task which the United Nations could do was to sponsor and finance research programmes on problems that are vital to underdeveloped countries. Such programmes are beyond the technical and financial resources of those countries. They need, for example, research to check the growth of their populations and therefore a cheap, easy, safe, and effective method of birth control. Another thing they need is a cheap fuel for cooking. If the United Nations could devote a few million dollars to research for such purposes and get results, that would make all the difference to the lives of the peoples of the underdeveloped countries.

The Group noted that there was overlapping in aid programmes. Even the fields of the various agencies of the United Nations were not altogether exclusive. At one time in Pakistan three different agencies were working in the same field. This lack of coordination was known to the United Nations which was trying to introduce some sort of discipline.

The Group considered that the procedures of the World Bank were also very rigid. The Bank insisted on very high standards, which, whatever their long range value to the underdeveloped countries, were extremely difficult for them to meet. As a result of these procedures and standards sometimes the funds promised by the Bank for a project arrived after it had been completed. This happened in the case of the Karnafuli Paper Mills in East Pakistan.

Another criticism of the Bank was that it levied a commitment charge of one per cent on every loan provided by it. Of course, this charge substantially adds to the resources of the Bank. However, the underdeveloped countries feel that the Bank could afford to go without it.

The Group recalled the oft-expressed view that what the Western countries gave in aid, they took away in trade. Through adverse terms of trade, the basic wealth of the underdeveloped countries was being gradually reduced in value and a very small part of it was being paid back in the form of grants or loans. The question regarding measures to improve the terms of trade, in order to stabilise the prices of the commodities produced by the under-developed countries, had been taken up by Pakistan in practically all the forums of the United Nations. A Commission on International Commodity Trade has been appointed but as has been noticed no concrete measures have emerged from it. Prices of manufactured goods continue to rise, because of the labour component involved in their manufacture; and wages in the advanced countries are allowed to go on increasing. The result is that for a given quantity of goods exported by the raw material producing countries, these countries get ever fewer manufactured goods in exchange. This is a major factor in the inability of those countries to make progress with their own resources.

The Group was strongly of the opinion that the quantity of foreign aid received by the underdeveloped countries was not sufficient to meet their needs. It was not by any means sufficient to lead to development on such a scale as would make an appreciable difference to the standard of living of the masses of the underdeveloped countries. To achieve that end, transfer of funds on a very large scale is necessary. This is absolutely necessary if there is to be a stable world order, and if the human race is to live in freedom and dignity. The United States made possible the miracle of the recovery of Germany by giving that country $5,000 million dollars over a short period of time. The wealthy nations have plenty and to spare. It would not be just generosity on their part if they gave in an ample measure to the people of Asia and Africa. These people produce so many of the raw materials whose utilisation is a factor in building up the superprosperity of the wealthy nations. For the latter, it is also the call of enlightened self-interest, concluded the Group.

chapter nine

Some "Cold War" Issues

ADMISSION OF NEW MEMBERS

A question which was for many years the subject of much acrimonious debate has been the admission of new members to the United Nations. The position as it emerged in 1947 was that neither side was willing that likely adherents of the other side should be admitted, unless its own friends were also brought in. Since Article 4 of the Charter provides that the admission of a new member is to be made by the General Assembly upon the recommendation of the Security Council, the Soviet Union was able to use its Council veto to block certain applications. On the other hand, the Western powers, commanding a majority in the Council, tended to take the view that unanimity of the five permanent members was not required for a "recommendation" by the Council and that even without such unanimity, the admission of a state to membership could be effected by a decision of the General Assembly. This view was rejected by the International Court of Justice in an advisory opinion given on 8 March 1950.

Speaking in the plenary meeting of the General Assembly in 1947, Sir Zafrulla Khan stressed the role of the Security Council in the admission of new members, holding that:

> ... He could not agree with the view expressed by the representative of Australia, that since the Charter merely required a recommendation from the Council, the real decision had to be taken by the Assembly and that the latter was therefore empowered to reverse a rejection by the Council. If the Charter had considered that the function of the Council was in any way inferior or ancillary to a decision by the Assembly, it would have been worded differently. It would have stated that the Assembly should take a decision after considering the opinion of the Security Council. The object of the Charter was clearly that successful applicants should have the approval of both organs.[1]

Sir Zafrulla also supported the view that:

> ... the admission of new members was not a procedural problem, and consequently the unanimity rule must apply. The great majority of decisions taken by the Security Council were in the nature of recommendations, but that did not mean that they were not substantive decisions.[2]

Opposing "horsetrading" in admitting new members, Sir Zafrulla declared that:

> ... he did not believe that a member of the Security Council was justified in opposing the admission of a State which it agreed was fully qualified, on the grounds that other States were not also accepted. That was not a valid argument and was contrary to the Charter. No member was justified in

---

[1] General Assembly, Official Records (G.A.O.R.): 2nd Sess., 1st Ctte., 100th Plenary Mtg., 8 Nov. 1947, p. 361.

[2] *Ibid.*

taking an unreasonable attitude, simply because another delegation was being unreasonable. . . .[3]

Pakistan supported the Polish proposal that the five permanent members of the Security Council, who had primary responsibility in the matter, should consult together in an effort to resolve their differences and arrive at a solution.

In 1947 the Assembly sought the advisory opinion of the International Court as to whether a member was juridically entitled to make its consent to admit a new member dependent upon conditions other than those laid down in the Charter, particularly if it made the condition that other states should also be admitted. The Court decided that a member was not so entitled. This was in consonance with the view advocated by Pakistan.

In the third session of the Assembly in 1948, Sir Zafrulla Khan declared that his delegation would always support an application for admission to the United Nations provided that the applicant was a sovereign state, that its statehood and sovereignty had been established, and that its application was not a means of establishing the legality of either of those factors. Moreover, the applicant must be a peace-loving state, able and willing to discharge the obligations placed upon member states by the Charter. His delegation would support such an application, irrespective of the bloc to which the state would adhere after it had been admitted to membership.[4]

However, the deadlock in the Security Council continued, and its members, notwithstanding the opinion of the Court, allowed themselves to be guided by political considerations rather than by what was clearly their legal duty, namely, to consider all pending applications for membership strictly on their merits. Sir Zafrulla addressing the 1950 session of the General Assembly asked:

> . . . Is there not a single applicant from among those who have hitherto been blocked, or, perhaps, at least one from

[3] *Ibid.*, p. 362.
[4] G.A.O.R., 3rd Sess., 176th Plenary Mtg., 8 Dec. 1948, p. 791.

r

each side, which may be regarded as fulfilling the conditions
laid down in Article 4, and whose admission may be recommended by the Security Council as a token of the fact that the
permanent members of the Security Council are now prepared
to move forward in respect of this question on some reason-
able basis?[5]

In 1952 the General Assembly appointed a Special Committee to
study the problem of the admission of new members but it could
produce no generally acceptable solution. A Committee of Good
Offices was appointed in 1954; it persevered in its efforts until the
following year. In 1955 sixteen states were admitted to the membership of the United Nations, Japan following in 1956. The applications of the Republic of Korea, the Republic of Vietnam, the People's
Republic of Korea, and the Democratic Republic of Vietnam were
debated by the Special Committee. Pakistan supported the applications of the Republic of Korea and the Republic of South Vietnam
but abstained on those of the People's Republic of Korea and the
Democratic Republic of Vietnam. There was nothing to prove,
said Mr. K. Ahmed, that the two latter states would accept the
obligations of the Charter. He concluded that:

> ... If, however, a draft resolution was presented to the Com-
> mittee indicating clearly that the Democratic People's Repub-
> lic of Korea and the Democratic Republic of Viet-Nam ac-
> cepted the obligations set forth in the Charter, particularly
> those of Articles 1 and 4, the Pakistani delegation would
> examine those applications and vote in accordance with the
> principles he had just outlined.[6]

Spain was one of the sixteen countries admitted to the United
Nations in 1955. In 1946 the General Assembly had passed a resolution barring Spain from membership in the United Nations
and from participation in its activities and calling upon member
states to sever diplomatic relations with it.[7]

---

5 G.A.O.R., 5th Sess., 283rd Plenary Mtg., 25 Sept. 1950, p. 97.
6 G.A.O.R., 11th Sess., Special Political Ctte., 20th Mtg., 28 Jan. 1957, p. 91.
7 General Assembly Resolution 39(I), 11 Dec. 1946.

In the resolution of 1946 the hope was expressed that the Fascist regime in Spain would end and that in its place there would be established a democratic government, deriving its authority from the consent of the people and respecting freedom of speech, of religion, and of assembly. Speaking in the First Committee of the second session of the General Assembly, Sir Zafrulla Khan had asked: "But what was a Fascist State? There was no particular definition for that; there was a tendency to describe whatever regime was disliked as a Fascist regime."[8]

Addressing the fifth session, Sir Zafrulla again referred to the ban placed on Spain through the Assembly's resolution. He said:

> ... To say the least, that resolution ignored realities. At its worst, it was capable of causing grave mischief. In any case it is incomprehensible what the object of that resolution was. Was it penal—to inflict some penalty upon Spain for having accepted its present regime? Or was it reformatory—passed in the hope that the moment the people of Spain learned of the resolution they would rise in revolt against that regime and set it aside? At the most it could but have been passed in some such hope, but no consequences of that kind have flowed from it. The General Assembly passed the resolution and the walls of Madrid did not fall.[9]

In 1955, as we have seen, the same Spain was admitted to the United Nations, some of its sponsors being the very powers that had supported the resolution of 1946.

As early as 1952 Pakistan had pleaded for the admission of Japan to the United Nations.[10] This plea was repeated in 1953.[11] It was not until the eleventh session that Japan was admitted to the United Nations.

---

8 G.A.O.R., 2nd Sess., 1st Ctte., 104th Mtg., 11 Nov. 1947, p. 405.

9 G.A.O.R., 5th Sess., 283rd Plenary Mtg., 25 Sept. 1950, p. 97.

10 G.A.O.R., 7th Sess., *Ad Hoc* Political Ctte., 46th Mtg., 16 Dec. 1952, p. 288.

11 G.A.O.R., 8th Sess., *Ad Hoc* Political Ctte., 10th Mtg., 13 Oct. 1953, p. 47.

THE KOREAN QUESTION

The United Nations' crucial decisions on the Korean question in June 1950 were taken in the Security Council, of which Pakistan was not at that time a member. These decisions were epoch-making, for under them the United Nations for the first time took action against aggression. For the first time soldiers and sailors fought, military aircraft flew sorties, guns thundered, and bombs fell in the name of the United Nations. As is well known, the absence of the Soviet Union's representative in the Security Council made this action possible at the time it was being considered. Arguing that the representatives of the Communist regime held sway over the whole of mainland China, rather than the representatives of the defeated Nationalist government, the Soviet representative had held that the Peking government should take the place of the Nationalists on the Security Council. By way of protest the representatives from the USSR had then withdrawn from the Security Council. If the Soviet member had been present in the Security Council, he would doubtless have cast a veto and prevented the action that was taken in Korea.

Pakistan's attitude towards the June 1950 resolutions on Korea is important in considering Pakistan's position in international affairs. Hitherto Pakistan, always a leader of the assault on colonialism, speaking and voting against the West on many vital questions, was regarded as altogether independent of the two power blocs. After the support that it gave to United Nations action in Korea, Pakistan came to be regarded in some quarters as pro-West. This support, according to the Pakistan view, was motivated by objective considerations. In later years, too, Pakistan has on a variety of issues voted against the West.

When the conflict over Korea broke out, the Prime Minister of Pakistan was on a visit to the United States. In a statement issued in Boston on 27 June 1950, he declared his government's support for the Security Council's resolutions of 25 June and 26 June and for any measures that the Council should decide to take to help South Korea against aggression from the north. Mr. Liaquat Ali Khan said that as a loyal member of the United Nations, it was Pakistan's duty to take that attitude. This policy was endorsed by the Pakistan Parliament through a resolution moved by the Prime Minister on 11 October 1950.

Articulate opinion in Pakistan was generally, though not universally, behind the government's Korean policy. In an editorial *Dawn* of Karachi, while pleading for cessation of fighting, said:

> If, however, this war goes on, peace-loving nations such as Pakistan will have no alternative but to tread the painful path of duty which their conscience dictates and their abhorrence of aggression in any shape or form, in any part of the world, naturally prompts them to follow. Pakistan has been the victim of aggression herself and is still seeking a peaceful solution of the Kashmir dispute through the intervention of the United Nations.

Dawn added that Pakistan in its turn:

> ... can do no less than give at the United Nations' call, her moral and material support, within her means, to any other country which may be the victim of similar aggression.[12]

Pakistan's military forces being insufficient even for its own defence needs, Pakistan was unable to send any troops to Korea. In response to the Security Council's resolution of 27 June 1950, Pakistan gave five thousand tons of wheat. Although all the members of the United Nations had been called upon to help, only sixteen of them sent military forces. These forces operated under the command of General Douglas MacArthur of the United States and the Military Staff Committee of the United Nations was completely by-passed.

When the General Assembly met in the autumn, North Korean aggression was condemned by the Foreign Minister of Pakistan. It was not, he said, the outcome of a chance or casual collision or conflict. Sir Zafrulla Khan declared:

---

[12] *Dawn* (Karachi), 22 July 1950.

In these circumstances the duty of the Security Council was clear, and for the first time in its history the Council gave an immediate and bold reply to the challenge so grave and impudent to the authority, nay, to the very existence of the United Nations, . . . [13]

In a statement issued in Ottawa, Sir Zafrulla Khan proclaimed Pakistan's support for the United States' view that there was nothing sacrosanct about the thirty-eighth parallel and that it should be crossed and the whole of Korea brought under the occupation of the United Nations forces.[14]

In the General Assembly, Pakistan was one of the sponsors of the resolution calling for measures for assuring stability throughout Korea, including the holding of elections under United Nations auspices, "to establish a united independent and democratic Government of Korea." The resolution also created the United Nations Commission for the Unification and Rehabilitation of Korea. Of this Commission, Pakistan was elected a member and also served as its Chairman. Pakistan abstained on the resolution branding Communist China as an aggressor in Korea as well as on the resolution imposing an embargo on the export of certain categories of goods to areas under the control of Communist China and North Korea. Pakistan was one of the sponsors of the resolution creating a good offices committee to bring about a cease-fire in Korea.

UNITED ACTION FOR PEACE

The "Uniting for Peace" resolution, passed by the General Assembly on 3 November 1950, was a child of the Korean crisis. The resolution provided, *inter alia*, that if the Security Council, because of lack of unanimity of its permanent members, fails to take action in any case where there appears to be a threat to or a breach of the peace or an act of aggression, the General Assembly should im-

---

[13] G.A.O.R., 5th Sess., 283rd Plenary Mtg., 25 Sept. 1950, p. 95.
[14] *Dawn* (Karachi), 3 Oct. 1950.

mediately consider the matter with a view to making appropriate recommendations to the members for collective measures, including, when necessary, the use of armed force to maintain or restore international peace and security. If not in session, the Assembly may meet in an emergency session, within twenty hours of being requested to do so.

The provisions of this resolution implied a readjustment of the powers and functions of the Security Council and the General Assembly for the maintenance of international peace and security. When it came before the First Committee, Sir Zafrulla Khan in his first statement said that his delegation had been unable to make up its mind with regard to its legality. However, he recognised that the Charter in itself was not a perfect document, based as it was upon compromises, calculated to set at rest certain misgivings. If the draft resolution[15] sought to confer on the General Assembly certain powers which had been actually withheld from it, that would constitute an attempt to amend the Charter by a mere resolution and would be unconstitutional. If on the other hand it was recognised that while the principal responsibility for the maintenance of international peace was vested in the Security Council, the General Assembly possessed all residual powers, then it could be reasonably construed that the Assembly had all the powers of the Council, if the latter failed to act, and the draft resolution merely elaborated them. If the Assembly was the residual depositary of the powers of the Security Council, where was the need for Article 14, which specifically conferred upon the Assembly, with regard to the pacific settlement of disputes, powers which had been conferred upon the Council under Chapter VI? Sir Zafrulla Khan noted that the resolution did not seek to confer upon the Assembly the power of direct action, but sought only to have it make recommendations. He made it clear that his delegation was in complete agreement with the aim of the resolution.[16]

---

[15] G.A.O.R., 5th Sess., Annexes: Vol. II, Agenda item 68, pp. 4-6.
[16] G.A.O.R., 5th Sess., 1st Ctte., Vol. I, 359th Mtg., 11 Oct. 1950, pp. 95-96.

Speaking five days later on 16 October 1950, Sir Zafrulla Khan told the First Committee that his delegation would support the draft resolution. On the considerations which he had set out in his previous speech he had not come to any definite clear-cut conclusions; but he had been influenced by an appraisal of the Organisation's position in dealing with threats to peace, breaches of peace, and acts of aggression. With regard to the limitation in Article 12, Sir Zafrulla Khan said that it should not raise much difficulty in reference to the scope of the draft resolution, since the resolution would come into operation only when the Council, because of the lack of unanimity among its permanent members, failed to act. This meant that the matter would have been considered by the Council and the provisions of Article 12 would have been complied with by means of a procedural vote. The way would then be clear for the operation of the provisions of Article 10, which were of a general character. The Assembly could then make recommendations to the members of the United Nations or to the Security Council. True, Article 24 specified the primary responsibility of the Security Council for the maintenance of international peace and security. But if the Council was unable or unwilling to take prompt and effective action, was it to be concluded that the responsibility of the Organisation as a whole was ended? Since there was no specific provision for that situation, it must be presumed that there are general powers for taking action towards the maintenance of international peace and security.

Sir Zafrulla Khan was of the opinion that under Article 11(2), action in the sense of enforcement action was in the domain of the Council alone. Recommendations could nevertheless be made by the Assembly, which could recommend action, including the use of armed forces. It would be justifiable, he said, to adopt the view that where the Council had been unable to act, the General Assembly had a responsibility to take action under Article 10.[17]

---

[17] *Ibid.*, 363rd Mtg., 16 Oct. 1950, pp. 126-27.

Pakistan voted in favour of the entire draft resolution,[18] which was adopted on 3 November 1950. Amongst its provisions, other than the principal ones referred to above, was the establishment of a Peace Observation Commission of which Pakistan was elected a member.

SEATING OF COMMUNIST CHINA

The defeat of the Chinese Nationalists and the establishment of a Communist government as the only effective power on the mainland of China inevitably raised the question as to who should represent China in the United Nations. Important in itself, the question was of far-reaching significance insofar as China was a permanent member of the Security Council. The Western view was that since the Communists had gained control over the country by force and violence, the government constituted by them was not entitled to be considered a legitimate government. In any event, it was argued that the Communists could not be expected to carry out the obligations attaching to the membership of the United Nations. Thus, there were objections to the character and composition of the Communist government and there were doubts about its future behaviour as a member of the United Nations. Sir Zafrulla Khan speaking in the 1950 session of the General Assembly declared that these considerations were irrelevant to the issue. It was also irrelevant, he pointed out, to consider whether the new government was peace-loving or not and whether it was able and willing to discharge its obligations under the Charter as required by its Annex 4. These provisions, he said, related to the admission of new members and not to the validity of representation, with which alone the Assembly was at that moment concerned. Sir Zafrulla Khan declared:

> . . . China is not applying for admission to the United Nations. It is a Member State, a permanent member of the Security

---

[18] General Assembly Resolution 377(V), 3 Nov. 1950.

Council, one of the Big Five. I do venture to submit that whether it is willing or not willing to discharge the obligations laid down in the Charter, it is entitled as of right to be represented in the United Nations like every other member State, until it is—a contingency that might apply to every other State also—expelled in accordance with the provisions of the Charter.[19]

The sole question, Sir Zafrulla said, is who is entitled to represent China?

... The government from which the delegation present here purports to draw its authority has for months ceased to exercise jurisdiction over any portion of the Chinese mainland. ...

The truth of the matter is that the General Assembly is unwilling to concede the existence of a fact, not because the fact has not been established, but because the majority regard it as unpleasant. It is easy to conceive what the verdict would have been had the position been reversed, and it is this reflection that is so disquieting. ...

Sir Zafrulla Khan went on to point out:

Instances have not been wanting in the past—and I need not further particularize the matter—where a State declared, while its application for admission was pending, that not only was it not willing but that it was determined not to carry out the obligations incumbent upon it under the Charter—the obligations which were the very foundation of that State being brought into being—and in the face of such a declaration, that State was admitted to membership.[20]

The reference obviously was to Israel.

Pakistan voted for the Indian resolution[21] asking for the seating of the Peking government. The resolution was rejected. In subsequent years Pakistan has voted for the Western-sponsored resolu-

---

19 G.A.O.R., 5th Sess., 283rd Plenary Mtg., 25 Sept. 1950, p. 97.
20 *Ibid.*
21 G.A.O.R., 5th Sess., 277th Plenary Mtg., 19 Sept. 1950 (A/1365), p. 2.

tion that consideration of the question of the representation of China in the United Nations be postponed. However, if a resolution asking for the seating of the People's Republic of China in the United Nations were to be voted on in the General Assembly, the presumption is that Pakistan would vote for it.

DISARMAMENT AND ATOMIC ENERGY

On the twin questions of control of atomic energy and disarmament, Pakistan has played but a modest part in the United Nations. The reason for it is obvious. A solution of these questions can emerge only out of an agreement between the great powers. From time to time Pakistan has urged the need for such an agreement and for bold decisions both on atomic energy and on disarmament. Thus Mr. K. Sarwar Hasan, addressing the *Ad Hoc* Political Committee of the fourth session of the General Assembly, referred to "the profound concern of all mankind regarding the most serious problem of atomic energy and its important implications as an instrument of destruction or benefit to humanity." He emphasised that "the constantly increasing anxiety of the peoples of the world could be allayed only by a genuine agreement providing for effective guarantees amongst the nations possessing atomic energy and atomic weapons."[22] It was the view of the delegation of Pakistan, he said, that the search for an agreement should continue, for the atomic bomb could be banished only if the great powers agreed to an arrangement whereby its use was abandoned. The conflicting attitudes of the great powers must be reconciled. Improvement in their political relations would facilitate an understanding between them on this issue. The representative of Pakistan also urged consideration of the question of the use of atomic energy for peaceful purposes, particularly in view of the difficult economic situation prevailing in the world.

---

[22] G.A.O.R., 4th Sess., *Ad Hoc* Political Ctte., 34th Mtg., 11 Nov. 1949, pp. 196-97.

It will be recalled that the Atomic Energy Commission had been established in January 1946 by a unanimous vote of the General Assembly. The Commission was constituted to provide for the exchange of knowledge about atomic energy between all nations, for its control, so that it is used only for peaceful purposes, for the elimination of atomic weapons from the nations' armaments, and for safeguards against violations and evasions through inspection and other means. The Commission consisted of the eleven members of the Security Council with Canada.

In February 1947 the Security Council set up the Commission on Conventional Armaments for the regulation and reduction of armaments and armed forces. But because of lack of agreement between the Soviet Union and the Western powers neither of the two Commissions, although they had numerous meetings, was able to report the conclusion of its task.

In the absence of a settlement the great powers continued to arm themselves and to spend more and more on armaments and on the production of yet more destructive weapons. It was not that they did not desire peace. The speeches made by the representatives of all countries, large and small, in the United Nations showed that there was full consciousness of the consequences of another war, most likely fought with nuclear and thermonuclear weapons; and there was an unmistakable desire to avert it. Thus Dean Acheson, United States Secretary of State, speaking in the General Assembly on 20 September 1950, said:

> ... Men and women everywhere are weighed down with fear, fear of war, fear that man may be begetting his own destruction.
>
> But man is not a helpless creature who must await an inexorable fate. It lies within our power to take action which, God willing, can avert the catastrophe whose shadow hangs over us. That terrible responsibility rests upon every man and every woman in this room. . . .[23]

---

[23] G.A.O.R., 5th Sess., 279th Plenary Mtg., 20 Sept. 1950, p. 25.

Mr. Andrei Vyshinsky, speaking for the Soviet Union, said:

> It is the duty of the United Nations to put an end to the atomic weapon and the other major weapons of mass slaughter of populations. This is what millions and millions of people are demanding.
>
> The Government of the Soviet Union deems it essential that the General Assembly should take all the steps in its power to implement the measures it has itself already approved in this matter, in order to achieve the unconditional prohibition of the atomic weapon and the condemnation as a war criminal of any government which is first to use the atomic weapon against another country.[24]

Thus we see the leaders of the two opposing camps unequivocally affirming their desire for peace and for the abolition of the weapons of mass destruction. However, in the words of Sir Zafrulla Khan, "with that affirmation the limits of peace are reached and disagreement starts."[25]

In the 1951 session, the First Committee had before it two resolutions, one submitted by the United Kingdom, the United States, and France, proposing the creation of a new Disarmament Commission, and the other, offered by the Soviet Union. The latter amended the Western proposal by asking, amongst other things, for a disarmament conference. Pakistan, along with Iraq and Syria, sponsored a resolution asking for a subcommittee, under the chairmanship of the President of the Assembly and consisting of the representatives of the USSR, the United Kingdom, and the United States. The task of the subcommittee would be to formulate agreed proposals, concerning the control and reduction of armed forces and armaments as well as the abolition of atomic and other weapons of mass destruction.[26] Sir Zafrulla Khan, on introducing the draft resolution, "implored the Great Powers to attempt to reach an

---

[24] *Ibid.*, p. 30.

[25] G.A.O.R., 6th Sess., 343rd Plenary Mtg., 14 Nov. 1951, p. 113.

[26] G.A.O.R., 6th Sess., Annexes: Agenda items 66 and 16, p. 7.

agreement which would serve mankind." Without such an agreement, he emphasised, "all the resolutions that could be adopted
would be of no use unless perhaps for purposes of propaganda."
Sir Zafrulla regretted that there was a contradiction between the
declared purposes of men and their actual behaviour and warned
that "the world was close to the abyss."[27] The joint Iraqi, Pakistani,
and Syrian resolution was adopted.

The subcommittee reported that while there was agreement or the
possibility of agreement on general objectives and, in general terms,
on the machinery for attaining those objectives, there was disagreement on the specific means and the principles which should be
applied to the guidance of the new Commission. The Assembly,
while rejecting the USSR amendment, adopted the three power
proposal to establish a Disarmament Commission. Not only was
this body to agree to the regulation, limitation, and balanced reduction of armed forces but it was also to provide for the international
control of nuclear energy that would assure the prohibition of
atomic weapons and the use of nuclear energy only for peaceful
pursuits. While wholeheartedly endorsing the purposes which the
three power draft resolution and the USSR amendment sought to
achieve, Pakistan abstained on both of them on the ground that the
terms of reference of the Disarmament Commission would not be
sufficiently flexible to enable the great powers easily to reach an
agreement.[28]

The three power resolution was passed and, as a result, the Atomic
Energy Commission and the Commission on Conventional Armaments were dissolved. A Disarmament Commission for dealing both
with atomic and other weapons was established. This Commission
consisted of all members of the Security Council together with
Canada when it was not a member of the Security Council. Pakistan,
by virtue of being a member of the Security Council, was a member
of the Commission.

27 G.A.O.R., 6th Sess., 1st Ctte., 454th Mtg., 26 Nov. 1951, p. 30.
28 G.A.O.R., 6th Sess., 1st Ctte., 468th Mtg., 17 Dec. 1950, p. 84.

During the two years (1952-54) that Pakistan was a member of the Disarmament Commission, there was little that Pakistan could do in it; indeed there was little that the Commission itself did. The Commission could not have achieved any results without an agreement among the great powers and such an agreement was not forthcoming. Because of this deadlock the Disarmament Commission in April 1954 passed on its task to a subcommittee consisting of Canada, France, the USSR, the United Kingdom, and the United States. The long drawn out proceedings of the subcommittee were marked by acute differences between the Soviet Union and the Western powers.

In May 1954 the Colombo Powers, of whom Pakistan was one, demanded that "no further explosions of hydrogen bombs should take place." In April 1955, at the Asian-African Conference at Bandung, Prime Minister Mohammed Ali pleaded for the outlawing of nuclear and thermonuclear weapons. The communiqué of the Bandung Conference, to which Pakistan was a party, declared:

> The Conference considered that effective international control should be established and maintained to implement such prohibition, and that speedy and determined efforts should be made to this end. Pending the total prohibition of the manufacture of nuclear and thermo-nuclear weapons, this conference appealed to all the Powers concerned to reach agreement to suspend experiments with such weapons.[29]

Addressing the First Committee of the General Assembly in 1955, Mr. Mohammed Ali reviewed the progress made by the Disarmament Sub-Committee and the problems that remained unsolved. He observed that:

> During the previous year, disagreement on certain measures of disarmament had been narrowed. There was agreement on ceilings for armed forces, on the implementation of the programme in progressive phases, on the timing of the pro-

---

[29] *Keesing's Contemporary Archives* (London: Keesing's Publications, 1955-1956), Vol. X, p. 14184.

hibition of nuclear weapons and on the establishment of a single permanent control organ. Unresolved were the questions of the subjection to the Security Council veto of the use of nuclear weapons in defence against aggression, of the discontinuance of tests of nuclear weapons, of the liquidation of military bases, of the reporting of violations of the disarmament treaty, and in particular of the rights, powers and functions of the control organ. Since the Sub-Committee had recessed its London session, formidable technical difficulties had appeared. It had been agreed that there was no infallible device for detecting nuclear stockpiles. It had, therefore, been concluded that complete control over the elimination of nuclear weapons was impossible. Further, the failure of the Conference of Foreign Ministers to reach agreement on political questions had further undermined international confidence.

The present situation, according to the representatives of the United States, the United Kingdom, France and Canada, was that, until science devised a means for finding hidden stockpiles, a plan of disarmament involving nuclear weapons had to be ruled out. On the other hand, the Soviet Union, while admitting the difficulties, maintained that the necessary elements for a disarmament agreement under effective safeguards still existed. The Pakistan view was that, if detection was not possible, the stage for prohibition of nuclear weapons had not been set. The dangers involved in the margin of error of detection were such as to make any responsible statesman hesitate to agree to a programme without watertight guarantees.

It had been emphasized that a disarmament agreement required unanimity, which did not exist; the impasse could only be resolved by science. Pakistan had wondered whether there had been sufficient reconciliation between the West and the Soviet Union to warrant the hope of an agreement on disarmament in the field of conventional weapons. There also was the question whether effective control was possible. It was reassuring to read a statement made by the representative of France at the 47th meeting of the Disarmament Commission in which he had asserted that the technical means to ensure complete control in the conventional field did exist. . . . The Soviet Union['s] emphasis in the past on sovereignty had discouraged the hope of a compromise. However, it should be possible to arrive at a synthesis, in which event it would be practicable to enforce any agreement on the reduction of armed forces and conventional armaments. The statements of the representatives of Sweden (799th meeting) and of the States members of the Sub-Committee supported that view. Thus, while there was an impasse on nuclear armaments, a large measure of disarmament was still feasible which might transform the international situation. Such a partial solution would enhance the prospects of a solution in the nuclear field.

Any disarmament plan had to be drawn up so that each stage increased the security of all parties and not of only one. Secondly, it should avoid a disequilibrium of power dangerous to international security. . . .[30]

In the same speech Mr. Ali referred to his government's support of the four power draft resolution[31] on a comprehensive disarmament plan although he regretted the omission of a proposal which would have diverted savings arising from disarmament to the improvement of underdeveloped areas. However, Pakistan fully concurred with those provisions in President Eisenhower's plan that were intended to prevent a nuclear war, just as it welcomed Marshal Nikolai Bulganin's proposal for control posts.

In August 1957 the Disarmament Sub-Committee ceased to function as a result of the withdrawal of the Soviet Union's representative from its deliberations. Thus the problem of disarmament was left unsolved. Speaking about it in debate in the General Assembly in 1957, Mr. Firoz Khan Noon, Foreign Minister of Pakistan, said:

I now turn to the fateful issue of disarmament. It is not necessary for me to elaborate upon the terrible prospect of mass annihilation which faces mankind as a result of the per-

---

[30] G.A.O.R., 10th Sess., 1st Ctte., 806th Mtg., 7 Dec. 1955, p. 261.
[31] G.A.O.R., 10th Sess., Annexes: Agenda items 17 and 66, p. 8.

s

fection of thermonuclear weapons and the means of their delivery. Warnings have been uttered during the past few years that the problem of disarmament is a race against time, since science and technology are placing weapons of mass destruction in the hands of man faster than his ability to devise measures of control or defence against them. The admission by the "nuclear" Powers that an adequate and reliable system of control over nuclear disarmament is not possible at the moment because of the impossibility of detecting hidden stockpiles of nuclear weapons is most disconcerting. Through frittering away precious time in mutual suspicion and distrust, have we been carried beyond the point of no return? However, nothing will more surely spell the doom of our existence than a fatal acceptance of that inevitability. All Members of the United Nations must therefore bend their urgent efforts to narrow the differences between the Western Powers and the Soviet Union over the question of achieving comprehensive disarmament under an effective system of inspection and control.

. . .

The Pakistan delegation attaches great importance to . . . a partial agreement. A reduction of armed forces and conventional armaments of the great Powers cannot but remain the first pre-occupation of those nations which are not among the "nuclear" Powers. If such a reduction could be agreed upon between themselves initially, appropriate reductions could be brought about in the armed forces and conventional armaments of all the nations of the world. Tensions would be relaxed and the danger of local wars which might develop into a world conflict would be reduced. A large part of the world would be relieved of the crushing burden of unproductive expenditures which could then be devoted to constructive purposes. . . .[32]

In the First Committee and the plenary meetings of the General Assembly in 1957, questions of disarmament and control of atomic energy were debated together. There was a detailed discussion of

---

[32] G.A.O.R., 12th Sess., 694th Plenary Mtg., 30 Sept. 1957, pp. 216-17.

the progress made by the Disarmament Sub-Committee and the attitudes of the various powers. In the First Committee, Pakistan voted against the Indian draft resolution which sought to create a scientific-technical commission of experts for recommending to the Disarmament Commission a system of inspection and supervision to render suspension of test explosions effective and to maintain other controls. The member states were to report to the scientific commission whenever they found any evidence of an explosion. This resolution was rejected both in the First Committee and in the Assembly.

Pakistan abstained on the Japanese resolution calling for a provisional suspension of test explosions, while parallel efforts were made to expedite agreement on unsettled points in evolving a system of supervision and inspection. The proposal was opposed both by the Western powers and the Soviet Union. The resolution was rejected by the First Committee. Pakistan voted against the Soviet draft resolution proposing the establishment of a permanent disarmament commission consisting of all member states of the United Nations. This resolution was rejected both in the First Committee and in the Assembly. Pakistan also voted against another Soviet resolution which proposed an experimental five-year moratorium on the use of hydrogen and atomic weapons. This resolution was rejected by the First Committee.

The latter resolution contradicted the Twenty-Four Power resolution, which was passed by the First Committee by 59 votes to 9, with 16 abstentions. This resolution embodied the proposals set out by the four Western powers to the Disarmament Sub-Committee in their working paper of 29 August 1957, which had occasioned the withdrawal from that Sub-Committee of the Soviet Union. To this draft resolution Norway and Pakistan jointly submitted two amendments, which were accepted by 61 to 9 votes with 10 abstentions. They proposed the study by groups of technical experts of an inspection system for disarmament measures on which agreement might be reached in principle and indicated how the groups should be constituted and the time within which they should report.

Introducing the amendments[33] in the First Committee Mr. G. Ahmed put forward the view of the Pakistan delegation on the Twenty-Four Power draft resolution[34] and commented on the progress made by the Disarmament Sub-Committee. He said:

> The general debate in this Committee has disclosed the extent of the narrowing down of differences between the Western Powers and the Soviet Union which has resulted from the Sub-Committee's deliberations in London on measures of partial disarmament represented by the first stage plan which, both sides agree, should be given priority in further negotiations. Specifically, the points on which agreement in principle exists are the suspension of test explosions of nuclear weapons, the reduction of armed forces and conventional weapons and the question of open inspection with ground and aerial components to guard against the possibility of surprise attack. The general debate has established beyond doubt the earnest desire of all Governments for continued negotiations between members of the Sub-Committee in order to break the present stalemate by reaching similar agreements in principle on the other measures of the first stage plan as set forth in the operative part of the twenty-four Power draft resolution. Also certain specific recommendations to salvage the negotiations have been made by a number of delegations, including my own. We have pointed out that the most promising way out of the dead end reached in the negotiations is to take out from the package proposals put forward by the Western Powers the two questions of reduction of levels of armed forces and conventional weapons and the establishment of an open inspection system against surprise attack and, having separated these two proposals from the package, to give them independent consideration. We have expressed the view that the interlinking of these questions with the proposals for nuclear disarmament is unnecessary and that insistence on simultaneous acceptance

[33] G.A.O.R., 12th Sess., Annexes: Agenda item 24, p. 15.
[34] *Ibid.*, p. 12.

of proposals in these two categories on an all or nothing basis would tend to freeze the present deadlock.[35]

Mr. Ahmed stressed the desirability of the nuclear powers' not taking up inflexible attitudes and welcomed the assurance of Canada that it would not regard the Western proposals as the last word on disarmament.

The Twenty-Four Power resolution was adopted by the General Assembly. While welcoming the narrowing down of the differences in the Disarmament Sub-Committee, it laid down principles for a disarmament agreement and asked the Sub-Committee to resume its efforts to evolve such an agreement and to report by 30 April 1958. The hope was also expressed that funds saved through disarmament would be spent on improving living conditions, "especially in the less developed countries."[36]

THE HUNGARIAN CRISIS

The Hungarian crisis called for another emergency session of the General Assembly and again for action under the "Uniting for Peace" resolution. Now the Soviet Union, which had been so vociferous in condemning imperialist aggression against Egypt, was in the dock. The United States, which had offended its principal Western allies and its West Asian protégé for their aggressive action in the Suez area, led them and others in their condemnation of Soviet intervention in Hungary.

Mr. Arkady Sobolev, the USSR representative, objecting to the inclusion in the agenda of the item "The situation in Hungary," said that since this was a matter of domestic jurisdiction, its discussion was barred by Article 2(7) of the Charter. He declared:

> ... By trying in contravention of the Charter, to involve the General Assembly in a discussion of the situation in Hungary,

---

[35] Original verbatim text. Summarized in G.A.O.R., 12th Sess., 1st Ctte., 889th Mtg., 4 Nov. 1957, p. 115.

[36] General Assembly Resolution 1184(XII), 14 Nov. 1957.

the United Kingdom and France, together with the United States, are attempting to gain time and to enable the British-French forces to settle accounts with the Egyptian people.[37]

On the other hand, the United States chief delegate, Henry Cabot Lodge, declared:

> ... After several days of ominous reports, the situation in Hungary has become all too clear. What is revealed is the sickening picture of duplicity and double-dealing. While this wholesale brutality by the Soviet Government was being perpetrated, the Soviet representative here in this hall was praising peace and non-aggression and raising his hands in horror against bloodshed in the Middle East. . . .[38]

Mr. Lodge submitted a draft resolution which while "condemning the use of Soviet military forces to suppress the efforts of the Hungarian people to reassert their rights," in its fourth operative paragraph asked:

> ... the Secretary-General to investigate the situation, to observe directly through representatives named by him the situation in Hungary, and to report thereon to the General Assembly at the earliest moment, and as soon as possible suggest methods to bring an end to the existing situation in Hungary in accordance with the principles of the Charter of the United Nations.[39]

Now precisely the same charges as were brought through this draft resolution against the Soviet Union in respect to Hungary, could be and indeed were being brought against France in respect to Algeria. However, France had always taken the position that affairs in its colonies fell within its domestic jurisdiction. France was not willing to see a precedent set up in the United Nations that would strengthen a possible demand for an investigation in Algeria. South

---

[37] G.A.O.R., 2nd Emergency Special Sess., 564th Plenary Mtg., 4 Nov. 1956, p. 2.

[38] *Ibid.*, p. 5.

[39] *Ibid.*, p. 7.

Africa, too, in view of its racial situation, was fearful of such a precedent. Accordingly the representative of France, with the promised support of South Africa, proposed that operative paragraph 4 be amended so that the Secretary-General "would investigate the situation caused by foreign intervention in Hungary" and would "suggest methods to bring to an end the foreign intervention in Hungary."[40] Mr. Lodge accepted the French amendment "in the interests of clarity."[41]

The draft resolution also called upon the governments of Hungary and the USSR to permit observers nominated by the Secretary-General to enter Hungary and to travel freely therein.[42] Fifty countries, including Pakistan, voted in favour of this resolution, the eight Communist governments voted against it, and fifteen states abstained.

Like France and South Africa, India, too, had to be careful in its attitude towards the Hungarian question, for India's role in Kashmir bore an unmistakable resemblance to that of the Soviet Union in Hungary. Not only did India abstain on the American draft resolution[43] but also, through an amendment[44] co-sponsored with Indonesia and Ceylon, India sought to modify the American draft resolution[45] in such a way as to remove from it all words attaching blame on the Soviet Union in respect of the situation in Hungary. The representative of Cuba was surprised to find that the representative of India should so enthusiastically defend the Soviet Union's part in Hungary.[46] The Cuban representative took a grave view of the thesis expounded by the Indian representative, namely, that what the Soviet Union had done in Hungary was legal

---

[40] *Ibid.*, p. 20.
[41] *Ibid.*
[42] *Ibid.*, p. 7.
[43] *Ibid.*, p. 20.
[44] G.A.O.R., 2nd Emergency Special Sess., 571st Plenary Mtg., 9 Nov. 1956, pp. 67-68.
[45] *Ibid.*, 570th Plenary Mtg., 9 Nov. 1956, pp. 47-48.
[46] *Ibid.*, 571st Plenary Mtg., 9 Nov. 1956, p. 48.

and proper and "that the United Nations must not react when confronted with an invasion launched by a Member State which by force, violence, and the use of its army, imposes a Government which does not reflect the wishes of the population."[47] India had done all that in Kashmir.

Mr. V. K. Krishna Menon had told the General Assembly that Soviet troops would be withdrawn from Budapest as soon as order was restored. The representative of Cuba drew the Assembly's attention to the alarming implication of that statement.[48] It will be recalled that Pandit Nehru had made an identical declaration about Indian troops in Kashmir.

The American draft resolution was adopted by the General Assembly as was also the draft resolution jointly proposed by Cuba, Ireland, Italy, Pakistan, and Peru.[49] This resolution condemned violent Soviet repression in Hungary, describing it as foreign intervention. Furthermore, it called for the immediate withdrawal of Soviet forces and for free elections under United Nations auspices to enable the people of Hungary to determine their own form of government. Explaining Pakistan's stand, Mr. Mir Khan said that his country had not joined in sponsoring the draft resolution to oblige its friends or to spite others, but out of respect for certain principles which were more sacred than any earthly friendship or animosities, the principles enshrined in the United Nations Charter and affirmed in the Bandung declaration.[50] India voted against operative paragraph 2 calling for free elections under United Nations auspices, abstained on all the other parts of the resolution, and voted against the resolution as a whole.

On 30 November the Secretary-General reported to the General Assembly that he had no information concerning compliance with the Assembly's decision regarding withdrawal of troops or related

---

[47] *Ibid.*, pp. 72-73.

[48] *Ibid.*

[49] *Ibid.*, pp. 77-80.

[50] *Ibid.*, 570th Plenary Mtg., 9 Nov. 1956, p. 48.

political matters.[51] He also stated that no permission had been given by the Hungarian authorities for observers to enter Hungary.

The stand taken on these two points by the General Assembly in its second emergency session was reaffirmed in the regular session through a resolution[52] of which Pakistan was a co-sponsor. Speaking in support of it, Begum Ikramullah said:

> In co-sponsoring this draft resolution, our delegation has been motivated by one desire alone, namely, to establish the authority of the United Nations. We feel that this Organization, by allowing its decisions to be flouted or ignored with equanimity in the past, has reached a stage when its own effective existence is in jeopardy. Its efficacy in the future depends on the manner in which it can handle the questions that are now engaging our attention.[53]

---

[51] G.A.O.R., 11th Sess., Annexes: Agenda item 67, p. 13.
[52] General Assembly Resolution 1130(XI), 4 Dec. 1956.
[53] G.A.O.R., 11th Sess., 606th Plenary Mtg., 4 Dec. 1956, p. 492.

chapter ten

The United Nations and its Future

When in September 1947 Pakistan was admitted to the United Nations, the "cold war" had already engulfed the Organisation. There was disillusionment about its effectiveness as a means of preserving world peace; and there were demands for changes in the Charter, then barely two years old. The situation was such that the leader of the Pakistan delegation, Sir Zafrulla Khan (not yet his country's Foreign Minister), in thanking the General Assembly for admitting Pakistan to the membership of the United Nations, felt constrained to say:

> The great nations which were able to pool their resources and their statesmanship for winning the war, appeared to be afflicted with an incapacity to come to a frank and wholehearted agreement on the lines upon which the foundations of peace should be laid.

Nevertheless Sir Zafrulla was convinced that the United Nations offered mankind its last chance of salvation and urged that "our united efforts ought to be directed towards strengthening the Organisation, discovering means of making it work in the spirit in which it was founded, and achieving the ideals which have been set as its goal."[1] Indeed the situation was thought to be so desperate that a few days earlier a South American representative had felt compelled to say: "Our diplomatic language is to some extent the language of our era, but our actions are still very similar to those which strewed the tragic paths of history with millions of corpses."[2]

It was not until 1954 that Pakistan aligned itself with the West. But, both before and after that, Pakistan had always urged upon the powers the need for mutual accommodation and co-operation in matters affecting the vital interests of mankind. Thus Sir Zafrulla Khan addressing the First Committee of the General Assembly in 1950 regretted that "the world was divided into rival camps, each arming at ever increasing speed for a conflict which to many appeared almost inevitable." Sir Zafrulla recognised that:

> . . . so long as society continued to be dynamic, there would be difference of opinions, methods and ideologies. Civilization would not eliminate those differences but, having recognised their existence, must make provision for their peaceful settlement. . . .

This, he said, could be done, in accordance with the Charter. He urged that: "By their deeds and conduct the members of the United Nations must put the Charter into effect and so bring it to life." Pleading for sincerity in speech and action Sir Zafrulla adduced that: "It was high time, therefore, that a common tongue was used so that words should not only say what they meant but should also mean the same thing to every one." In the face of the ideological conflict, the Foreign Minister of Pakistan advised that:

---

1 General Assembly, Official Records (G.A.O.R.): 2nd Sess., 92nd Plenary Mtg., 30 Sept. 1947, pp. 317-18.
2 G.A.O.R., 2nd Sess., 82nd Plenary Mtg., 17 Sept. 1947, p. 17.

... Tolerance and understanding must be shown to those who cherished different faiths and aspirations, unless and until it was demonstrated beyond all doubt that those aspirations were contrary to peace, in which case the most resolute resistance must be shown.

Urging the importance of better international understanding, Sir Zafrulla said that until that had been achieved, "no resolution adopted in favor of peace would serve any purpose."[3]

Thus Pakistan's view was that the two blocs should recognise the existence of and show tolerance to each other and that in the interest of peace there should be understanding and co-operation between them. Speaking before the General Assembly in 1955 Mr. Mohammed Ali said: "Until the basic antagonism between East and West is removed, we cannot expect the United Nations to become that potent instrument for the maintenance of international peace and security which the authors of the Charter intended it to be."[4]

As a consequence of the rivalry between the Communists and the anti-Communists there came into existence in the General Assembly and all its Committees, as well as in the Security Council, two groups of members. Led respectively by the United States and the Soviet Union, these groups voted as blocs. "Only too often," said Sir Zafrulla Khan, the

... approach towards grave problems, in some instances of tragic import, is determined by "who says this" rather than by the merits of what is said, suggested or proposed. In too many instances, actions and proposals are dictated by the desire to manœuvre for position or the effort to build up prestige rather than by the just requirements of the problems to be resolved.[5]

However, Pakistan's voting in the United Nations, the late Mr. Liaquat Ali Khan claimed, had not been influenced by any con-

---

3 G.A.O.R., 5th Sess., 1st Ctte., 378th Mtg., 27 Oct. 1950, p. 213.

4 G.A.O.R., 10th Sess., 531st Plenary Mtg., 3 Oct. 1955, p. 208.

5 G.A.O.R., 7th Sess., 395th Plenary Mtg., 12 Nov. 1952, p. 237.

sideration except the merits of each case. "Sometimes we agreed with the Western bloc and sometimes with the Communist bloc, as the situation and the matter under discussion demanded."[6]

That this is still generally true is borne out from the record of Pakistan's activities in the United Nations as summarised in this study. This is true particularly in respect to the vast sector of those activities which relate to colonial problems and the economic problems of underdeveloped countries. In some matters, however, Pakistan has noticeably changed its stand. While recognising Communist China, Pakistan does not insist that it should be immediately seated in the United Nations and in recent years has voted for the postponement of the question.

Support for or opposition to Communism is not the only basis of grouping in the United Nations. There are other bases too. There is the Latin American group which generally supports the United States in non-colonial political and security matters and is sympathetic towards the Latin countries of Europe, namely, Spain, France, and Italy. There is also the Commonwealth group, consisting of Australia, Canada, Ceylon, India, New Zealand, Pakistan, the Union of South Africa, and the United Kingdom. The so-called European group comprises the non-Communist countries of Europe.

The largest group in the United Nations, however, is the Asian-African group which in 1958 had within its fold around thirty member states. The Soviet group, comprising only nine states, is by itself small. But in a number of matters it is always helped by the affirmative vote or the abstention of some members of the Asian-African group. The Soviet group supports the Asian-African group in its encounters with the Western powers. These powers, in the discussions on colonial problems, have consistently sought to take refuge behind Article 2(7) of the Charter, which places outside United Nations competence all matters essentially within the domestic jurisdiction of a state. This plea by the colonialists has

---

[6] *Dawn* (Karachi), 9 Mar. 1951.

always led to fierce dispute in the United Nations, with the Soviet group supporting the Asian-Africans.

The forerunner of the Asian-African group was the Arab group, which began functioning informally in 1946. In 1952, with the election of Pakistan to the Security Council, the group assumed its present name and became more formally organised. Professor Ahmed S. Bokhari chaired the group's meetings for ten months. Thereafter, the chairing of these conclaves has rotated alphabetically every month among its member states.

The Asian-African group has no constitution, written or unwritten. It has no arranged schedule of meetings: they may be called by any of its members at short notice. The decisions of the group are not binding on the members and no minutes of the proceedings are kept.

The group has not been consistently active. Nor because of its heterogeneity has it been consistently effective. Apart from the fact that some of its members are aligned with the West, while others are "neutralist," there are in it such differences as those between India and Pakistan and the differences *inter se* amongst the countries of the Middle East. Turkey was invited to join the group in July 1955 when it was a member of the Security Council and when, having participated in the Bandung Conference, it had renounced its total isolation from Asia. Since then, Turkey has attended some, but not all, the meetings of the group.

The common bond amongst the members of the group is their opposition to colonialism and their interest in the economic development of their regions. If it could draw its members closer together, it might have an even greater influence in the United Nations than it has at present.

The West has an overwhelming majority in the Security Council and the General Assembly. The Soviet bloc, which is in the minority in both those organs, makes use of the right of veto possessed by the Soviet Union as a permanent member of the Security Council. The veto is available and has been resorted to over the years also by the Western powers which are members of the Security Council.

The first major deadlock amongst the powers took place in 1947 on the question of the organisation of United Nations armed forces as required by Article 43 of the Charter. This was a crucial requirement and was visualised as an essential part of the enforcement procedure provided for under Chapter VII. Other questions on which there was, even in those early days, a wide divergence of views amongst the great powers were the admission of new members, disarmament, and atomic energy.

As early as the first session of the General Assembly, the First Committee was called upon to consider a proposal for a general conference of members under Article 109 of the Charter in order to eliminate the so-called "veto privilege" and another for a similar conference under the same Article for the wider purpose of reviewing the Charter. Both resolutions were rejected. But the Assembly did adopt a resolution requesting the permanent members of the Security Council to avoid the use of their special voting privilege in a manner likely to delay or impede the work of the Council and recommended the adoption by the Council of such practices and procedures as would secure that end.[7]

Now the Charter can be amended only in accordance with the procedure laid down in its Chapter XVIII. According to this procedure an amendment can be adopted only if it is supported by the vote of two-thirds of the members of the Assembly including all the permanent members of the Security Council. Therefore, for any amendment, agreement amongst those five permanent members is indispensable. In the absence of such an agreement, any talk of amending the Charter is wasted effort. It was for this reason, no doubt, that when the question again came up in the second session of the General Assembly, Pakistan took no part in the discussion although it had been just admitted as a member. Likewise when a similar proposal came up before the General Assembly in the third session Pakistan was again silent.

---

7 General Assembly Resolution 40(1), 12 Dec. 1946.

To remedy the situation created by the deadlock amongst the great powers in the Security Council, the General Assembly established the Interim Committee or the so-called "Little Assembly" with functions of an important character relative to the maintenance of peace and security. Created for one year in 1947, its life was prolonged for another year in 1948. In 1949 it was established for an indefinite period. Except in the early years of its existence, the Interim Committee has not been an active body largely because the Communist states considered its creation illegal and never attended its meetings. Their view has been that the Interim Committee has no place in the structure of the United Nations (all of whose organs are enumerated in the Charter) and that it was brought into being by the Western powers to convert the United Nations into their obedient tool.

Introducing the draft resolution for the creation of the Interim Committee, Mr. John Foster Dulles explained to the First Committee why the new body was being set up. He argued that it would be a perfectly legal body and that its functions would be entirely consistent with the Charter. "Competent handling of the agenda," said Mr. Dulles, "required more preparatory work, and continuous Assembly work ten months of the year." Mr. Dulles added: "The Interim Committee was expected to respect fully the primary responsibility of the Security Council for the maintenance of international peace and security, and thus would not study or deal with any dispute or situation on the current agenda of the Council."[8] Mr. Dulles further added:

> To avoid raising constitutional doubts, the United States proposal did not contemplate any delegation by the Assembly of any substantive discretionary authority given by the Charter. The interim committee would be only an internal organ of the Assembly, similar to others already created to study questions, and to report and make recommendations to the Assembly, and not to Member States or any organs of the United Nations.

---

[8] G.A.O.R., 2nd Sess., 1st Ctte., 74th Mtg., 14 Oct. 1947, pp. 130-31.

The only novel authority proposed was that of prior study of possible future agenda items for a plenary session.[9]

Mr. Andrei Vyshinsky, on the other hand, contended that it was "a new attempt to get rid of the 'veto' by creating an organ parallel to the Council." "That," said Mr. Vyshinsky, "would circumvent the principle of unanimity."[10] According to him, Mr. Dulles' remarks on the jurisdictional aspects of the matter "showed that actually the relations in question were not those between a principal and a subsidiary organ, but between two sovereign bodies, the Assembly and the interim committee, or the Assembly and the Council."[11]

Speaking in the same debate Sir Zafrulla Khan said that his government was not at that stage prepared to express its views about "the legal and constitutional aspects of the establishment of an interim committee." He however did not see any sinister motives behind the proposal; nor did it seem to him to be a matter "of grave and imminent urgency."[12] He welcomed the Australian proposal for referring the matter to a subcommittee.

When the question came up for discussion in the plenary session, Sir Zafrulla supported the proposal for the creation of the Interim Committee. A good many of the doubts with regard to the legality of the proposal, he said, had been resolved in the subcommittee.[13] Justifying the creation of the Interim Committee, Sir Zafrulla said:

> Now the position has changed. Until the dead-locks, which so often, so unfortunately and so unhappily continue to arise in the Security Council can be resolved, and the members of the Security Council can work together more amicably and more effectively towards the discharge of their functions, the General Assembly will have to deal with a larger volume of security and peace matters.

9 *Ibid.*, p. 131.
10 *Ibid.*, p. 134.
11 *Ibid.*, p. 135.
12 G.A.O.R., 2nd Sess., 78th Mtg., 10 Oct. 1947, p. 166.
13 G.A.O.R., 2nd Sess., Vol. II, 110th Plenary Mtg., 13 Nov. 1947, p. 799.

t

He added:

> Let us suppose that the General Assembly could be kept in
> session throughout the year, or for the greater part of the
> year. If it were practicable—and I submit it is not—to have
> the General Assembly in permanent session, as the Security
> Council is in permanent session, there would be no need, of
> course, for an interim committee. . . .

With regard to the constitutionality of the proposal, Sir Zafrulla
observed:

> So far as it has been able to study this resolution and its im-
> plications, the delegation of Pakistan does not find that it is
> proposed to vest the interim committee with any power that
> the General Assembly itself does not possess. As a matter
> of fact, the powers with which it is proposed to vest the
> interim committee are only a portion of the powers possessed
> by the General Assembly. . . .[14]

However, he sounded a note of warning when he said: "I have
still graver doubts as to whether the interim committee will be able
to justify itself as an experimental measure if all States do not co-
operate in making it a success."[15] The Pakistan delegation voted in
favour of the resolution for the creation of the Interim Committee.

When the proposal for the re-establishment of the Interim Committee came up before the General Assembly in 1949, Colonel
Abdur Rahim Khan, speaking for Pakistan in the *Ad Hoc* Committee, drew attention to the factors which had seriously hampered
the effectiveness of the Interim Committee, namely, the non-
participation in its work by a group of member states, the failure of
the General Assembly to entrust even non-political matters to it,
and the hesitation of member states to bring disputes before that
Committee, which was conclusive proof that it was not considered
really useful. Said Colonel Khan:

---

[14] *Ibid.*, pp. 800-01.

[15] *Ibid.*, p. 804.

... The delegation of Pakistan was prepared to vote in favour of the continuance of the Interim Committee for one additional year if necessary, in order to provide an opportunity for achieving universal participation. It could not, however, agree to the continuance of the Interim Committee as it stood, either on a permanent basis or for an indefinite period. ... [16]

The draft resolution[17] for establishing the Interim Committee for an indefinite period was adopted by the *Ad Hoc* Committee, Pakistan being the only non-Communist country to vote against it.

A remarkable development in the working of the Charter has been the practice evolved in the Security Council in respect to the abstention or absence of a permanent member. Under Article 27(3), decisions of the Council are to be made by an affirmative vote of seven members, including the concurring votes of the permanent members, except on procedural matters provided under Article 27(2) and with the qualification that a party to a dispute has to abstain from voting on decisions under Chapter VI and paragraph 3 of Article 52. There is no definition in the Charter of "procedural matters." Yet, over the years, the practice of the Security Council has resulted in certain matters being regarded as procedural.[18]

However, seemingly non-procedural decisions have been adopted by the Security Council by a vote in which one or more permanent members abstained. One such decision was to admit Israel to the United Nations. The admission of new members was looked upon by Pakistan as a non-procedural question. Accordingly Sir Zafrulla Khan, speaking in the *Ad Hoc* Political Committee, argued that:

... the decision to recommend the admission of Israel was not in conformity with the specific conditions prescribed in Article 27. A careful reading of the Article left the Committee

---

[16] G.A.O.R., 4th Sess., *Ad Hoc* Political Ctte., 17th Mtg., 14 Oct. 1949, p. 74.
[17] G.A.O.R., 4th Sess., *Report of the Interim Committee of the General Assembly (31 January - 17 August 1949)*, Supple. No. 11 (A/966), Annex III, pp. 27-28.
[18] These are enumerated with the history of each case in the *Repertory of United Nations Practice* (New York: United Nations, 1955), Vol. II, Art. 27, paras. 12-44, pp. 68-81.

no option but to conclude that the Council had not been in a position to make that recommendation or that it had in fact agreed that the applicant State should not be admitted to membership inasmuch as its application had obtained the concurring votes of only four permanent members of the Council.[19]

The Chairman of the Committee ruled that "it was beyond the competence of the Committee to question the regularity of the vote in the Security Council and the validity of the decision taken."[20] General Andrew G. L. McNaughton (Canada) fully supported the Chairman's ruling and expressed the view that "it would not be in order for the Committee to question the process by which the Council had arrived at its decision."[21] However, Mr. Rodolfo Muñoz (Argentina), while holding the view that "abstention in the Security Council by any of the five permanent members was a desirable system, since it constituted voluntary abandonment of the veto," objected to their doing so when it was in their own interest, "on an arbitrary basis and without considering the desires of the rest of the Organization."[22]

The permanent member that had abstained on Israel's application was the United Kingdom. Its representative, Sir Terence Shone, explained to the Committee:

> In addition to the laws and rules which governed the conduct of the various United Nations organs, they had established certain practices which had acquired great force. Since July 1946, a practice had been created in the Security Council whereby a permanent member could, by abstaining from the vote, permit the Council to take action which that member did not affirmatively support, provided that such action had been approved by the affirmative votes of seven members.

---

19 G.A.O.R., 3rd Sess., *Ad Hoc* Political Ctte., 42nd Mtg., 3 May 1949, p. 183.
20 *Ibid.*
21 *Ibid.*, p. 184.
22 *Ibid.*, p. 185.

That procedure had been explicitly sanctioned by all five permanent members on various occasions.[23]

Sir Terence quoted the representative of Syria as saying:

> I think it is now jurisprudence in the Security Council—and the interpretation accepted for a long time—that an abstention is not considered a veto, and the concurrent votes of the permanent members mean the votes of the permanent members who participate in the voting. Those who abstain intentionally are not considered to have cast a veto. That is quite clear.[24]

Thus in this case, as in some other cases, otherwise regarded as non-procedural, it came to be recognised as an unwritten rule in the practice of the United Nations that abstention of a permanent member did not preclude the fulfillment of the requirements of Article 27(3) concerning "the concurring votes of permanent members."

In 1953 the General Assembly referred to the Sixth Committee proposals for the publication of documents and preparatory studies in connection with a possible review of the Charter. The Sixth Committee adopted the Six-Power draft resolution, of which Pakistan was one of the co-sponsors; the others being Argentina, Canada, Cuba, the Netherlands, and New Zealand. Their original draft resolution[25] was modified by amendments and its requirement that member states "submit, preferably not later than 31 March 1955, their preliminary views with regard to the possible review of the Charter," was deleted. Amongst other material that it asked the Secretary-General to prepare and circulate was a repertory of the practice of the United Nations organs. In the course of the debate in the Sixth Committee, the representatives of the Communist states argued that the proposal, if accepted, would tend to undermine the United Nations. The Communist representatives argued

---

[23] G.A.O.R., 3rd Sess., 43rd Mtg., 4 May 1949, p. 200.

[24] *Ibid.*

[25] G.A.O.R., 6th Sess., Annexes: Agenda item 58, pp. 11-12.

that the real object of undertaking the proposed preparatory work was to abolish the principle of unanimity of the five permanent members of the Security Council, which was the basis of the Charter. They contended that the draft resolution had been submitted at the instigation of one of the great powers. Contradicting these allegations, the representative of Pakistan said that "the proposal reflected the spontaneous feelings of the smaller countries."[26] The resolution was adopted by the General Assembly.[27]

The question of the review of the United Nations Charter came up in earnest at the General Assembly in 1955. Speaking in the general debate, the leader of the Pakistan delegation, Mr. Mohammed Ali, said:

> At this session, we are required to take a decision whether a general conference of the Member States of the United Nations should be convened for the purpose of reviewing the Charter. The Pakistan delegation does not believe that the Charter is a perfect instrument. There is, for example, the right of veto, which militates against the concept of the sovereign equality of States, one of the fundamental principles of the United Nations. But what is even more to be deplored is the manner in which this prerogative has been exercised in the history of the Organization. . . .[28]

However, Mr. Ali emphasised that "it would be unrealistic to believe that the ills which beset the organization can be cured by merely altering its constitution. The causes of the *malaise* lie much deeper."[29] He listed two causes, namely, the failure of the Organisation to carry out its own resolutions on the grave problems affecting international peace and security and the basic antagonism between East and West. While Mr. Ali did not think that in the prevailing international climate alterations in the fundamental provisions of the Charter were possible, he expressed his delegation's desire to

[26] G.A.O.R., 8th Sess., 6th Ctte., 374th Mtg., 23 Oct. 1953, p. 75.
[27] General Assembly Resolution 796(VIII), 27 Nov. 1953.
[28] G.A.O.R., 10th Sess., 531st Plenary Mtg., 3 Oct. 1955, p. 208.
[29] *Ibid.*

eliminate the power of veto in connection with the admission of new members and to enlarge the non-permanent membership of the Security Council "so as to give more adequate representation to certain regions in Asia and Africa." He voiced the hope "that attempts in this direction would not be frustrated by a resort to the veto."[30]

Mr. Ali was careful to point out that Pakistan would not favour an increase in the number of permanent seats, for that had nothing to do with the principle of equitable geographical representation of all areas in the Security Council. Indeed in the question of permanent seats was involved a principle of doubtful validity, namely, that of the recognition of great power status. Mr. Ali said: "Enlargement of the number of permanent seats would result not only in a further derogation from the concept of sovereign equality, but would also add to the number of States enjoying the veto power in the Security Council."[31]

Considering all the circumstances, Mr. Ali said that his delegation would support the Secretary-General's proposal that the Assembly should decide in favour of a review conference, leaving open for the time being the question when it should be convened.

When the question regarding a Charter review conference came up for discussion in the General Assembly, Mr. A. K. Brohi, speaking for Pakistan, felt compelled to go beyond the proposals adumbrated by his leader. Mr. Brohi declared that the entire Charter would have to be jettisoned. He said:

> There is nobody who is so unsophisticated as to say that the economic or political situation of ten years ago is the same today, and that the assumption upon which the structure of the charter was based remains unchallengeable. Therefore I shall not go into that question. The operation of the provisions of the Charter is a clear commentary on the fact that the concept which was launched into existence and made the bed-

---

[30] *Ibid.*, p. 209.
[31] *Ibid.*

rock of the whole Charter has not been observed in the spirit and manner in which it was intended and expected to be observed.

As for the alternative, Mr. Brohi said:

> I grant that, in our present thinking, we have no cut-and-dried solution to the problem of defining the assumption on which the new charter is to be based, in order to ensure that world peace and security are brought about in the manner in which the principles of the present Charter say they should be brought about. What I certainly cannot grant is that such a concept cannot be found. The review conference, therefore, would be of an exploratory character. It might declare to us at the end that probably there was no better charter than the one we had and that, as a matter of painful necessity, we must carry on with it. That finding is not precluded. On the other hand, the conference members, sitting together as honourable men, might well discover another assumption which was less pretentious, perhaps, but which was of greater pragmatic relevance for the purpose of building the edifice of the new charter. . . .[32]

The General Assembly adopted a resolution deciding in principle to hold a general conference to review the Charter; the date, place, procedure and organisation of the Conference to be decided at its 1957 session. After the vote the representatives of the USSR and Poland stated that their delegations would not participate in any action aimed at revising the Charter.

The Study Group of the Pakistan Institute of International Affairs on Pakistan's attitude towards the United Nations examined the question of the future of the United Nations Charter. The Group came to the conclusion that while there was room for improvement in the Charter, the failures of the United Nations were due not to defects in the Charter, but to the manner in which it had been applied. The Group thought that in every instance where the United Nations had failed, the reason for such failure had been

---

[32] G.A.O.R., 10th Sess., 545th Plenary Mtg., 18 Nov. 1955, pp. 338-39.

that one or more of the great powers had blocked action through the veto in the Security Council, the use of their majority in the Assembly, and the exercise of their influence generally behind the scenes to prevent a decision or to procure a wrong decision. Particularly deplorable was the fact that in a number of cases decisions already taken by the General Assembly or the Security Council were not enforced because that did not suit the purposes of some great power or powers.

To give a few examples: the boundaries of the Arab and Jewish states to be carved out of Palestine were laid down in the General Assembly's resolution of 29 November 1947. True, the resolution, passed under pressure from both the power blocs, was contrary to the principles of the Charter. But after fighting had broken out in Palestine and the Jews had established a state embracing some of the areas allotted to the Arabs by the General Assembly, no effort was made to compel the Jews to confine their state to the boundaries expressly laid down for it in the General Assembly's resolution. In fact, that state was admitted to the United Nations although it had already possessed itself of excess territory in defiance of the Assembly's resolution.

The General Assembly's resolution also provided for the internationalisation of Jerusalem. Indeed, a statute for Jerusalem had been drawn up for it by the Trusteeship Council. The refusal of the governments of Israel and Jordan to carry out the statute was reported to the General Assembly but nothing further was done about it.

Likewise on the Kashmir question there are definite and mandatory decisions in the resolutions of the United Nations Commission on India and Pakistan. These resolutions were accepted both by India and Pakistan and endorsed by the Security Council. India, playing for time to consolidate its hold over Kashmir, first delayed and then refused to carry out its obligations under the resolutions. The Security Council did nothing about it. Thus, the fault lies not with the Charter but with the powers that control the Organisation.

The Group rejected as impractical suggestions for scrapping the United Nations and for setting up an altogether new organisation. It refused to consider proposals for establishing a world government, whatever its constitution or powers. The Group regarded these proposals as premature in the prevailing circumstances of the world: the rivalry between the two ideological blocs; the different levels of political, economic, and social development in various countries of the world; and the absence of a general desire in the international community for a world government particularly worked against the foundation of a superstate.

In the opinion of the Group, the only basic change needed in the Charter was the elimination altogether of the "permanent" members of the Security Council. However, insofar as amendment of the Charter itself was subject to the veto, the Group saw no hope at all of the veto privilege being taken away from any of the powers that had it. The Group felt strongly that in no case should the number of permanent members of the Security Council be added to, for to do so would be tantamount to giving further recognition to the principle of inequality of members and enlarging the opportunity for the use of the veto with all its attendant consequences. In any event, the assumption that the great powers would be jointly responsible for policing the world and should therefore have the veto to prevent, if they should wish to, their forces being committed to war-like action, had been irretrievably destroyed. Consequently there was no moral justification for the right of veto and much less for adding to the number of member states that possessed it.

To give adequate representation to Asia and Africa the Group favoured increasing the number of non-permanent members of the Security Council. It felt that this was an amendment that would probably be adopted, for none of the great powers would wish to antagonise Asian-African opinion by vetoing the measure.

The Group considered the argument against small countries, with tiny populations and practically no developed resources, having the same one vote as large, powerful, and influential countries like the United States, the Soviet Union, the United Kingdom, or Japan. The argument was not without force, thought the Group. But the Charter system was based on "the sovereign equality of all nations, large and small." The alternative was a totally new system, founded on the representation of the human race, irrespective of national groups, or representation of those groups, on a population basis. If either of these alternatives were accepted, it would not only necessitate far reaching changes in the structure of the Organisation but also completely alter the world political situation in a manner that would clearly not be to the liking of most of the member states.

While the Group recognised that the scope for a formal amendment of the Charter was extremely limited, it felt that it might be modified in certain respects without such amendment. In the past, practice had served to modify the Charter. An instance, already noted, of such modification has been the Security Council's understanding that the absence of a permanent member should not be regarded as a veto while the requirement of the concurring vote of the permanent members under Article 27(3) should only apply to the votes of those permanent members who participate in the voting. The area of procedural matters could be extended to include some of the matters that are now regarded as substantive. Through its resolution adopted on 14 April 1949, the General Assembly had asked the members of the Security Council to forbear exercising their right of veto in 35 types of decisions recommended by it.[33] The Group felt that there was more hope in a proposal like that than in attempts to amend the Charter. In particular, it was desirable to have an agreement that the veto would not be used to block proposals for peaceful solutions of disputes.

The Group examined the two positive attempts made in the past to by-pass the veto, namely the establishment of the Interim Committee and the passage of the "Uniting for Peace" resolution. The Interim Committee failed for reasons that have already been ex-

---

[33] General Assembly Resolution 267(III), 14 Apr. 1949.

amined. The "Uniting for Peace" resolution has been successful. Under it the General Assembly can exercise practically as much power as the Security Council. According to the letter of the law, the Assembly can only recommend. Yet the difference between recommendation and action is very thin and ceases to exist in the appropriate circumstances. In fact the action taken by the Assembly in the 1956 Suez crisis proves beyond doubt that the Assembly can in practice exercise extensive powers and recommend enforcement measures which, under the terms of the Charter, were regarded as the exclusive field of the Security Council. Nor is the General Assembly, in advising enforcement action, bound by such restrictive details of procedure as are laid down in Chapters VI and VII of the Charter for the Security Council. The resolutions of the Assembly on Suez were clearly based on the assumption that it was plenipotentiary in this particular case. The Group felt that the Assembly ought to be resorted to more and more in matters requiring adjustment of disputes or enforcement action. Not only would there be no veto in the Assembly, but also its decisions would be more satisfying to the more numerous smaller nations who lay so much store by the principles of equality for all states in the United Nations. The Group noted that, at the time the "Uniting for Peace" resolution was passed, the Soviet Union declared it to be illegal. Nevertheless, the USSR had voted under that resolution when it supported a Yugoslav proposal to refer the Suez question to the General Assembly. This was taken to indicate that the Soviet Union regarded the procedure provided for under the "Uniting for Peace" resolution as an established fact. In any case, the veto did not apply when a proposal was made to the Security Council to refer a matter to the General Assembly for action under that resolution.

The Group next considered whether there was need for modifying Article 2(7), which barred consideration by the United Nations of matters that fell within the domestic jurisdiction of a state. The Group came to the conclusion that there was no such need and that the General Assembly or the Security Council should decide in each case whether a matter was or was not essentially within a state's domestic jurisdiction. In any event it would be found that no action had been taken even in those cases where the plea of domestic jurisdiction advanced by a state had been rejected by an organ of the United Nations. Thus, in the case of the racial question in the Union of South Africa, after South Africa's plea of domestic jurisdiction had been rejected by the General Assembly, no action was taken against the Union Government and it continues to defy the United Nations.

After discussing the various cases in which United Nations decisions had been defied by member states, the Group considered whether it was necessary, to deal with such situations, to amend the Charter or alter the machinery or the procedures of the United Nations. To this question the answer of the Group was that no such amendment or alteration was necessary. What was needed was a firm practice that all resolutions of the United Nations should be implemented. The enforcement measures in the Charter, including those short of war, should be carried out. If the Security Council is deadlocked, recourse should be had to the General Assembly under the procedures that are now part of the normal system of the United Nations. If in the domestic sphere of a nation a decision by a competent authority were defied by some citizens, that authority would take action against them; if it did not, other citizens would defy it too and it would cease to be the authority. That had happened only too often in the United Nations. If determined action were taken, there would be an all-round increase in respect for the United Nations. Once the United Nations passed a resolution, it ought to be implemented.

The Group regretted that not enough use was made by the United Nations of the International Court of Justice, which was designed to be the principal judicial organ of the United Nations. A number of states were not parties to the Statute of the Court; others had made extensive reservations in their declarations under Article 36 of the Statute. Some states that were parties to the Statute had either totally withdrawn or modified their declarations with the object of preventing the Court from taking cognizance of their disputes with other states. This tendency, the Group thought, was greatly to be deplored in view of the urgent need for the establishment of the rule of law in international affairs.

An illustration of that tendency, the Group noted, was afforded by the fact that India had totally ceased to be a party to the Statute of the Court. This had been a gradual process. India had inherited from the pre-independence regime acceptance of the compulsory jurisdiction of the Court, subject to conditions set out in the declaration signed on 28 November 1940.[34] Pakistan accepted the compulsory jurisdiction of the Court subject to conditions contained in its declaration signed on 22 June 1948.[35] India's original declaration contained a reservation which prevented the Court from dealing with any disputes between India and other members of the Commonwealth. Pakistan, in its declaration, made no such reservation. On 7 January 1956 India modified its declaration, excluding from the jurisdiction of the Court disputes with "any country which on the date of this Declaration is a member of the Commonwealth of Nations."[36] Thus, if Pakistan should decide to secede from the Commonwealth and wish to have its legal disputes with India adjudicated upon by the International Court of Justice, that Court would be without jurisdiction. Pakistan did not modify its declaration. In a letter dated 8 February 1957, the Permanent Representative of India to the United Nations informed the Secretary-General of his government's decision to terminate the declaration of 7 January 1956.[37] The letter contained an assurance that "a fresh declaration will shortly be filed on behalf of the

---

[34] International Court of Justice, *Year Book 1947-1948*, p. 136.

[35] *Ibid.*, p. 138.

[36] *United Nations Treaty Series* (New York: United Nations, 1956), Vol. 226, No. 3116, p. 236.

[37] *United Nations Treaty Series* (New York: United Nations, 1957), Vol. 260, p. 459.

Government of India." Until the middle of 1958 no such declaration had been filed. On 23 May 1957 Pakistan renewed its original declaration without any modification, accepting as compulsory the jurisdiction of the Court. Clearly India knew that in its disputes with Pakistan it was on the wrong side of the law and that if any of those disputes went to the Court, the judgement of the Court would be against it. That explains why India first modified and later altogether denounced its acceptance of the compulsory jurisdiction of the Court.

The Study Group was of the view that acceptance of the compulsory jurisdiction of the Court in all legal disputes, without any reservations, should be a *sine qua non* for membership in the United Nations. This could be accomplished by an amendment of the Charter or without it, if all the members voluntarily signed the "optional clause." If this were done, whether through a Charter amendment or by the members *suo moto*, a large number of matters that now go to the other already overburdened organs of the United Nations would go, instead, to the Court. It was, however, realised by the Group that prevailing political atmosphere of the world engendered little hope that all the members would agree to sign the "optional clause" without reservations or agree to amend the Charter to make the compulsory jurisdiction of the Court a necessary qualification of United Nations membership. In fact, as already noted, most of the members of the United Nations, including the Soviet Union, had not accepted the compulsory jurisdiction of the Court at all and even the United States, which had accepted, had done so subject to extensive reservations.

With regard to the advisory jurisdiction of the Court, the Group noted that it had not been used as frequently as it might have been. Many a case would have been resolved if the opinion of the Court had been obtained and the legal questions involved in the case made the basis for decision. The Group regretted that in some cases the opinion of the Court had been flouted by member states and no action taken against them.

In a word, the Group attached the utmost importance to ways and means being found for making greater use of the International Court of Justice through resort either to its compulsory or its advisory jurisdiction. In most disputes that came up before the United Nations, legal issues were involved but these issues were obscured by political arguments in the course of the lengthy debates that took place. If the legal issues could be adjudicated by the Court and United Nations decisions based upon the Court's findings, a great deal of the time of other United Nations organs would be saved and their decisions would be just and free from the taint of political considerations. Precisely the same would be the gain if questions of fact could also be decided by the Court.

The Group favoured the setting up of an international Criminal Court and noted that the government of Pakistan had favoured the creation of such a court with jurisdiction to try any offender, in any state, in respect to any act which was an offence under recognised international law. The Court's jurisdiction was not to be dependent on a particular state's consent to submit its nationals to that body.

The members of the Group, all of whom had had experience of United Nations work, recalled that a great deal of time was wasted in the Security Council, the General Assembly and its Committees, through delegates making lengthy and repetitious speeches. However unimportant the point, a delegate was free to speak on it as long as he liked. Most of the speeches were made with an eye to their publication in the press of the speaker's country. It was always desirable to correct this situation, but it was all the more necessary to do so now that there were 82 member states. All these states were represented in the General Assembly and in each one of its Committees. To enable each representative to have his say, apart from other reasons, it was necessary that there should be a rigid time limit for all speeches. Except for stating a case in which a delegate's country was directly interested, no delegate should make a main speech of longer than twenty minutes duration. Other speeches should not exceed ten minutes. These restrictions should apply not only to speeches in the Security Council and the Committees of the General Assembly, but also to those in the plenary sessions, including the addresses of the heads of delegations in the general debate. These opening addresses as a rule contain little more than vague statements of national attitudes towards problems before the United Nations.

The Group next examined the idea of creating a permanent United Nations Force. Pakistan is a strong supporter of the proposal. Mr. Firoz Khan Noon, speaking in the general debate in the 1956 session of the General Assembly, observed:

> The General Assembly's prompt action in setting up the United Nations Emergency Force encourages my delegation in the hope that without undue delay the International Force envisaged in Chapter VII of the Charter will be established on a permanent basis for enforcing the rule of law in all international disputes. Even though this permanent international force may not be stronger than the national armed forces, its moral force, with the backing of the whole civilized world, would be an effective deterrent to any potential aggressor. This international force, comprising for the present the units made available to the United Nations by the armed forces of Member States under General Assembly resolution 377(V), should eventually be recruited and paid for by this Organisation and located, under its own commanders, in various strategic areas of the world. . . .[38]

Mr. Noon, adverting to the subject in his address to the twelfth session, said in 1957:

> Pakistan is a strong supporter of the concept of a United Nations peace force which, in the words of the Secretary-General, "could be activated on short notice in future emergencies to serve in similar ways." Until such time as unanimity of the permanent members of the Security Council makes it possible for the Security Council to have at its disposal the armed forces to be made available by Member States under Chapter VII of the Charter, a United Nations peace force

---

[38] G.A.O.R., 11th Sess., 601st Plenary Mtg., 29 Nov. 1956, p. 417.

u

would be a practical, if not a wholly adequate, substitute. Such a force could be created through appropriate action by the General Assembly in furtherance of the primary objective of the United Nations to maintain peace and tranquility. It need not be a large force. When deployed with the moral authority of the United Nations behind it, it will not be an ineffective deterrent to a potential aggressor. It will enhance the effectiveness of the United Nations in achieving peaceful adjustment of disputes and emergency situations.[39]

These propositions were examined by the Study Group which was constituted by the Pakistan Institute of International Affairs to consider Pakistan's attitude towards the United Nations. The Group came to the conclusion that it was not possible to create a United Nations force capable of intervening in or preventing a conflict between the major powers; the problems of finance, organisation, and armaments needed for such a force being insuperable. The Group, however, felt strongly that the force visualised in Chapter VII and advocated by Mr. Noon in his address before the General Assembly in 1956, ought to be constituted as early as practicable. However, since the unanimity of the permanent members of the Security Council indispensable to the creation of such a force was not likely to be forthcoming in the foreseeable future, the Group supported the creation of a United Nations peace force as proposed by Mr. Noon in his address before the General Assembly in 1957. This force would be analogous to the "emergency international United Nations force," which was set up by the resolution of 4 November 1956. Established "with the consent of the nations concerned," this force was "to secure and supervise the cessation of hostilities."[40] In effect it was not a fighting force, but a force which was intended to perform police functions of an international character during the period of transition from war to peace, other operations incidental to that transition, or duties specially assigned to it. The "peace force" advocated by Mr. Noon would be created

[39] G.A.O.R., 12th Sess., 694th Plenary Mtg., 30 Sept. 1957, p. 216.
[40] G.A.O.R., 1st Emergency Special Sess., 4 Nov. 1956 [998(ES-I)], p. 2.

on a more permanent basis by the General Assembly. It would not be a large force, though its members might exceed those of UNEF which consists of 6,000 men. It would be equipped with conventional weapons. In addition to performing such functions as were assigned to UNEF, it would be available for other duties such as guarding truce lines, occupying disputed territories, and supervising plebiscites and elections. More significantly, the permanent force would be deployed in the name of the United Nations on the soil of any country that is menaced by aggression. The expectation was that the aggressor would be deterred not by the size of the force, but by the moral authority of the world community behind it. It might even be agreed that should an aggressor attack the force, the member states of the United Nations would make war on him. The Security Council and the General Assembly would have, under their respective procedures, concurrent authority to order deployment of the force.

The problems involved in the creation of such a United Nations force have been admirably examined by William R. Frye, who notes that "The Kashmir case has placed severe obstacles in the way of creating a permanent UN police force."[41] For should such a force come into existence, it would at least be available to the United Nations to facilitate the holding of a plebiscite in Kashmir. On that account, no doubt, India's V. K. Krishna Menon opposed the idea of a police force in Egypt in a private meeting of the Asian-African bloc.[42] However, the Indian permanent representative, Arthur S. Lall, had already committed his country to such a force. Frye notes:

> ... Mr. Krishna Menon has even bristled at the suggestion that UNEF's life be prolonged in Egypt and has specifically criticized the idea that it might be regarded as "a kind of nucleus of a future force." ...[43]

---

[41] William R. Frye, *A United Nations Peace Force* (New York: Oceana Publications for the Carnegie Endowment for International Peace, 1957), p. 37.

[42] *Ibid.*, p. 7.

[43] *Ibid.*, p. 38.

As regards the composition of the force, the Study Group thought that it should, like UNEF, consist of contingents contributed by member states other than the permanent members of the Security Council, though the personnel of the contingents might change from time to time. The UNEF precedent in regard to the political control of the force by the Secretary-General should also be adopted.

In Frye's book there is a discussion by him, and in an appendix to it by Richard L. Plunkett, on the feasibility of the use of a United Nations force to resolve the Kashmir dispute. "The difficulty with the proposal," says Frye, "is not that it would fail, but, paradoxically, that it might succeed too well."[44] Despite his original commitment Nehru resists it as he wishes to avoid a plebiscite in Kashmir for fear of losing it. The world community would not put pressure on India because the United States and certain other members of the United Nations do not wish to annoy India. Having made these observations, Frye expresses the opinion (not his own) that a United Nations force, stationed on the Pakistani side of the cease-fire line in Kashmir, "probably would not be able to prevent border crossings by Indian 'peace brigades' (fanatic agitators and terrorists) determined to cow the electorate."[45] It might be pointed out that these "terrorists" are hirelings and not "fanatic agitators," that they are capable only of terrorising unarmed Kashmiris under conditions of Indian military occupation, and that they would not take such risks as are involved in border crossings when the border is guarded by a military force.

Plunkett too upholds the view that a United Nations force might have helped to obtain the demilitarisation of Kashmir, necessary for the holding of a plebiscite. "Existence of a UN force would have strengthened UNCIP's hand in the negotiations . . ."[46] Then the force would have been used to secure demilitarisation, guarding and directing a staged withdrawal of the armed forces, directing

---

[44] *Ibid.*, p. 36.
[45] *Ibid.*, p. 37.
[46] *Ibid.*, p. 141.

a partial disarmament of the *Azad* Kashmir forces as well as the pro-Indian civil militia. The next phase would have involved the creation of preconditions of law and order for the plebiscite.[47]

Plunkett concludes:

> Within the framework of the political agreement reached by UNCIP, a UN Force might have played an active and valuable role in ending the Kashmir dispute through implementing the agreed means to a final settlement. Demilitarization and the plebiscite are the stumbling blocks which have obstructed the settlement of the Kashmir crisis over the past eight years: a decision of the Security Council to send in a UN Force might have made possible a final peaceful settlement.[48]

According to Pakistani opinion what a United Nations force "might" have done, it could still do. Addressing the Security Council on 16 January 1957, Mr. Noon pleaded:

> ... The functions of protecting the State and ensuring internal security should be entrusted by the Council to a United Nations Force, which should be introduced into the area at once. Let all other forces—Indian, Pakistani, and local— be disbanded and non-Kashmiri nationals even in the police forces be removed. . . .[49]

We have in this Chapter given a picture of the Pakistani view, both as officially stated and unofficially considered, of the working of the Charter system, the changes that are required in it, and the possibilities of effecting those changes. This view is based on Pakistan's experience of the United Nations, both in matters which are of direct interest to it and those with which Pakistan has been concerned as a member of the United Nations. That experience as examined in this study indicates the range of Pakistan's part in the activities of the world organisation.[50]

---

[47] *Ibid.*, pp. 141-42.

[48] *Ibid.*, p. 143.

[49] Security Council, Official Records: 12th Year, 761st Mtg., 16 Jan. 1957, p. 20.

[50] For Pakistan's participation in United Nations bodies, see Appendix.

As adumbrated by this study, it would appear that Pakistan's effort in respect to the United Nations, and in international organisations generally, has by no means been small. Nor indeed was it avoidable, for the United Nations, together with other international organisations, today constitutes the framework of human society. This is the great international revolution of our times. International organisations participate in a number of facilities that are essential for the life of a country while membership in the United Nations has become an important concomitant of statehood.

In his maiden speech before the General Assembly, at Pakistan's admission to the United Nations on 30 September 1947, Sir Zafrulla Khan assured the Assembly that the Pakistani government would:

> ... make the utmost contribution of which it is capable towards securing and maintaining lasting peace. It would also be ever ready, and indeed anxious, to make its due contribution towards the alleviation of all forms of human suffering and distress and the promotion of beneficient cooperation among the nations for the general raising of standards of living and the fostering of liberty and tolerance throughout the world.[51]

In a statement on the morrow of the establishment of Pakistan, Mr. Liaquat Ali Khan declared:

> If today we come into our heritage of freedom, it is because the sufferings and sacrifices of many nations, particularly during the two World Wars, have extended the bounds of human liberty, reduced, if not altogether eliminated, the scope for power politics and made it impossible any longer for one nation to hold another in subjection. We are conscious of this fact and therefore conscious of our obligations to the great world family of nations, the security and orderly progress of each one of whom is essential for our own security and our own progress. We firmly believe that world peace is a condition precedent to the peace and prosperity of Pakistan, and we shall therefore unreservedly co-operate with the

---

[51] G.A.O.R., 2nd Sess., Vol. I, 92nd Plenary Mtg., 30 Sept. 1947, p. 318.

United Nations in every possible way in the great task of establishing world peace.[52]

Mr. Jinnah, broadcasting to the people of the United States of America in February 1948, said:

> Our foreign policy is one of friendliness and goodwill towards all the nations of the world. We do not cherish aggressive designs against any country or nation. We believe in the principle of honesty and fair play in national and international dealings and are prepared to make our utmost contribution to the promotion of peace and prosperity among the nations of the world. Pakistan will never be found lacking in extending its material and moral support to the oppressed and suppressed peoples of the world and upholding the principles of the United Nations Charter.[53]

The United Nations is not, of course, an end in itself. It is merely a means to the ends that have been set out in the preamble of the Charter. Having subscribed to the Charter, Pakistan naturally desires the establishment of a world order which safeguards fundamental human rights, assures the dignity and worth of the human person, and equal rights of men and women and of their nations, large and small. Said Mr. Mohammed Ali:

> We want one world order, not one world super-state. We want a world in which all nations, small ones and big ones, can live together in peace, accord and amity, free from any kind of fear of political domination or economic exploitation.[54]

The chief obstacle in the way of creating such a world order is the moral chaos that prevails in international affairs. In the words of Sir Zafrulla Khan:

> ... The great fault of international relations was the assumption that men could act with evil intent on behalf of a nation with impunity and even with advantage. . . .[55]

---

52 *The Statesman* (Delhi), 18 Aug. 1947.
53 *Quaid-e-Azam Speaks* (Karachi: Pak Publicity, n.d.), p. 93.
54 *Dawn* (Karachi), 23 Dec. 1953.
55 G.A.O.R., 4th Sess., 1st Ctte., 326th Mtg., 14 Nov. 1949, p. 270.

To remedy that deplorable situation, Sir Zafrulla Khan called for "the application to the conduct of nations of those simple standards in individual life which entitled a man to be called honourable."[56]

But moral precepts are not enough. For that reason the Pakistani bent is all in favour of a system under which rights and duties are not merely declared but also enforced.[57] Pakistan desires to see established, through the United Nations, a world order which is based upon law and justice.

---

[56] *Ibid.*

[57] See the speech of Mr. Firoz Khan Noon, G.A.O.R., 11th Sess., 601st Mtg., 29 Nov. 1956, p. 417.

Appendix

18. United Nations Children's Fund—   1953 to-date
    Executive Board
19. Special Committee on the Question of   1953-54
    Defining Aggression
20. Commission on Human Rights   1954-56
21. Commission on the Status of Women   1954-57, 58-60
22. Commission on International Commodity   1954-57
    Trade
23. Committee on South West Africa   1954 to-date
24. Special Committee on Review of   1955
    Administrative Tribunal Judgments
25. *Ad Hoc* Committee on a Special United   1955-57
    Nations Fund for Economic Development
26. Advisory Committee to the Secretary-   1956
    General on UNEF
27. Advisory Committee on the United   1956 to-date
    Nations Emergency Force
28. UNICEF Committee on Administrative   1956 to-date
    Budget
29. Committee on Control and Limitation of   1957 to-date
    Documentation
30. Preparatory Committee on a Special United   1957 to-date
    Nations Fund for Economic Development

Index

B

Baghdad Pact, 74-7, 161, 183
Bahrein, 57
Bajpai, Sir Girja Shankar, 141
Bakshi, Ghulam Mohammed, 148-9, 150, 157
Balfour Declaration, 166, 167-8, 173
Balkan Sub-Commission, 303
Baluchistan, 29
Bandung Communiqué (1955), 188, 270
Bandung Conference (1955), 69, 70-4, 261, 276
Bantu Education Act, 221
Batala *tehsils*, 43
Bazaz, Pandit Prem Nath, 89, 91n, 92n, 95n, 97n, 100, 105, 107, 108n
B.B.C., 150
Beas river, 43, 46
Belgium, 133, 185
Ben Gurion, David, 154
Bengal, 22
Bevin, Ernest, 195
Bevin-Sforza agreement, 189
Bharatpur state, 92, 96, 126
Big Five, 11, 18
    see also Great powers.
Big Four, 6
Birdwood, Lord, 43, 95n, 99, 102, 107, 111, 137n
Birth control, 225, 242
Black, Eugene, 45
Black Sea, 2
Boer War, 216
Bogor Communiqué (1954), 188
Bokhari, Ahmed S.
    and Asian-African group, 276
    and Palestine question, 166
    and race questions in South Africa, 212-3, 218-20, 222

and Tunisian question, 194-5
Bolitho, Hector, 27n
Bolivia, 201
Boundary Commissions, 38, 42, 43
Bourguiba, Habib, 193
Brandon, Dorothy, 37n
Brazil, 11, 161, 185, 195
British Cabinet Mission's Plan (3 June 1947), 33, 34, 36, 79-80, 91
British Commonwealth
    Commonwealth Group, 275
    and International Court of Justice, 292
    and Pakistan, 183
    Prime Ministers' Conference (1951), 144
British Indian Empire
    and Burma, 49
    and Indian states, 80
    and Pakistan, 20-6
    plans for liquidation, *see* British Cabinet Mission's plan.
Brohi, A. K., 285-6
Bulganin, Nikolai, 76, 185, 263
Bulgaria, 19
Burma
    and Asian-African Conference, 71
    British withdrawal, 3, 65,
    and Colombo powers conference, 69
    and former Italian colonies, 191
    origins, 20
    relations with India and Pakistan, 49
    and West Irian question, 188

C

Cambodia, 71
Campbell-Johnson, Alan, 37n, 133n
Canada, 27-8
    and aid to Pakistan, 46, 235, 239, 240

M

Soviet Union (*Continued*)
and former Italian colonies, 10
group in UN led by, 274-5
and Hungarian crisis, 267-71
and Israel, 54
and Kashmir question, 54, 76, 134, 162
and Marshall plan, 19
military alliances in Eastern Europe, 64
and Moscow declaration, 6
and Palestine question, 172
relations with China, 64
relations with Pakistan, 54-5, 64
and seating of Communist China, 250
and Soviet wives of foreign nationals, 217
and Suez question, 185
trade with Pakistan, 41
and Tunisian question, 195
and United States military aid to Pakistan, 62
and "Uniting for Peace" resolution, 290
and veto, 76, 153, 245, 276
and World War II, 2, 4
and Yalta Conference, 10
Spain, 41, 49, 248-9, 275
Special United Nations Fund for Economic Development (SUNFED), 227-30, 241, 304
Speeches, curtailment of, 294-5
Spheres of influence, 7, 8, 9
Srinagar, 108, 114
Stalin, Joseph, 6, 7, 8, 10, 11, 54
Standstill Agreement, 92, 93, 105
Statesman, The (Calcutta), 95n, 96n, 98
Statesman, The (New Delhi)
and Asian-African Conference, 74n

and creation of Pakistan, 32n, 34n
and Kashmir question, 92n, 98, 148n
and Middle East Defense Organization, 58n
and Pakistan and world peace, 301n
and Pakistan's alliance with the West, 62n
Stephens, Ian, 92n, 98, 108
Stettinius, Edward R., 7n, 8n, 9-10
"Stimson Doctrine," 3
Strategic areas, 9, 14, 15
Sudan, 71
Suez Canal Company, 181
Suez Canal question, 58, 69-70, 181-5, 290
Suez Canal Users' Association, 182
Suhrawardy, Hussein Shaheed, 70
Sukarno, President, 71
SUNFED, *see* Special United Nations Fund for Economic Development.
Sutlej river, 43, 44, 46
Sweden, 49, 162, 239, 263
Switzerland, 64
Sykes-Picot agreement, 173
Symonds, Richard, 95
Syria, 12, 71, 175, 188n, 220, 259, 260

T

Tanneries, 34
Technical assistance
expanded programme, 230, 241
Libya, 192-3
Pakistan, 231, 240, 241
see also Economic development.
Technical Assistance Administration, 241
Technical Assistance Board, 241
Technical Assistance Committee, 224, 241, 303